WRITERS OF THE AMERICAN WEST

WRITERS OF THE AMERICAN WEST

MULTICULTURAL LEARNING ENCOUNTERS

JOHN STANSFIELD

2002
TEACHER IDEAS PRESS
Libraries Unlimited
A Division of Greenwood Publishing Group, Inc.
Greenwood Village, Colorado

Copyright © 2002 John Stansfield
All Rights Reserved
Printed in the United States of America

No part of this publication may be reproduced, stored in a retrieval system, or transmitted, in any form or by any means, electronic, mechanical, photocopying, recording, or otherwise, without the prior written permission of the publisher. An exception is made for individual librarians and educators, who may make copies of activity sheets for classroom use in a single school. Other portions of the book (up to 15 pages) may be copied for in-service programs or other educational programs in a single school or library. Standard citation should appear on each page.

TEACHER IDEAS PRESS
Libraries Unlimited
A Division of Greenwood Publishing Group, Inc.
7730 E. Belleview Ave., Suite A200
Greenwood Village, CO 80111
1-800-237-6124
www.lu.com/tip

Library of Congress Cataloging-in-Publication Data

Stansfield, John, 1947-
    Writers of the American West : multicultural learning encounters / John Stansfield.
      p. cm.
    Includes bibliographical references and index.
    ISBN 1-56308-801-0
      1. American literature--West (U.S.)--Study and teaching. 2. American literature--West (U.S.)--Activity programs. 3. West (U.S.)--In literature--Study and teaching. 4. West (U.S.)--In literature--Activity programs. 5. Authors, American--West (U.S.)--Biography. 6. Multicultural education--Activity programs. I. Title.

PS271 .S73 2002
810.9'978'071--dc21

2001050561

CREDITS

We gratefully acknowledge the following authors, illustrators, and publishers for use of their work in *Writers of the American West*:

Indian Boyhood by Charles A. Eastman, courtesy of Dover Publications, Inc.

American Indian Stories and *Old Indian Legends* by Zitkala-Ša, courtesy of the University of Nebraska Press, publisher.

High, Wide and Lonesome by Hal Borland, reprinted by permission of Frances Collin, Literary Agent. Copyright © 1956 by Hal Borland. Copyright © renewed 1984 by Barbara Dodge Borland.

A Bloomer Girl on Pike's Peak 1858, used by permission of the Denver Public Library, Western History Collection.

Text and illustrations reprinted from *Man of the Family* by Ralph Moody by permission of University of Nebraska Press. Copyright 1951 by Ralph Moody. Copyright renewal © 1979 by Ralph Moody.

The Story of My Boyhood and Youth by John Muir, reprinted by permission of Sierra Club Books.

Text excerpted from *Two in the Far North*, text by Margaret E. Murie, copyright 1997, with permission of Alaska Northwest Books, an Imprint of Graphic Arts Center Publishing Company.

A Girl from Yamhill, copyright © 1988 by Beverly Cleary. Used by permission of HarperCollins Publishers.

Quotation. Copyright © 1990 by Scholastic, Inc. from *A Fire in My Hands* by Gary Soto, used by permission.

"Fear" copyright © 1985 by Gary Soto from the book *Living up the Street* (Dell, 1992), used by permission of the author.

Excerpt. Reprinted with the permission of Simon & Schuster Books for Young Readers, an imprint of Simon & Schuster Children's Publishing Division from *The Lost Garden* by Laurence Yep. Copyright © 1991 Laurence Yep.

DEDICATION

This book is dedicated to:

    John and Sally Stansfield, my parents, who brought me West and share it with me still.

    Carol Wood Stansfield, my wife and partner in exploring the West and its literature.

    The writers of the West who make the effort to re-create the times and places of their childhoods.

    The teachers and students who make the effort to learn from the incomparable geographic and cultural landscapes of western North America.

CONTENTS

ACKNOWLEDGMENTS xiii

INTRODUCTION xv

A USER'S GUIDE TO *WRITERS OF THE AMERICAN WEST* xvii

STORYTELLERS

CHARLES A. EASTMAN (OHIYESA) 3
   An Appreciation of the Writer 3
   In His Own Words 4
   The Writer's Life 9
      Hakadah, the Pitiful Last 9
      Ohiyesa, the Winner 10
      Charles Alexander Eastman 10
      Man of Medicine 11
      The Name Giver 11
      Man of Letters 12
   Teaching Advice for Charles A. Eastman (Ohiyesa) 12
      Autobiographical Writings 12
      Age Appropriateness 12
      Elaine Goodale Eastman, Literary Collaborator 13
      Lakota, Dakota, Nakota? 13
      Native American, American Indian, First People? 13
      Ohiyesa and Zitkala-Ša 13
   Learning Horizons 14
      Literature Aloud Experiences 14
      Language Arts Experiences 16
      Social Studies Experiences 17
   Charles A. Eastman Resources 23
      Selected Eastman Books 23
      Eastman Biographies 23
      Electronic Sources 23

ZITKALA-ŠA (GERTRUDE SIMMONS BONNIN) ... 24
An Appreciation of the Writer ... 24
In Her Own Words ... 25
The Writer's Life ... 33
    A Time of Upheaval ... 33
    Caught Between Two Worlds ... 33
    Creative Self-Expression ... 34
    A Life of Purpose ... 35
Teaching Advice for Zitkala-Ša ... 35
    Autobiographical Writings ... 35
    Age Appropriateness ... 35
    Meeting the Devil ... 36
    Lakota, Dakota, Nakota? ... 36
    Native American, American Indian, First People? ... 36
    Zitkala-Ša and Ohiyesa ... 36
Learning Horizons ... 37
    Literature Aloud Experiences ... 37
    Language Arts Experiences ... 39
    Social Studies Experiences ... 42
Zitkala-Ša Resources ... 45
    Zitkala-Ša Books ... 45
    Selected Zitkala-Ša Educational Materials ... 45
    Electronic Resources ... 45

PIONEERING YOUNG PEOPLE

HAL BORLAND ... 49
An Appreciation of the Writer ... 49
In His Own Words ... 52
The Writer's Life ... 54
    The Homestead ... 55
    The Prairie Town ... 57
Teaching Advice for Hal Borland ... 58
    Autobiographical Writings ... 58
    Age Appropriateness ... 58
    Borland and Moody ... 58
    Touchy Terminology ... 58
    Out of Print ... 59
Learning Horizons ... 59
    Literature Aloud Experiences ... 59
    Language Arts Experiences ... 61
    Social Studies Experiences ... 62
    Multidisciplinary Language Arts and Social Studies Experiences ... 64
Hal Borland Resources ... 69
    Selected Borland Books ... 69
    Audio Resources ... 69

JULIA ARCHIBALD HOLMES ... 70
- An Appreciation of the Writer ... 70
- In Her Own Words ... 71
- The Writer's Life ... 84
  - Kansas Emigrants ... 84
  - Headed West ... 85
  - Headed East ... 87
- Teaching Advice for Julia Archibald Holmes ... 88
  - Autobiographical Writings ... 88
  - Age Appropriateness ... 88
  - Women's Rights Then and Now ... 89
  - Notable Names ... 89
  - Slavery ... 89
  - Touchy Terminology ... 89
- Learning Horizons ... 90
  - Literature Aloud Experiences ... 90
  - Language Arts Experiences ... 92
  - Social Studies Experiences ... 95
- Julia Archibald Holmes Resources ... 101
  - Selected Holmes Biographies ... 101
  - Audio Resources ... 101
  - Electronic Resources ... 102

RALPH MOODY ... 103
- An Appreciation of the Writer ... 103
- In His Own Words ... 104
- The Writer's Life ... 108
  - Little Britches: Father and I Were Ranchers ... 108
  - Man of the Family ... 109
  - The Home Ranch ... 110
  - Mary Emma and Company ... 111
  - The Fields of Home ... 111
- Teaching Advice for Ralph Moody ... 113
  - Autobiographical Writings ... 113
  - Age Appropriateness ... 113
  - Literary License ... 113
  - Borland and Moody ... 113
  - Touchy Terminology ... 113
- Learning Horizons ... 114
  - Literature Aloud Experiences ... 114
  - Language Arts Experiences ... 116
  - Social Studies Experiences ... 120
- Ralph Moody Resources ... 122
  - Selected Books by Moody ... 122
  - Electronic Resources ... 122
  - Rodeo Resources—Text ... 122
  - Rodeo Resources—Electronic ... 123

YOUNG NATURALISTS

JOHN MUIR 127
   An Appreciation of the Writer 127
   In His Own Words 129
   The Writer's Life 133
      Scotland 133
      Wisconsin 134
      The World 136
   Teaching Advice for John Muir 137
      Autobiographical Writings 137
      Age Appropriateness 137
      Muir's Spirituality 137
      Scotland and Wisconsin, Western? 137
   Learning Horizons 138
      Literature Aloud Experiences 138
      Language Arts Experiences 140
      Social Studies Experiences 144
   John Muir Resources 147
      Selected Books by Muir 147
      Selected Muir Resources 147
      Electronic Resources 148
      Video Resources 149
      Audio Resources 149

MARGARET MURIE 151
   An Appreciation of the Writer 151
   In Her Own Words 152
   The Writer's Life 157
      Up to Alaska 157
      Travels Together 158
      Wyoming and the Nation 159
   Teaching Advice for Margaret Murie 160
      Autobiographical Writings 160
      Age Appropriateness 160
      Touchy Terminology 161
   Learning Horizons 161
      Literature Aloud Experiences 161
      Language Arts Experiences 162
      Social Studies Experiences 168
   Margaret Murie Resources 171
      Selected Books by Murie 171
      Selected Murie Biographies and Resources 171
      Electronic Resources 171
      Video Resources 172

WRITERS OF THE NEW WEST

BEVERLY CLEARY 175
   An Appreciation of the Writer 175
   In Her Own Words 178
   The Writer's Life 181
      Yamhill 181
      Portland 181
      High School 182
      College and Career 183
   Teaching Advice for Beverly Cleary 184
      Age Appropriateness 184
      Touchy Terminology 184
   Learning Horizons 184
      Literature Aloud Experiences 184
      Language Arts Experiences 186
      Social Studies Experiences 190
   Beverly Cleary Resources 195
      Selected Books by Cleary 195
      Selected Cleary Biographies and Resources 195
      Electronic Resources 195

GARY SOTO 197
   An Appreciation of the Writer 197
   In His Own Words 198
   The Writer's Life 201
      Growing Things 201
      Growing Up 202
      Growing in New Directions 203
   Teaching Advice for Gary Soto 204
      Autobiographical Writings 204
      Age Appropriateness 205
      Touchy Terminology 205
      Mexican, Chicano, Latino? 205
   Learning Horizons 206
      Literature Aloud Experiences 206
      Language Arts Experiences 208
      Social Studies Experiences 212
   Gary Soto Resources 215
      Selected Books by Soto 215
      Electronic Resources 215
      Video Resources 216

LAURENCE YEP 217
An Appreciation of the Writer 217
In His Own Words 218
The Writer's Life 220
Living over the Store 220
Puzzle Solver 221
Teaching Advice for Laurence Yep 223
Autobiographical Writings 223
Touchy Terminology 223
Yep on His Writing and the Writing Process 223
Learning Horizons 224
Literature Aloud Experiences 224
Language Arts Experiences 225
Social Studies Experiences 228
Laurence Yep Resources 231
Selected Books by Yep 231
Selected Yep Resources 232
Electronic Resources 232
Video Resources 232

ADDITIONAL READINGS AND LEARNING EXPERIENCES IN THE AUTOBIOGRAPHIES OF WESTERN WRITERS 233

APPENDIX 249
Topographic Map Symbols 249
Meters–Feet Conversion Table 250

AUTHOR/TITLE INDEX 251

SUBJECT INDEX 255

ABOUT THE AUTHOR 261

ACKNOWLEDGMENTS

Writing a book is like undertaking a long journey on foot. Along the way, there are many steps, many ideas, many stops and starts, and many words, pages, and chapters to the story before the end is reached. Sometimes the going gets tough. But when the going gets easy, it is usually because someone is there to offer help. Among the many people who provided assistance with this book, I especially want to recognize:

> Gladys Bueler and Stephen Trimble, for guidance in author selection.
>
> Kendall Haven, for writing process strategies.
>
> Mark Madison, U.S. Fish and Wildlife Service; Lorena Donohue, Littleton Historical Museum; and Lori Swingle and staff, Denver Public Library Western History Department, for assistance with research and graphics.
>
> Jean C. Smith, for much technical support with graphics.
>
> Esther Acosta, for her insight on culture and language.
>
> Paula Campbell, for a thorough background in Six-Trait Writing.
>
> Clay Jenkinson, for his perspective on western exploration and Lewis and Clark.
>
> Gary Soto, for manuscript guidance and professional respect.
>
> Jerry Flack and Norma Livo, two remarkable writers, mentors, and role models.
>
> Carol Wood Stansfield, for long-term support and naturalist information, as well as countless helpful reviews and discussions.

INTRODUCTION

THE WESTERN CRAZY QUILT

To say that the North American West of Canada, the United States, and northern Mexico is remarkable is an understatement as big as the land itself. There exists no other region remotely like it on earth. The West presents astounding geology, including numerous mountain ranges, the Grand Canyon and other fantastic canyons on the region's rivers, and some of the world's highest and lowest terrain. Its natural communities are diverse, from Arctic tundra to tall prairie grass, from rainforest to desert. Some of these ecosystems still function primarily by nature's rules, a rarity and treasure in a world of increasing human population and development. The human cultures of the West span more than 25,000 years and reflect both the bounty and the scarcity of its natural resources.

It is not surprising that so spectacular, extreme, and diverse a landscape as western North America would uniquely shape the lives of its human inhabitants, including children. In his groundbreaking book, *Growing up with the Country: Children on the Far Western Frontier* (Albuquerque: University of New Mexico Press, 1989), historian Elliott West argues that an understanding of the lives of western young people, though often overlooked, is critical to a full understanding of the region. He describes how western landscape and culture molded nineteenth-century children of the region in different ways than their brothers and sisters in other parts of the world. It is not that western children are inherently unusual. What makes their life experience and perspective different from other children, West claims, is facing the region's distinctive challenges and opportunities. This quality is certainly evident in the childhood autobiographies of the writers featured in this book.

If a complete story of the North American West could ever be written, it would be like a crazy quilt composed of millions of unique pieces assembled on a gigantic landscape. Each piece is a person, a special place, or a living thing that adds to the ancient and ongoing story. As with a crazy quilt, some pieces are larger, more finely colored, or more elaborately textured than others. Perhaps these pieces represent the writers, the autobiographers, the personal storytellers. Their pieces contribute more significantly to the quilt because the writers take time and care to add the detail of their remembrances.

MOTIVATED BY AUTOBIOGRAPHY

Teaching students about the value of primary sources has never been more important. *Writers of the American West* uses primary sources (i.e., autobiography) and, specifically, youthful recollections, as a touchstone to stimulate student involvement in oral expression, language arts, and social studies. Educators, parents, and writers know that children like to read and learn about people their own age. For that reason, this book features 10 authors who have written about their childhood and young adult lives in the western United States and Canada. Their selection for this book is based on three factors:

- They spent at least part of their growing years in western North America.
- They created autobiographies of their youths in a style and content generally appropriate for young people.
- With one exception, they wrote other works of fiction or nonfiction that provide students with further opportunities for reading and learning.

Each chapter of this book presents autobiographical excerpts, learning experiences, and author biographies and media resources designed to stimulate student exploration and discovery about the writers and their world. Skills of oral expression and memory are highlighted in the Literature Aloud Experiences. Reading, writing, and speaking skills are especially emphasized in the language arts activities. The social studies activities focus on geography, speaking, and multimedia reporting skills. The Young Naturalists section can be integrated into the curriculum for science.

Educational research bears out that some of the most effective learning takes place when students become actively involved. In many of the learning experiences in this book, students participate in real-life situations with measurable, observable outcomes.

The intent of *Writers of the American West* is that young people and their teachers, whether they live in the West or not, come to better understand and respect the land, people, and history of western North America. I hope that everyone, especially the young people, will add notable pieces of their own life stories to the pattern of the western quilt.

A USER'S GUIDE TO WRITERS OF THE AMERICAN WEST

In chapter 8 you will find a learning experience based on seven questions—what?, who?, whom?, where?, when?, why?, and how?—answered by successful writers in preparation for writing. As you prepare to use this book, it is only fair to give you my answers for the same seven questions.

What is the book's purpose? To engage students and assist educators in exploring the lives and works of notable people who share valuable stories of childhood and young adult experience in western North America.

Who is the intended audience for this book? Educators, in the broadest sense of the word: classroom and resource teachers, school and public librarians, historical and environmental interpreters, leaders of community youth groups, and, last but definitely not least, parents—both those who homeschool their children and those who do not.

With whom is the book best used? Young people, especially those from age nine to fourteen, in fourth to eighth grades. In addition, much of the text is appropriate for slightly younger, gifted children and older students of all ability levels.

Where can the book be used? Anywhere in the world, not just the West, including school classrooms and libraries, homes, public libraries, nature centers and parks, youth group meetings, historical sites, indoors, outdoors, and wherever creativity leads you.

When can this book be used? Anytime. It is not a curriculum, but is designed to supplement learning in literature, oral expression, language arts, and social studies.

Why use this book? Because the autobiographies of Western writers are exceptional teaching tools in themselves and are pathways for student exploration and discovery of the North American West, which is a living classroom and one of the most remarkable regions of the world.

How Do I Use This Book? Here is the whole picture in one paragraph:

Writers of the American West is organized into four topical sections: **STORYTELLERS, PIONEERING YOUNG PEOPLE, YOUNG NATURALISTS**, and **WRITERS OF THE NEW WEST**. Sections are arranged chronologically. Each is prefaced with brief commentary about the featured authors and educational applications of their writings. Within each section, chapters explore the lives of two or three writers and their autobiographical works of childhood experience.

Each chapter contains the following divisions:

- **An Appreciation of the Writer** introduces the subject of each chapter in his or her role as writer, including details about their writing process, literary accomplishments, and awards. (*This division is intended for use by teachers and students.*)

- **In His/Her Own Words** presents an excerpt from the featured writer's autobiography. Sometimes activities from **Learning Horizons** segments relate to the excerpt. (*This division is intended for use by teachers and students.*)

- **The Writer's Life** is a biographical sketch of the author, often focused on his or her childhood and adolescence. In most cases, it is a "nutshell" version of the life recounted at length in the author's work. (*This division is intended for use by teachers and students.*)

- **Teaching Advice** offers information designed to help educators prepare to teach about each writer. This background information includes: *Autobiographical Writings*, a review of the author's personal writings; *Age Appropriateness*, suggestions for what ages might benefit from reading and listening to the autobiographies; *Touchy Terminology*, an alert to profanity or mature content in the autobiographical text, which may require preliminary review by the teacher, as well as possible explanation to students; and, other topics pertinent to each writer. (*This division is intended as preparatory information for teachers.*)

- **Learning Horizons** contains student educational activities based on the writers' lives and works. The variety of learning experiences results from the fact that they are based on the diverse lives and works of the featured writers. Three types are presented here:

    Literature Aloud Experiences involve students and teachers in oral expression—public speaking, storytelling, reading aloud, poetry recitation, historical reenactment, readers theater—and in performance events to showcase the art forms for audiences.

    Language Arts Experiences focus on the connections between reading, speaking, and writing.

    Social Studies Experiences explore the cultural, historical, geographic, and political contexts in which the featured authors lived, as well as those of the students.

Each learning experience is written as a guide for teachers, in preparation for implementing it with students. Educators are encouraged to adapt or augment the activities to meet the needs of their particular students or the urges of their own creativity. Many of the experiences are presented in reproducible format so they can be used easily in the classroom.

Each learning experience comprises the following parts:

Title

Level: Indicates the grade levels suggested as appropriate for the experience.

Student Learning Opportunities: This section lists concepts, skills (including Six-Trait Writing techniques), and tasks students use in each activity from which teachers can develop their own objectives or anticipated outcomes, as necessary in planning. These components are linked to **Teacher Evaluation Opportunities**, below.

Background: Provides basic information that teachers, and often students, need at the outset of the learning experience.

Basics: Presents a list of the numbered steps necessary to accomplish the fundamental purpose of the learning experience.

Extensions: Offer additional activities related to the learning experience. Some directly continue the concept(s) established in **Basics**, while others are supplementary.

Teacher Evaluation Opportunities: Suggest elements of the learning experience appropriate for formal or informal evaluation. Teachers should feel free to add to or subtract their own elements for evaluation from the list, based on educational standards, grading system, personal preference, or other criteria.

The **Resources** division, at the end of each chapter, is a selected and annotated bibliography of book, audio, video, and Internet materials appropriate for use by teachers and students.

A NOTE ABOUT SIX-TRAIT WRITING

In the **Student Learning Opportunities** and **Teacher Evaluation Opportunities** segments of many learning experiences, you will find reference to Six-Trait Writing. This common-sense model of writing instruction and assessment was developed in recent years by educators, including Vicki Spandel and others, at the Northwest Regional Educational Laboratory (NWREL) in Portland, Oregon.

Many teachers throughout North America now incorporate Six-Trait Writing in their classroom writing programs because it is a comprehensive, well-organized system, which applies to writing in any subject area and produces excellent student results. What are the six traits? They are universal building blocks of effective composition:

1. **Ideas**, which motivate writing that is clear in theme and content, as well as original, interesting, and convincing.

2. **Organization**, which structures writing from an inviting beginning through a logical sequence of events, assertions, or information to a well-defined conclusion.

3. **Voice**, which expresses the unique point of view of the writer and elicits a meaningful response from the reader.

4. **Word choice**, which involves selection of language that is vivid, direct, and well-chosen to match the content of the writing.

5. **Sentence fluency**, which uses a variety of sentence beginnings, as well as simple and complex sentence structures. A good test of a sentence that flows is that it reads well aloud.

6. **Conventions**, which apply correct writing mechanics through capitalization, punctuation, paragraphing and headings, spelling, grammar, and word use. Proofreading and editing (revision) are the tasks that reinforce conventions.

Recently, the folks at NWREL added another trait to the list: **presentation**. This is how written text appears on the page, a trait that includes handwriting and spatial organization. All together, these traits work well when applied to all of the following five forms of prose writing. (A handy acronym for the prose writing forms is, appropriately enough, I 'D PEN.)

- **Imaginative**—developing new, original characters, situations, and viewpoints; also called creative writing.
- **Descriptive**—creating believable images, imaginary or real, for the reader with words
- **Persuasive**—stating an effective argument through logic, evidence, and passion.
- **Expository**—writing that explains, "exposing" the reader to new information.
- **Narrative**—telling a story, fact or fiction, that presents conflict and somehow resolves it.

An excellent guide to the trait-based writing model is *Creating Writers Through 6-Trait Writing Assessment and Instruction* by Vicki Spandel (3d ed. New York: Longman, 2000). Further information can be found at the Northwest Regional Educational Laboratory Web site: http://www.nwrel.org/eval/writing/ (Accessed January 10, 2001).

FOR SPEAKING OR TELLING, READING, RECITING, SINGING (TAKE YOUR PICK) ALOUD

The educational activities in this book encourage many types of verbal expression. This is partly because the author is more than 20 years a professional storyteller. But, beyond that, these verbal ventures, generically called oral expression or oral language experiences, hold great benefit for adults and, especially, for young people. They help build verbal skills, memory, creativity, self-confidence, and self-esteem. They are also a lot of fun.

Acquiring oral language (oral literacy) early in life is fundamental to the later development of visual language skills—reading, writing, mathematics, and other symbol-based languages. Consider the research on the connections between oral literacy and visual literacy. In the "old days," hundreds or thousands of years ago, educators understood this connection. What do we do today, however, when kids are in school, especially the upper grades? We "forget to save a dance for the one that brung ya." We often ignore the powerful learning pathways that involve listening, speaking, and memory, in favor of educational strategies dominated by visual literacy. Our young people need all of the literacy skills they can master—including oral literacy. In our early years and throughout our lives, we all need a well-balanced diet of both visual and oral skills to be educationally well-nourished. (I will now step down from my soapbox.)

READER COMMENTS

A book does not have to be a one-way street, going only from writer to reader. As an educator (and, therefore, a lifelong learner), I will benefit greatly from any thoughtful evaluation of the contents of this book. It would be helpful to know what you and your students find most or least useful, what you like or do not like, what you would add or subtract. Contact me with comments, queries, fights, doubts, confusions, or what have you, at P.O. Box 588, Monument, CO 80132. In the spirit of our West, best wishes to you all!

STORYTELLERS

Charles A. Eastman (Ohiyesa)
Zitkala-Ša (Gertrude Simmons Bonnin)

Young people raised in primarily oral cultures experience distinctly different forms of education than those raised with written traditions. Oral literacy emphasizes learning through speaking, listening, and remembering. The more modern visual literacy features learning through reading and writing symbols. Both forms of literacy teach effectively. Oral forms of education rely on cultural and individual memory to store and transmit vast quantities of information. Story and storytelling are fundamental. Visual forms, which dominate contemporary education, are often less personal than oral forms and depend on books and electronic media.

The two individuals featured in this segment, Charles A. Eastman (Ohiyesa) and Zitkala-Ša (Gertrude Simmons Bonnin), both Lakota, were children of the oral tradition and became adept storytellers. By extensive effort on their parts, they also mastered visual literacy as they grew older. However, neither Eastman nor Zitkala-Ša forgot the value of their early oral education. Later in their lives, they worked diligently to transmit to the outside world, in writing, factual and fictional stories from the oral tradition.

In describing the forms of early education he received, Charles Eastman says, in *Indian Boyhood*, "This sort of teaching at once enlightens the boy's mind and stimulates his ambition." These are worthwhile ends for the education of any boy or girl, anywhere. What characterizes the "sort of teaching" to which he refers? Most important is the oral sharing of story, which immerses children in story listening and storytelling from an early age.

Through the medium of story, personal experience, imaginary creation, cultural values, ethics, history, mythology, and more pass between generations.

Eastman lists other attributes of effective education, as well:

- ◈ Fostering deep understanding of and respect for nature.
- ◈ Training in strength, stoicism, patience, survival skills, and respect for elders.
- ◈ Constant sharpening of childrens' powers of observation and decision-making.
- ◈ Providing opportunities for children to learn by experience, often by trial and error.

No matter the forms of education through which children learn, these attributes are as important today as they were for Eastman and Zitkala-Ša. The readings and **Learning Horizons** divisions of the chapters in **Storytellers** strive to blend oral and visual forms of literacy, often with physical experiences, offering teachers and students a variety of learning formats.

CHARLES A. EASTMAN (OHIYESA)

Born in 1858 near Redwood Falls, Minnesota. Died January 8, 1939 in Detroit, Michigan. Childhood and young adult autobiography describes Minnesota, Manitoba, Saskatchewan, North Dakota, and South Dakota.

Figure 1.1. Charles A. Eastman (Ohiyesa).

AN APPRECIATION OF THE WRITER

Very early the Indian boy assumed the task of preserving and transmitting the legends of his ancestors and his race. Almost every evening a myth, or a true story of some deed done in the past, was narrated by one of the parents or grandparents, while the boy listened with parted lips and glistening eyes. On the following evening, he was usually required to repeat it.

—Charles A. Eastman from *Indian Boyhood*, chapter 2, "An Indian Boy's Training."

~~~

As his names imply, Charles Alexander Eastman (Ohiyesa) was a man who lived in two worlds. Until the age of 15 he lived in the traditional lifestyle of the Dakota. (Also called Santee or Eastern Sioux. Dakota is a division of the Lakota, or Sioux tribe.) Thereafter, Eastman lived amidst the cultural diversity and rapid change of nineteenth- and twentieth-century American society. Building bridges between cultures often means being run over. His accomplishments in two such startlingly different worlds are a testament to his strength, adaptability, and intelligence. His writings create a legacy for all Americans.

In all, Eastman wrote 11 books. Taken together with his many articles and speeches, they represent his desire to educate an often unknowing and uncaring world in two particular areas. Eastman's writings focus on Native American cultures and individuals and on the sacredness and bounty of the natural world.

Eastman's two autobiographies reflect the distinct phases of his life. *Indian Boyhood* presents recollections of his "thrilling wild life," growing up in the nomadic, hunter–warrior culture of the Dakota. *From the Deep Woods to Civilization: Chapters in the Autobiography of an Indian* continues with the story of Eastman's schooling and his professional life in medicine, education, and public affairs, as well as elements of his personal and family life. His collections of stories, *Wigwam Evenings: Sioux Folk Tales Retold*, co-written with his wife Elaine Goodale Eastman, and *Old Indian Days*, are interesting for their traditional Lakota tales and for the pictures of the people's life and culture that they portray. Had someone other than Eastman written his *Indian Heroes and Great Chieftains*, which provides biographies of Native American leaders, Eastman would undoubtedly have been included, given all that he accomplished in his long life.

IN HIS OWN WORDS

The skills of storytelling were some of the most significant gifts given Ohiyesa in his boyhood. Until the age of 15, the oral stories of his family and people were the "textbooks" from which he studied. In this chapter from *Indian Boyhood*, Eastman re-creates one of the traditional stories heard in his youth. Note that he presents the all-important cultural context of the storytelling, as well as the story itself. Key elements of this context include: the season of the year and time of day of the telling; the child successfully recounting a traditional tale; the elder's role as storyteller; and appropriate story listening etiquette.

NOTE: *The following is excerpted as punctuated and spelled in the original manuscript.*

Manitoshaw's Hunting

It was in the winter, in the Moon of Difficulty (January). We had eaten our venison roast for supper, and the embers were burning brightly. Our teepee was especially cheerful. Uncheedah sat near the entrance, my uncle and his wife upon the opposite side, while I with my pets occupied the remaining space.

Wabeda, the dog, lay near the fire in a half doze, watching out of the corners of his eyes the tame raccoon, which snuggled back against the walls of the teepee, his shrewd brain, doubtless, concocting some mischief for the hours of darkness. I had already recited a legend of our people. All agreed that I had done well. Having been generously praised, I was eager to earn some more compliments by learning a new one, so I begged my uncle to tell me a story. Musingly he replied:

"I can give you a Sioux-Cree tradition," and immediately began:

"Many winters ago, there were six teepees standing on the southern slope of Moose Mountain in the Moon of the Wild Cherries (September). The men to whom these teepees belonged had been attacked by the Sioux while hunting buffalo, and nearly all killed. Two or three who managed to get home to tell their sad story were mortally wounded, and died soon afterward. There was only one old man and several small boys left to hunt and provide for this unfortunate little band of women and children.

"They lived upon teepsinna (wild turnips) and berries for many days. They were almost famished for meat. The old man was too feeble to hunt successfully. One day in this desolate camp a young Cree maiden—for such they were—declared that she could no longer sit still and see her people suffer. She took down her dead father's second bow and quiver full of arrows, and begged her old grandmother to accompany her to Lake Wanagiska, where she knew that moose had often been found. I forgot to tell you that her name was Manitoshaw.

"This Manitoshaw and her old grandmother, Nawakewee, took each a pony and went far up into the woods on the side of the mountain. They pitched their wigwam just out of sight of the lake, and hobbled their ponies. Then the old woman said to Manitoshaw:

" 'Go, my granddaughter, to the outlet of the Wanagiska, and see if there are any moose tracks there. When I was a young woman, I came here with your father's father, and we pitched our tent near this spot. In the night there came three different moose. Bring me leaves of the birch and cedar twigs; I will make medicine for moose,' she added.

"Manitoshaw obediently disappeared in the woods. It was a grove of birch and willow, with two good springs. Down below was a marshy place. Nawakewee had bidden the maiden look for nibbled birch and willow twigs, for the moose loves to eat them, and to have her arrow ready upon the bow-string. I have seen this very place many a time," added my uncle, and this simple remark gave to the story an air of reality.

"The Cree maiden went first to the spring, and there found fresh tracks of the animal she sought. She gathered some cedar berries and chewed them, and rubbed some of them on her garments so that the moose might not scent her. The sun was already to set, and she felt she must return to Nawakewee.

"Just then Hinhankaga, the hooting owl, gave his doleful night call. The girl stopped and listened attentively.

" 'I thought it was a lover's call,' she whispered to herself. A singular challenge pealed across the lake. She recognized the alarm call of the loon, and fancied that the bird might have caught a glimpse of her game.

"Soon she was within a few paces of the temporary lodge of pine boughs and ferns which the grandmother had constructed. The old woman met her on the trail.

" 'Ah, my child, you have returned none too soon. I feared you had ventured too far away; for the Sioux often come to this place to hunt. You must not expose yourself carelessly on the shore.'

"As the two women lay down to sleep they could hear the ponies munch the rich grass in an open spot near by. Through the smoke hole of the pine bough wigwam Manitoshaw gazed up into the starry sky, and dreamed of what she would do on the morrow when she would surprise the wily moose. Her grandmother was already sleeping so noisily that it was enough to scare away the game. At last the maiden, too, lost herself in sleep.

"Old Nawakewee awoke early. First of all she made a fire and burned cedar and birch so that the moose might not detect the human smell. Then she quickly prepared a meal of wild turnips and berries, and awoke the maiden, who was surprised to see that the sun was already up. She ran down to the spring and hastily splashed handsful of the cold water in her face; then she looked for a moment in its mirror-like surface. There was the reflection of two moose by the open shore and beyond them Manitoshaw seemed to see a young man standing. In another moment all three had disappeared.

" 'What is the matter with my eyes? I am not fully awake yet, and I imagine things. Ugh, it is all in my eyes,' the maiden repeated to herself. She hastened back to Nawakewee. The vision was so unexpected and so startling that she could not believe in its truth, and she said nothing to the old woman.

"Breakfast eaten, Manitoshaw threw off her robe and appeared in her scantily cut gown of buckskin with long fringes, and moccasins and leggings trimmed with quills of the porcupine. Her father's bow and quiver were thrown over one shoulder, and the knife dangled from her belt in its handsome sheath. She ran breathlessly along the shore toward the outlet.

"Way off toward an island Medoza, the loon, swam with his mate, occasionally uttering a cry of joy. Here and there the playful Hogan, the trout, sprang gracefully out of the water, in a shower of falling dew. As the maiden hastened along she scared up Wadawasee, the kingfisher, who screamed loudly.

" 'Stop, Wadawasee, stop—you will frighten my game!'

"At last she had reached the outlet. She saw at once that the moose had been there during the night. They had torn up the ground and broken birch and willow twigs in a most disorderly way."

" 'Ah!' I exclaimed, 'I wish I had been with Manitoshaw then!'

" 'Hush, my boy; never interrupt a storyteller.'

"I took a stick and began to level off the ashes in front of me, and to draw a map of the lake, the outlet, the moose and Manitoshaw. Away off to one side was the solitary wigwam, Nawakewee and the ponies.

"Manitoshaw's heart was beating so loud that she could not hear anything," resumed my uncle. "She took some leaves of the wintergreen and chewed them to calm herself. She did not forget to throw in passing a pinch of pulverized tobacco and paint into the spring for Manitou, the spirit.

"Among the twinkling leaves of the birch her eye was caught by a moving form, and then another. She stood motionless, grasping her heavy bow. The moose, not suspecting any danger, walked leisurely toward the spring. One was a large female moose; the other a yearling.

"As they passed Manitoshaw, moving so naturally and looking so harmless, she almost forgot to let fly an arrow. The mother moose seemed to look in her direction, but did not see her. They had fairly passed her hiding-place when she stepped forth and sent a swift arrow into the side of the larger moose. Both dashed into the thick woods, but it was too late. The Cree maiden had already loosened her second arrow. Both fell dead before reaching the shore."

" 'Uncle, she must have had a splendid aim, for in the woods the many twigs make an arrow bound off to one side,' I interrupted in great excitement.

" 'Yes, but you must remember she was very near the moose.'

" 'It seems to me, then, uncle, that they must have scented her, for you have told me that they possess the keenest nose of any animal,' I persisted.

" 'Doubtless the wind was blowing the other way. But, nephew, you must let me finish my story.'

"Overjoyed by her success, the maiden hastened back to Nawakewee, but she was gone! The ponies were gone, too, and the wigwam of branches had been demolished. While Manitoshaw stood there, frightened and undecided what to do, a soft voice came from behind a neighboring thicket:

" 'Manitoshaw! Manitoshaw! I am here!'

"She at once recognized the voice and found it to be Nawakeewee, who told a strange story. That morning a canoe had crossed the Wanagiska carrying two men. They were Sioux. The old grandmother had seen them coming, and to deceive them she had pulled down her temporary wigwam, and drove the ponies off toward home. Then she hid herself in the bushes near by, for she knew that Manitoshaw must return there.

" 'Come, my granddaughter, we must hasten home by another way,' cried the old woman.

"But the maiden said, 'No, let us go first to my two moose that I killed this morning and take some meat with us.'

" 'No, no, my child; the Sioux are cruel. They have killed many of our people. If we stay here they will find us. I fear, I fear them, Manitoshaw!'

"At last the brave maid convinced her grandmother, and the more easily as she, too, was hungry for meat. They went to where the big game lay among the bushes, and began to dress the moose."

" 'I think, if I were them, I would hide all day. I would wait until the Sioux had gone; then I would go back to my moose,' I interrupted for the third time.

" 'I will finish the story first; then you may tell us what you would do,' said my uncle reprovingly.

"The two Sioux were father and son. They had come to the lake for moose; but as the game usually retreated to the island, Chatansapa had landed his son, Kangiska, to hunt them on the shore while he returned in his canoe to intercept their flight. The young man sped along the sandy beach and soon discovered their tracks. He followed them up and found blood on the trail. This astonished him. Cautiously he followed on until he found them both lying dead. He examined them and found that in each moose there was a single Cree arrow. Wishing to surprise the hunter if possible, Kangiska lay hidden in the bushes.

"After a little while the two women returned to the spot. They passed him as close as the moose had passed the maiden in the morning. He saw at once that the maiden had arrows in her quiver like those that had slain the big moose. He lay still.

Figure 1.2. The Courtship of Manitoshaw.
Illus. by E. L. Blumenschein.

"Kangiska looked upon the beautiful Cree maiden and loved her. Finally he forgot himself and made a slight motion. Manitoshaw's quick eye caught the little stir among the bushes, but she immediately looked the other way and Kangiska believed that she had not seen anything. At last her eyes met his, and something told both that all was well. Then the maiden smiled, and the young man could not remain still any longer. He arose suddenly and the old woman nearly fainted from fright. But Manitoshaw said:

" 'Fear not, grandmother; we are two and he is only one.'

"While the two women continued to cut up the meat, Kangiska made a fire by rubbing cedar chips together, and they all ate of the moose meat. Then the old woman finished her work, while the young people sat down upon a log in the shade, and told each other all their minds.

"Kangiska declared by signs that he would go home with Manitoshaw to the Cree camp, for he loved her. They went home, and the young man hunted for the unfortunate Cree band during the rest of his life.

"His father waited a long time on the island and afterwards searched the shore, but never saw him again. He supposed that those footprints he saw were made by Crees who had killed his son."

" 'Is that story true, uncle?' I asked eagerly.

" 'Yes, the facts are well known. There are some Sioux mixed bloods among the Crees to this day who are descendants of Kangiska.'

End of excerpted manuscript.

THE WRITER'S LIFE

Hakadah, the Pitiful Last

Hakadah, the Pitiful Last was the name given the child at his birth on a Dakota reservation, near Redwood Falls, Minnesota, in 1858. His plight was pitiful, in part, because his mother died within days of his birth. Hakadah was the last of four sons and a daughter born to Mary Nancy Eastman and Many Lightnings. Fortunately for Hakadah, Many Lightnings's mother, Uncheedah (grandmother), stepped forward to raise him.

Uncheedah was a notable person. As Eastman describes her in *Indian Boyhood*, she was "remarkably active for her age (she was then fully sixty), and possessed of as much goodness as intelligence." Uncheedah was small, but strong and very brave. She possessed great skills as a midwife, nature educator, and herbalist. Uncheedah had great hopes for her grandson. She once said, "I hope (Hakadah) will be a great medicine man when he grows up."

Ohiyesa, the Winner

Even as a toddler, Hakadah disliked his name. At age four, he served as mascot for his people, the Wahpetonwan (Dwellers Among the Leaves) Dakota, in a great lacrosse match. When they won, a medicine man gave him the name, Ohiyesa. This pleased the boy greatly. It is customary for Dakota to bear several different names during their lives.

In that same year, 1862, a few among the Dakota in Minnesota lashed out against ill-treatment and broken treaty promises by the U.S. government. Ultimately, hundreds, on both sides, died in the fighting that ensued. Separated from his father and two oldest brothers, Ohiyesa's family fled to Canada. More than 300 Santee were arrested and sentenced to hang. Though most were pardoned by President Lincoln, 38 were executed. Ohiyesa's family believed that Many Lightnings and his sons were among the dead.

The boys' uncle, Mysterious Medicine, then became the stepfather for Ohiyesa and his older brother Chatanna. Under the direction of his uncle and grandmother, Ohiyesa grew mentally, physically, and spiritually. He grew to be an ever-vigilant observer. He endeavored to live in harmony with the forests, plains, rivers, and, especially, the other animals in his environment. For the next 10 years, through both play and work, Ohiyesa developed the traditional skills of tracker, hunter, and warrior, needed by a Dakota man. The boy learned to have a great animosity toward the *Wasichu*, "the rich" white people, who took Dakota lands and the lives of his father and brothers. Then, in only one day's time, his life and perspective almost completely were changed.

Figure 1.3. Ohiyesa, right, and his brother Chatanna. Illus. by E. L. Blumenschein.

Charles Alexander Eastman

In September 1873, as Ohiyesa returned to his village in Canada from a solitary hunt, his uncle and an unknown man wearing white man's clothing approached him. Eastman asked:

"What does this mean, uncle?"

"My boy, this is your father, my brother, whom we mourned as dead. He has come for you."

My father added: "I am glad that my son is strong and brave. Your brothers have adopted the white man's way; I came for you to learn this new way, too; and I want you to grow up a good man."

Obediently—at first, uncomfortably—Ohiyesa donned clothes like his father's. He and his grandmother accompanied his father, now known as Jacob Eastman, to their homestead farm in

Flandreau, South Dakota. Jacob had converted to Christianity while in prison with his sons after the 1862 battles. After their release and a brief stay on a reservation, Jacob concluded that the traditional Dakota lifestyle was doomed. He believed his family must adapt to the agricultural way of life and the American culture that was rapidly converting the face of the West after the Civil War.

Jacob borrowed the name of Eastman from his wife's father, Seth. Seth Eastman, later a well-known artist, was a U.S. Army captain during the 1830s in Minnesota where he met and married Cloudman's daughter, a Santee Dakota. They had four sons and one daughter, Nancy Mary Eastman, Ohiyesa's mother. Before his Christian baptism, Ohiyesa received the name Charles Alexander Eastman.

Charles struggled to speak, read, and write in English. It was not easy to decide if the path his father had chosen was also right for him. With Jacob's guidance, Charles concluded that his skills as a warrior and hunter could be used to explore a new world—the world of knowledge.

Man of Medicine

Over the next 14 years, Eastman moved on the path of knowledge. It was often a difficult path. His second education began at the mission school in Flandreau and the Santee Normal School in Santee, Nebraska, where his brother, John, was a teacher. After attending Beloit College and Knox College, Charles graduated with honors in 1887 from Dartmouth College.

Fulfilling his grandmother's prophetic wish, Eastman received an M.D. degree from Boston University Medical School in 1890, and became one of the first Native American doctors. He was soon hired by the government as doctor for the Pine Ridge Agency on the Sioux Reservation in South Dakota. The job brought him among his people again and into the middle of an impending storm of violence.

Government Indian agents feared outbreaks of trouble among the Sioux, spawned by the newly popular Ghost Dance religion. They called the U.S. Cavalry to Pine Ridge. Sioux leader, Sitting Bull, and 13 others were killed in a dispute between his supporters and Indian police. On December 29, 1890, the Cavalry attempted to disarm Big Foot's band at Wounded Knee Creek. Fighting broke out. That morning, 153 Sioux men, women, and children were killed, with 44 wounded. Among the Cavalry, 25 soldiers died and 34 were wounded.

Eastman was the only doctor available for the wounded Sioux, few of whom survived. Massachusetts native Elaine Goodale worked beside Charles in his temporary clinic, the mission chapel. The 22-year-old Goodale served as supervisor of Indian schools in Nebraska and the Dakotas. She was an ardent proponent of American Indian education. Through these difficult times, Charles and Elaine grew close. They married in June of 1891 and eventually had six children. Elaine edited each of Charles's 11 books and much of his other writings.

The Name Giver

Throughout the rest of his life, Eastman never hesitated to speak honestly for his people and himself and against the prevalent ill-treatment of the Sioux and other Native Americans. His stints with the government, in service to his people, numbered five. Most were brief, two to three years, due to his forthright stands. His longest tenure, 1903–1909, grew out of the recognition by Charles and others that the Sioux did not fairly and universally receive allotments of money and land due to them from treaty settlements and other laws. President Roosevelt appointed him to revise allotment procedures. To do this, Charles carefully devised appropriate first and last names for more than 25,000 Lakota. Up to that time, the Sioux did not trace family lineage through a surname. As a sign of recognition of their trust in his work, Sioux people, in turn, gave Ohiyesa a new moniker—The Name Giver.

Man of Letters

Charles Eastman's most lasting public legacies are in the books he wrote and the organizations he helped craft. Among these groups are the YMCA, the Society of American Indians, the Camp Fire Girls, and the Boy Scouts. The scouting organizations were cofounded by writer–naturalist Ernest Thompson Seton, a close friend of Eastman. Seton and Eastman shared common bonds of experience, growing up at the same time, not many miles apart, in the woods and prairies of southern Canada. Through their writings for all ages, both shared a great appreciation for nature and Native American peoples.

Even after the age of 70, Eastman remained active. The well-known author–lecturer toured England in 1928, speaking on the cultures of Native America. That same year, he moved to a cabin on the shore of Lake Huron in Ontario, where he could canoe, fish, swim, observe wildlife, and write. Charles Alexander Eastman (Ohiyesa) died at the age of 80 on January 8, 1939.

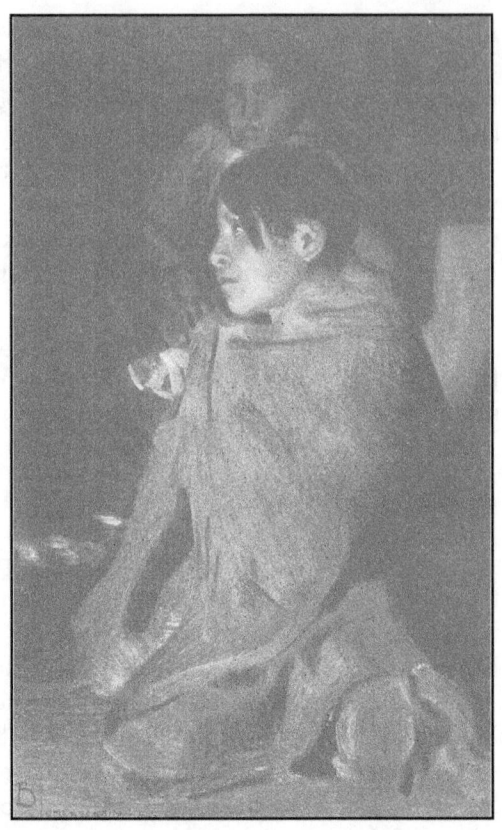

Figure 1.4. Evening in the Lodge. Illus. by E. L. Blumenschein.

TEACHING ADVICE FOR CHARLES A. EASTMAN (OHIYESA)

Autobiographical Writings

With *Indian Boyhood* and *From the Deep Woods to Civilization*, Charles A. Eastman was not the first American Indian to publish his personal history. But, at the time they appeared and after, his books were widely read in the United States, Canada, and around the world. Through his writings and speeches, Ohiyesa had a profound impact on the ways in which other people viewed the Lakota and Native peoples in general.

Age Appropriateness

Indian Boyhood is appropriate reading and listening for children, young adults, and adults. Young adults and adults will appreciate the more sophisticated content of *From the Deep Woods to Civilization*, either by itself or as a sequel to *Indian Boyhood*.

Elaine Goodale Eastman, Literary Collaborator

Charles A. Eastman often struggled to write fluently in his adopted language of English. Throughout most of his writing career, his wife Elaine worked closely with him on all aspects of his manuscripts. They jointly published one book, *Wigwam Evenings*. She often subordinated her own literary talent to the important tasks of developing Charles's stories and interpreting the Lakota people to the world. She did publish seven books of her own, most notably *Sister to the Sioux: The Memoirs of Elaine Goodale Eastman, 1885–1891* (Lincoln, NE: University of Nebraska Press, 1985).

Lakota, Dakota, Nakota?

The Lakota-oyate, or Sioux, culture is composed of many subgroups, some of which speak different dialects of their language. One tribal member describes the meaning of Lakota-oyate as "many tribes in one nation." Ohiyesa's people are the Dakota, sometimes also called the Eastern or Santee, as well as by the name of their individual band, in his case, Wahpeton. Zitkala-Ša's (see chapter 2) group is the Nakota and she belonged to the Yankton band. The final group is the Lakota, which is also the overall name for the culture. The name Sioux, commonly used to refer to the Lakota, was given to them by people outside of the culture.

Native American, American Indian, First People?

In the United States, the appropriate term of reference for Native people may be Native American for some, American Indian, or First American for others. In Canada, First People may be appropriate. Since there is a variety of preferred racial and cultural reference among Native peoples today, this text uses the terms somewhat interchangeably for variety's sake, but with respect for all. The most important thing to remember is that groups of people and individuals should be free to refer to themselves in any way they find appropriate and that others should respect those preferences.

Ohiyesa and Zitkala-Ša

An interesting project for students is to compare the writings of Ohiyesa and Zitkala-Ša (covered in chapter 2). There is sharp contrast between the more detailed, affirmative writings of Charles A. Eastman and those of his fellow Lakota and friend Zitkala-Ša, written in an impressionistic, often bitter autobiographical style. (See Zitkala-Ša, chapter 2.) What unifies their writings is a mutual desire to sympathetically portray the humanity and value of their native culture to an oppressive, often racist, outside world.

14 STORYTELLERS

LEARNING HORIZONS

Literature Aloud Experiences

◆ STORYTELLING CONNECTIONS

Level: Grades four and higher.

Student Learning Opportunities: Reading; Story selection; Individual and group rehearsal; Memory; Performance.

Background: An exciting way to enliven the instruction of Charles Eastman's life and works is to retell one of the traditional Dakota folktales that he learned as a boy. A good selection of these stories is found in both *Indian Boyhood* and *Wigwam Evenings*. The process for preparing a story for telling, figure 1.5, was borrowed from storytellers, who borrowed it from storytellers on back to the Dark Ages. So, have fun with it, as you make the story come to life.

Basics: Figure 1.5 presents a tried-and-true process for preparing a story for telling.

Extensions: See **Intergenerational Storytelling**, below, and **Making the Story Your Own** in **Literature Aloud Experiences**, chapter 2.

Teacher Evaluation Opportunities: Story selection; Story rehearsal; Cooperation; Performance.

◆ INTERGENERATIONAL STORYTELLING

Level: Grades four to eight.

Student Learning Opportunities: Listening; Memory; Retelling; Cooperation.

Background: Just as Ohiyesa did from his elders, students can learn and retell stories from a version presented orally by an adult.

Basics:
1. Tell or read aloud a short, simple traditional folktale from any culture or source. Repeat the story if necessary to assure the students' basic understanding.

2. Have students use "Preparing a Story for Telling" in **Literature Aloud Experiences** in this chapter to prepare the story for retelling.

3. Have students present their first retelling to partners. Urge them to be brief and to share constructive comments with each other.

4. Ask for volunteers to present their brief version of the story again to a larger group.

5. Ultimately, students will share their retelling with other adults and/or children at home or in other settings.

PREPARING A STORY FOR TELLING

1. Choose a story you feel comfortable learning and *like*.

2. Read or listen to it several times. Look for the two basic elements of each story:

    a. the order of events—"the skeleton."

    b. the language and detail of the story—"the flesh and blood."

3. Practice the story in your own words, alone or with a partner, until you can tell it smoothly. Retell it on tape or before a mirror, if you wish.

4. *Do* memorize specific rhymes, phrases, facts, descriptions or whole stories you desire to tell as written. Otherwise, *don't* memorize.

5. Note material you want to remember on cards to help you through trouble spots.

6. Tell your story for the first time to a sympathetic audience!

7. As the story evolves, develop appropriate facial expressions, body motions, and hand gestures for it.

8. Bring personal elements of characterization, dialect or accent, vocal presentation and control, audience participation, and additional content you may research into the story. Exercise your personal creativity. Grow with the story!

9. Find complementary materials for building a thematic program in poetry, song, dance, creative movement, puppets, and so forth, if you wish.

10. TELL IT. TELL IT. TELL IT. IF YOU DON'T USE IT, YOU'LL LOSE IT.

    And remember, ALWAYS:

    - Prepare yourself for each storytelling.
    - Tell in a comfortable, quiet location.
    - Arrange your listeners as you want them.
    - Strive to maintain eye contact at all times.

Figure 1.5. Preparing a Story for Telling.

16 STORYTELLERS

Extensions:
1. Tell or read aloud a number of Ohiyesa's stories. Have students select and prepare their own version of one of Ohiyesa's traditional stories or life experiences, using *Indian Boyhood*, *Old Indian Days*, and *Wigwam Evenings* as sources.
2. Organize a special event through which the students share their stories. Possibilities include tellings in other classrooms, senior citizen centers, and at evening family events at school.

Teacher Evaluation Opportunities: Cooperation; Retellings of oral tales; Retellings of tales selected from Eastman texts.

Language Arts Experiences

◈ THE NAME-GIVER

Level: Grades four to eight.

Student Learning Opportunities: Discussion; Family inquiry; Research; Expository written reporting; Oral reporting; Six-Trait Writing—Ideas, Voice, Sentence Fluency, Conventions.

Background: Hakadah, Ohiyesa, The Name-Giver—Charles A. Eastman had a number of meaningful names in his life. Names hold special individual and social significance. They also provide students with an opportunity for original research and creativity.

Basics:
1. Read aloud or have students read the last three paragraphs (or more) of the chapter, "A Midsummer Feast" and the naming segment from the chapter, "The Boy Hunter," from *Indian Boyhood*. These relate to the renaming of Hakadah and others. Discuss the stories in the naming of Eastman, his friends, and family.
2. Ask students to explore the stories behind their own names. By whom were they named? Were they named after anyone? What are the meanings of their first, middle and last names? Are stories connected to those names? What are the ethnic origins of their last names? Encourage students to do family inquiry and other research to find answers.
3. Have students write a report or nonfiction story that answers these and other questions that arise.
4. Have students orally present their name-stories to the group.

Extensions: Names are significant. Dakota names are sometimes accidentally derived and sometimes intentionally created. Either way, when names are bestowed, it is an important, sometimes life-changing process for the recipient.

1. Have students create an English version of a Dakota-style name for themselves. Names such as Many Lighnings, White Rabbit, Cloud Man, and Sleepy Eye are found throughout *Indian Boyhood*. Ask them to think seriously about memorable events in their lives, big or small. Can they use an event to suggest a Dakota-style name? Can they explain why it is relevant to them? Is it a name they would want to carry for the rest of their lives?

2. Discuss the students' Dakota-style name choices and the stories about their origins.

3. Have students write brief two-to-six paragraph explanations of the origin of their new names, including answers to the questions in step one.

Teacher Evaluation Opportunities: Participation in discussion; Research procedure; Written reports; Oral presentation of reports; Use of Six-Trait Writing techniques.

Social Studies Experiences

◈ *A SENSE OF PLACE—OHIYESA*

Level: Grades four to eight.

Student Learning Opportunities: Map analysis; Map making; Text analysis—Place Names.

Background: Skills in map analysis and navigation pay lifelong dividends for students.

Basics:
1. While reading *Indian Boyhood*, make or have the students make a list of specific geographic places and features identified by Eastman. Note both the Dakota and contemporary place names, if possible. Remember that it is difficult to locate some Dakota place names, as they may not be the names used today. Look for locations, especially in the beginning of later chapters. Examples are Redwood Falls in Minnesota, the Assiniboine and Mouse (Souris) rivers in Manitoba, and Turtle Mountain(s) in Manitoba and North Dakota.

2. Obtain detailed maps of the states of Minnesota, North Dakota, South Dakota, and the Province of Manitoba. The map, figure 1.6, can help in finding locations near Ohiyesa's birthplace.

3. Have students find identifiable locations from the list of place names and mark them on individual maps, or on a group map if they are working in teams.

4. Using the map, figure 1.6, verbally guide students on an imaginary journey around Ohiyesa's homelands. Can they follow your directions? Can students be the guides on later map journeys as well? Use other maps to expand the scope of imaginary treks.

Extensions: Though it may be challenging, students may be able to trace some of the movements of Ohiyesa and his family from clues on their marked maps and in the text. (Historians do this kind of detective work in their attempts to re-create the past.)

1. Have students create their own maps and trace Ohiyesa's movements either from scratch or by using an outline map of states and provinces.

2. In the same manner, have them create a map tracing their own family's movements during their lifetime or before.

Teacher Evaluation Opportunities: Map-reading skills; Map-making skills; Family mapping.

18 STORYTELLERS

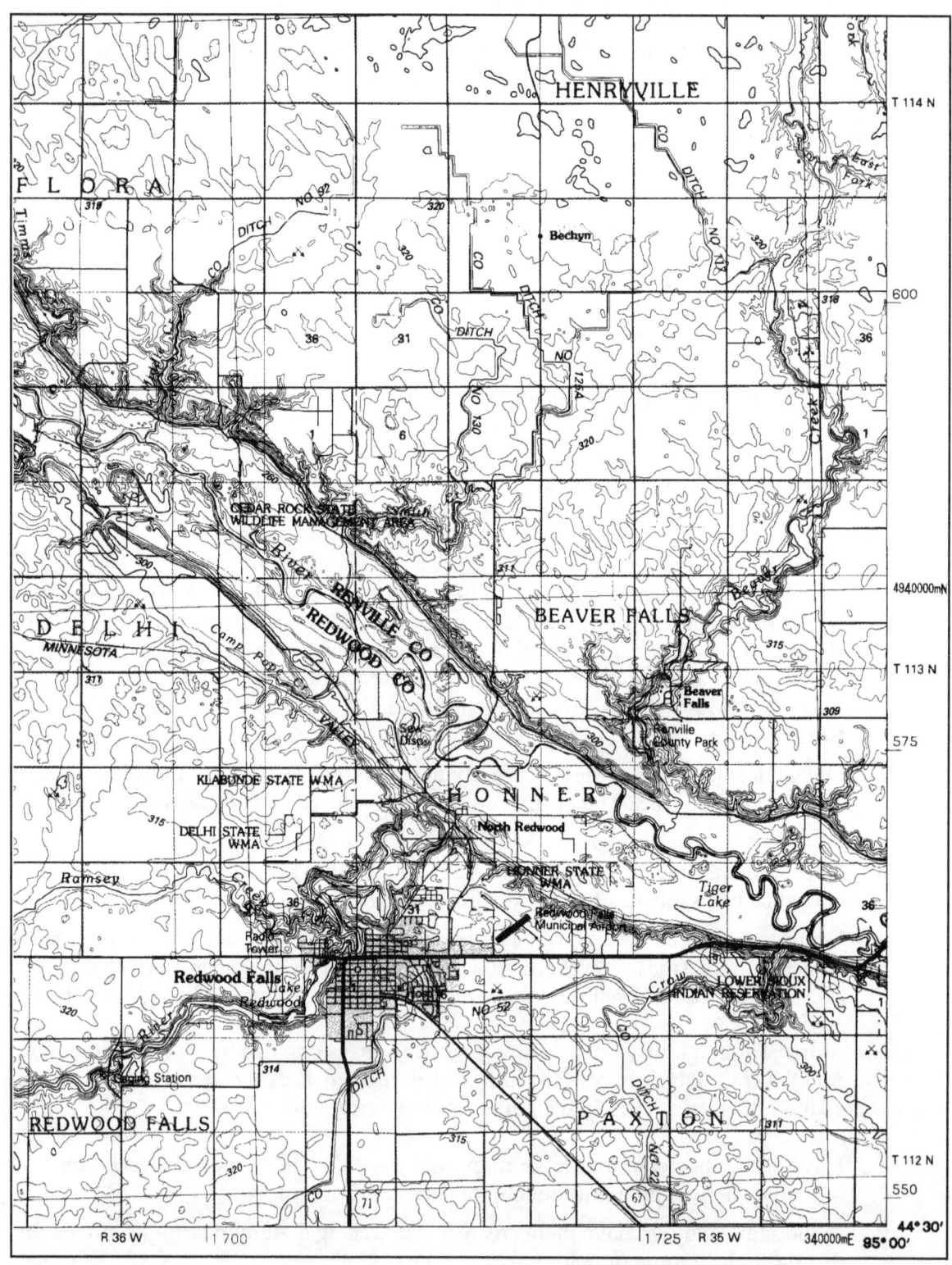

Figure 1.6. Contemporary map of the area of Charles A. Eastman's birth, near Redwood Falls, Minnesota. Public Domain, courtesy of U.S. Geological Survey.

◈ *LIFE SKILLS SELF-INVENTORY*

Level: Grades six to eight.

Student Learning Opportunities: Skills identification; Skills self-assessment.

Background: The skills our children need to survive and prosper in their environment may be the same as or quite different from those needed by Ohiyesa. From "An Indian Boy's Training" in *Indian Boyhood* and other writings, we know that Eastman had a clear picture at a young age of what his world required of him. Can your students identify what training is required of them by their environment? **The Life Skills Self-Inventory**, figure 1.9, page 21, helps them to quantify and assess their own life skills needs.

Basics:
1. Prior to beginning the Self-Inventory form, discuss the three general environments in which skills are needed for the students' survival and well-being: Home and Family, Education, The Outside World.

2. Review with students how the 10- to 15-year-old Ohiyesa might have identified skills required for the education portion of his life, as in figure 1.7. Through discussion, identify additional skills students find important in their education, such as reading, writing, and using technology, and have them explain the reasons why.

3. Students can identify their own individual skills by completing a **Life Skills Self Inventory Form**, figure 1.9. Encourage them to make answers general rather than too specific. For example, "work habits," rather than "dish washing" or "room cleaning."

Ohiyesa's Educational Life Skills Self-Inventory

Student Name: Ohiyesa

Environment—Education

Skills Needed

1) observation

2) memory

3) speech

4) hunting

5) manners

6) strength and endurance

More? plant and animal identification; problem-solving; patience.

Figure 1.7. Life Skills Self-Inventory.

20 STORYTELLERS

Extensions:
1. Upon completion of the first phase of the Life Skills Self-Inventory, have students assess their proficiency in each skill. Have them mark two or three letters after the skills they listed for each environment, based on the following criteria:

    a) For a skill necessary for physical survival, mark "S".

    b) For a skill that provides benefit for human life, beyond physical survival, mark "A".

    c) Finally, mark *only one of the following* after each skill:
    For a skill in which students feel they are still learning the basics, mark "B".
    For a skill in which students feel they are competent, mark "C".
    For a skill in which students feel they excel, mark "E".

    For example, Ohiyesa might have annotated his Self-Inventory, figure 1.8, in this manner:

Ohiyesa's Annotated Life Skills Self-Inventory

Student Name: Ohiyesa

Environment—Education

Skills Needed

1) observation—S, A, C

2) memory—S, A, B

3) speech—S, A, C

4) hunting—S, B

5) manners—S, A, C

6) strength and endurance—S, A, C

More? plant and animal identification—S, A, C; problem-solving—S, A, B; patience—S, B

Figure 1.8. Annotated Life Skills Self-Inventory.

Teacher Evaluation Opportunities: Group discussion; Life Skills Self-Inventory—skills identification and assessment of proficiency; Discussion of Self-Inventory results with individual students.

Life Skills Self-Inventory Form

Student Name:

Environment—Home and Family

Skills Needed

    1)
    2)
    3)
    4)
    5)
    6)

More?

Environment—Education

Skills Needed

    1)
    2)
    3)
    4)
    5)
    6)

More?

Environment—The Outside World

Skills Needed

    1)
    2)
    3)
    4)
    5)
    6)

More?

Figure 1.9. Life Skills Self-Inventory Form.

◆ O AND M WALK

Level: Grades four to eight.

Student Learning Opportunities: Discussion; Observation; Memory; Retelling; Descriptive, narrative, and/or expository writing; Six-Trait Writing—Ideas, Word Choice.

Background: Experience is often the best teacher. Just like Ohiyesa, your students can heighten their powers of observation and memory, as well as oral and written skills of description, with Observation and Memory (O and M) walks.

Basics:
1. Read aloud or have students read the section from "An Indian Boy's Training" in *Indian Boyhood*, describing Ohiyesa's training by his uncle. Discuss what Ohiyesa learned.
2. Give each student a general category of natural or man-made objects to look for, carefully observe, and remember on the walk. Some examples of observable items found in many locales are birds, trees, buildings, cars, trucks, mammals, or distinctive human characteristics.
3. Take a walk in the environment of your school and neighborhood.
4. Upon return, ask students to describe their observations—aloud at first, and then, in complete sentences in writing, using specific nouns and strong verbs. As his uncle did for Ohiyesa, remind them that, at first, naming something is not as important as describing its characteristics and the details of the place where it was seen. For example, a student's response, "I saw a black bird," says little about the bird and nothing about its environment. A better response might be, "A large, all-black bird with a big beak squawked at me from the top of a tall tree in somebody's front yard."
5. Identification (naming) and research activities follow from the students' descriptions. For example, have students work to determine the kind of bird and tree; the bird's eating and nesting habits; the tree's flowers, fruit, or seeds; and so forth.

Extensions:
1. Take more O and M walks in various seasons. Students can assemble O and M walk journals with accumulated observations for later reference.
2. Stretch student observation powers and memory by giving them several natural or man-made items to observe and remember at the same time.
3. Tie the walks in with content from other subjects of instruction, if desired.
4. Encourage students to take O and M walks in different environments, outside of school time. Stress safety awareness during these walks. Have students prepare written evaluations of their walks and keep them in O and M walk journals.

Teacher Evaluation Opportunities: Discussion; Cooperation (during walks); Quality and quantity of observations; Identification and research findings; O and M walk journals; Use of Six-Trait Writing techniques in journals.

CHARLES A. EASTMAN RESOURCES

Selected Eastman Books

Eastman, Charles A. *From the Deep Woods to Civilization: Chapters in the Autobiography of an Indian.* Lincoln, NE: University of Nebraska Press, 1977 (1916).

    First published in 1916, this book continues Eastman's life story beyond age 15. Though written for adults, it is easily accessible to young adult readers of *Indian Boyhood* who desire a sequel.

———. *Indian Boyhood.* Illustrated by E. L. Blumenschein. New York: Dover, 1991 (1902).

    Eastman shows the benefit of his early training in observation and memory through his powerful recollections. In presenting his own story, he preserves a rare picture of mid-nineteenth-century Dakota culture. It is the most important book for young people studying Eastman. The text is also available electronically (see below).

———. *Old Indian Days.* Lincoln, NE: University of Nebraska Press, 1991 (1907).

    Retells traditional stories and oral history of the Dakota in pre-reservation times in a manner suitable for young adult and adult readers. The text is also available electronically (see below).

Eastman Charles A., and Elaine Goodale Eastman. *Wigwam Evenings: Sioux Folk Tales Retold.* Lincoln, NE: University of Nebraska Press, 1990 (1909).

    A collection of 27 traditional tales ripe for storytelling or reading aloud by fourth to eighth graders and adults. It is an excellent complement to the folktales in *Indian Boyhood*.

Eastman Biographies

Anderson, Peter. *Charles Eastman: Physician, Reformer, and Native American Leader*, People of Distinction Series. Chicago: Childrens Press, 1992.

    A thorough, 110-page biography appropriate for fourth- to eighth-grade students. It concentrates on Eastman's three roles mentioned in the title, with less emphasis on his role as writer. Illustrated with 16 historic photographs.

Ross, Michael Elsohn. *Wildlife Watching with Charles Eastman*, Naturalist's Apprentice Series. Illustrated by Laurie A. Caple. Minneapolis, MN: Carolrhoda Books, 1997.

    Though this book focuses on Eastman as naturalist, it briefly covers all significant aspects of his life in 48 pages. The text is generously interspersed with Caple's accurate wildlife illustrations and 12 historic photographs. Format is especially appropriate for fourth to sixth graders. Special features include the wildlife field guide entries and detailed children's nature activities, for those who want to follow Ohiyesa's path as a naturalist.

Electronic Sources

Eastman, Charles A. *Indian Boyhood.* Copyright 1999. The Gutenberg Project. Available: http://promo.net/pg/ (Accessed November 15, 2000).

    This free, e-text service also provides Eastman's *Indian Heroes and Great Chieftains, Old Indian Days,* and *The Soul of the Indian.*

ZITKALA-ŠA (GERTRUDE SIMMONS BONNIN)

CHAPTER 2

Born February 22, 1876 in South Dakota. Died January 26, 1938 in Washington, D.C. Childhood and young adult autobiography describes South Dakota, Nebraska, and Indiana.

Figure 2.1. Zitkala-Ša (Gertrude Simmons Bonnin).

AN APPRECIATION OF THE WRITER

I loved best the evening meal, for that was the time old legends were told. I was always glad when the sun hung low in the west, for then my mother sent me to invite the neighboring old men and women to eat supper with us. . . . As each in turn began to tell a legend, I pillowed my head in my mother's lap; and lying flat on my back, I watched the stars as they peeped down upon me, one by one. The increasing interest of the tale aroused me, and I sat up eagerly listening to every word.

—Zitkala-Ša from American Indian Stories, "The Legends," page 13.

It was Arizona writer Joseph Wood Krutch who said, "There is all the difference in the world between looking at something and living with it." The wisdom of this statement becomes clear when we explore the work of American Indian writer Zitkala-Ša (Red Bird), also known as Gertrude Simmons Bonnin. At first glance, her writing style seems easily accessible to older children and adults. Her stories and essays are simple in structure and direct in message. The term, "American Indian writer," is quite familiar to us today. There are many writers in North America who fit that description—Joseph Bruchac, Leslie Marmon Silko, Michael Dorris, Louise Erdrich, Scott Momaday, Luci Tapahonso, Sherman Alexie, Paula Gunn Allen, and others.

But the culture that Zitkala-Ša (zeet-ka-la sha) was "living with" in the United States, more than a century ago, was very different. At that time, the terms "American Indian" and "writer" bore little connection in most peoples' minds. Native cultures, as Zitkala-Ša describes above, were still primarily oral cultures, with scant written tradition, if any. There were few Indian writers—and no women Indian writers until Zitkala-Ša.

For young, college-educated Zitkala-Ša, writing about herself and her people represented a bold step into little-known lands. She became the first American Indian woman to write without help from an interpreter, ethnographer, or editor. Though her career in writing for mass-circulation publication was relatively brief, it was impressive. From 1900 to 1902, Zitkala-Ša published numerous essays in such notable magazines as *Harper's* and *Atlantic Monthly*. Her collection of traditional Sioux tales, *Old Indian Legends,* appeared in 1901. In 1921, she compiled her magazine essays, including several autobiographical pieces, into the book, *American Indian Stories.*

With her writing, Zitkala-Ša endeavored to interpret her Native culture to an American people who were often bent on annihilating it. Her example and encouragement prompted writing by other American Indians, including Charles A. Eastman (see chapter 1). Through the power of her pen, Zitkala-Ša became a lifelong advocate for her people and all Native Americans.

IN HER OWN WORDS

The Quaker missionaries and staff of White's Manual Training Institute, the boarding school that Zitkala-Ša first attended, had an arguably more liberal, less dogmatic approach than that of other Indian schools of the era. However, they still adhered to the policy of rapid assimilation of Indian young people promoted by the U.S. government. The initial effects of the boarding school experience were startling and strange for most American Indian children. In these excerpts, Zitkala-Ša paints a stark picture of herself as a naive little girl coming to terms with the shocking changes in her life.

The following segments, beginning on page 27, are excerpted from "Impressions of an Indian Childhood" and "The School Days of an Indian Girl," pages 39 to 56, in *American Indian Stories.*

26 STORYTELLERS

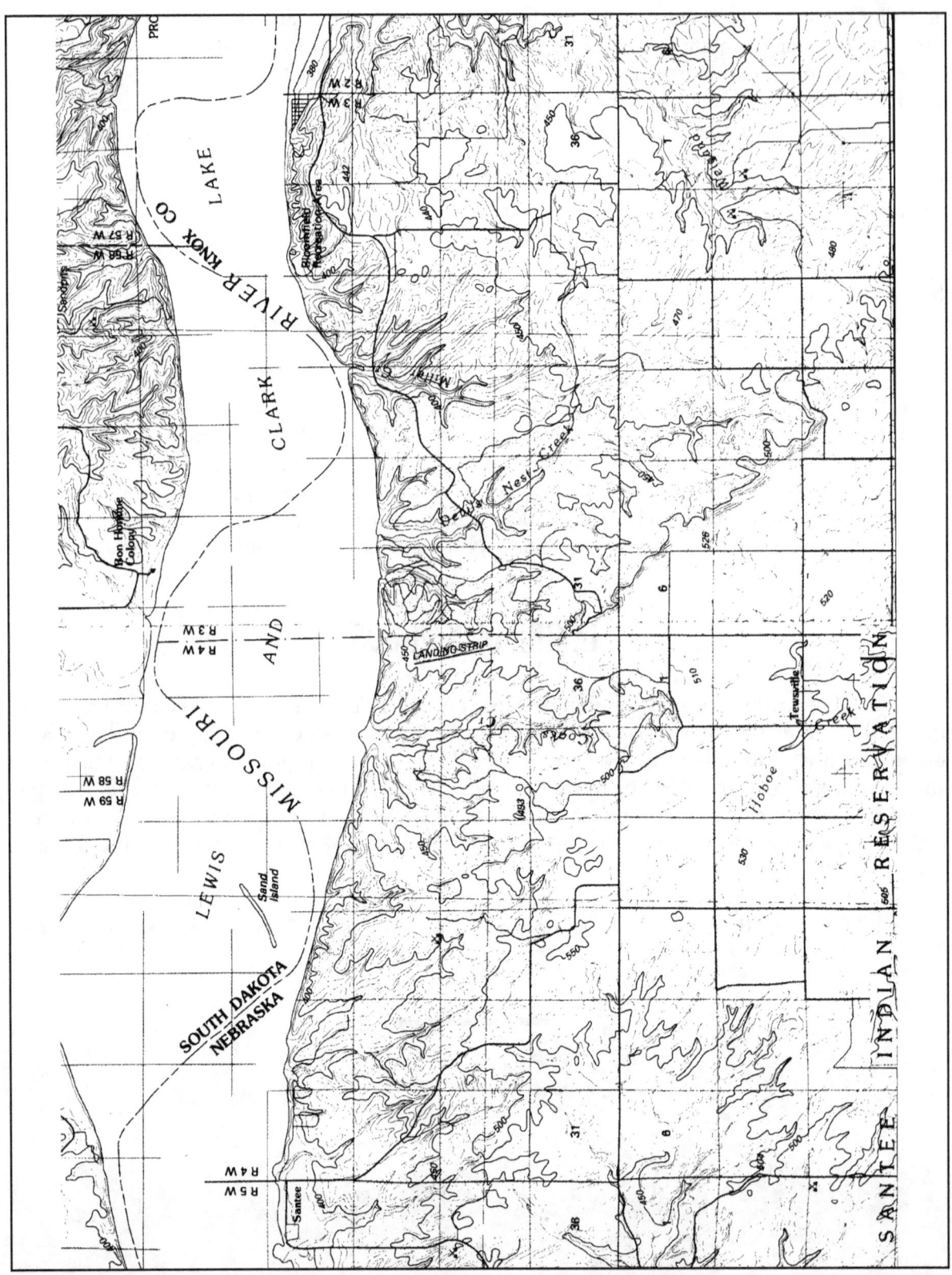

Figure 2.2. Contemporary map of the Missouri River country of South Dakota and Nebraska, land of Zitkala-Ša's childhood. Public domain, courtesy of U.S. Geological Survey.

Note: The following is excerpted as punctuated and spelled in the original manuscript.

The Big Red Apples

The first turning away from the easy, natural flow of my life occurred in an early spring. It was in my eighth year; in the month of March, I afterward learned. At this age I knew but one language, and that was my mother's native tongue.

From some of my playmates I heard that two paleface missionaries were in our village. They were from that class of white men who wore big hats and carried large hearts, they said. Running direct to my mother, I began to question her why these two strangers were among us. She told me, after I had teased much, that they had come to take away Indian boys and girls to the East. My mother did not seem to want me to talk about them. But in a day or two, I gleaned many wonderful stories from my playfellows concerning the strangers.

"Mother, my friend Judéwin is going home with the missionaries. She is going to a more beautiful country than ours; the palefaces told her so!" I said wistfully, wishing in my heart that I might go.

Mother sat in a chair, and I was hanging on her knee. Within the last two seasons my big brother Dawée had returned from a three years' education in the East, and his coming back influenced my mother to take a farther step from her native way of living. First it was a change from the buffalo skin to the white man's canvas that covered our wigwam. Now she had given up her wigwam of slender poles, to live, a foreigner, in a house of clumsy logs.

"Yes, my child, several others besides Judéwin are going away with the palefaces. Your brother said the missionaries had inquired about his little sister," she said, watching my face very closely.

My heart thumped so hard against my breast, I wondered if she could hear it.

"Did he tell them to take me, mother?" I asked, fearing that Dawée had forbidden the palefaces to see me, and that my hope of going to the Wonderland would be entirely blighted.

With a sad, slow smile, she answered: "There! I knew you were wishing to go, because Judéwin has filled your ears with the white man's lies. Don't believe a word they say. Their words are sweet, but, my child, their deeds are bitter. You will cry for me, but they will not even soothe you. Stay with me, my little one! Your brother Dawée says that going East, away from your mother, is too hard an experience for his baby sister."

Thus my mother discouraged my curiosity about the lands beyond our eastern horizon; for it was not yet an ambition for Letters that was stirring me. But on the following day the missionaries did come to our very house. I spied them coming up the footpath leading to our cottage. A third man was with them, but he was not my brother Dawée. It was another, a young interpreter, a paleface who had a smattering of the Indian language. I was ready to run out to meet them, but I did not dare to displease my mother. With great glee, I jumped up and down on our ground floor. I begged my mother to open the door, that they would be sure to come to us. Alas! They came, they saw, and they conquered!

Judéwin had told me of the great tree where grew red, red apples; and how we could reach out our hands and pick all the red apples we could eat. I had never seen apple trees. I had never tasted more than a dozen red apples in my life; and when I heard of the orchards of the East, I was eager to roam among them. The missionaries smiled into my eyes and patted my head. I wondered how mother could say such hard words against him.

"Mother, ask them if little girls may have all the red apples they want, when they go East," I whispered aloud, in my excitement.

The interpreter heard me, and answered: "Yes, little girl, the nice red apples are for those who pick them; and you will have a ride on the iron horse if you go with these good people."

I had never seen a train, and he knew it.

"Mother, I am going East! I like big red apples, and I want to ride on the iron horse! Mother, say yes!" I pleaded.

My mother said nothing. The missionaries waited in silence; and my eyes began to blur with tears, though I struggled to choke them back. The corners of my mouth twitched, and my mother saw me.

"I am not ready to give you any word," she said to them. "Tomorrow I shall send you my answer with my son."

With this they left us. Alone with my mother, I yielded to my tears, and cried aloud, shaking my head so as not to hear what she was saying to me. This was the first time I had ever been so unwilling to give up my own desire that I refused to hearken to my mother's voice. There was a solemn silence in our house that night. Before I went to bed I begged the Great Spirit to make my mother willing I should go with the missionaries.

The next morning came, and my mother called me to her side. "My daughter, do you still persist in wishing to leave your mother?" she asked.

"Oh, mother, it is not that I wish to leave you, but I want to see the wonderful Eastern land," I answered.

My dear old aunt came to our house that morning, and I heard her say, "Let her try it."

I hoped that, as usual, my aunt was pleading on my side. My brother Dawée came for my mother's decision. I dropped my play, and crept close to my aunt.

"Yes, Dawée, my daughter, though she does not understand what it all means, is anxious to go. She will need an education when she is grown, for then there will be fewer real Dakotas, and many more palefaces. This tearing her away, so young, from her mother is necessary, if I would have her an educated woman. The palefaces, who owe us a large debt for stolen lands, have begun to pay a tardy justice in offering some education to our children. But I know my daughter must suffer keenly in this experiment. For her sake, I dread to tell you my reply to the missionaries. Go, tell them that they may take my little daughter, and that the Great Spirit shall not fail to reward them according to their hearts."

Wrapped in my heavy blanket, I walked with my mother to the carriage that was soon to take us to the iron horse. I was happy. I met my playmates, who were also wearing their best thick blankets. We showed one another our new beaded mocassins, and the width of the belts that girdled our new dresses. Soon we were being drawn rapidly away by the white man's horses. When I saw the lonely figure of my mother vanish in the distance, a sense of regret settled heavily upon me. I felt suddenly weak, as if I might fall limp to the ground. I was in the hands of strangers whom my mother did not fully trust. I no longer felt free to be myself, or to voice my own feelings. The tears trickled down my cheeks, and I buried my face in the folds of my blanket. Now the first step, parting me from my mother, was taken and my belated tears availed nothing.

Having driven thirty miles to the ferryboat, we crossed the Missouri in the evening. Then riding again a few miles eastward, we stopped before a massive brick building. I looked at it in amazement, and with a vague misgiving, for in our village I had never seen so large a house. Trembling with fear and distrust of the palefaces, my teeth chattering from the chilly ride, I crept noiselessly in my soft moccasins along the narrow hall, keeping very close to the bare wall. I was as frightened and bewildered as the captured young of a wild creature.

The Land of Red Apples

There were eight in our party of bronzed children who were going East with the missionaries. Among us were three young braves, two tall girls, and we three little ones, Judéwin, Thowin, and I.

We had been very impatient to start on our journey to the Red Apple Country, which, we were told, lay a little beyond the great circular horizon of the Western prairie. Under a sky of rosy apples we dreamt of roaming as freely and happily as we had chased the cloud shadows on the Dakota plains. We had anticipated much pleasure from a ride on the iron horse, but the throngs of staring palefaces disturbed and troubled us.

On the train, fair women, with tottering babies on each arm, stopped their haste and scrutinized the children of absent mothers. Large men, with heavy bundles in their hands, halted near by, and riveted their glassy blue eyes upon us. I sank deep into the corner of my seat, for I resented being watched. Directly in front of me, children who were no larger than I hung themselves on the back of their seats, with their bold white faces toward me. Sometimes they took their forefingers out of their mouths and pointed at my moccasined feet. Their mothers, instead of reproving such rude curiosity, looked closely at me, and attracted their childrens' further notice of my blanket. This embarrassed me, and kept me constantly on the verge of tears.

I sat perfectly still, with my eyes downcast, daring only now and then to shoot long glances around me. Chancing to turn to the window at my side, I was quite breathless on seeing one familiar object. It was a telephone pole which strode by at short paces. Very near my mother's dwelling, along the edge of a road thickly bordered with wild sunflowers, some poles like these had been planted by white men. Often I had stopped, on my way down the road, to hold my ear against the pole, and, hearing its low moaning, I used to wonder what the palefaces had done to hurt it. Now I sat watching for each pole that glided by to be the last one.

In this way I had forgotten my uncomfortable surroundings, when I heard one of my comrades call out my name. I saw the missionary standing very near, tossing candies and gum into our midst. This amused us all, and we tried to see who could catch the most of the sweetmeats. Though we rode several days inside of the iron horse, I do not recall a single thing about our luncheons

It was night when we reached the school grounds. The lights from the windows of the large buildings fell upon some of the icicled trees that stood beneath them. We were led toward an open door, where the brightness of the lights within flooded out over the heads of the excited palefaces who blocked our way. My body trembled more from fear than from the snow I trod upon.

Entering the house, I stood close against the wall. The strong glaring lights in the large whitewashed room dazzled my eyes. The noisy hurrying of hard shoes upon bare wooden floor increased the whirring in my ears. My only safety seemed to be in keeping next to the wall. As I was wondering in which direction to escape from all this confusion, two warm hands grasped me firmly, and in the same moment I was tossed high in midair. A rosy-cheeked woman caught me in her arms. I was both frightened and insulted by such trifling. I stared into her eyes, wishing her to let me stand on my own feet, but she jumped me up and down with increasing enthusiasm. My mother had never made a plaything of her wee daughter. Remembering this I began to cry aloud. They misunderstood the cause of my tears and placed me at a white table loaded with food. There our party were united again. As I did not hush my crying, one of the older (children) whispered to me, "Wait until you are alone in the night." It was very little I could swallow besides my sobs, that evening.

"Oh, I want my mother and my brother Dawée! I want to go to my aunt!" I pleaded; but the ears of the palefaces could not hear me.

From the table we were taken along an upward incline of wooden boxes, which I learned afterward to call a stairway. At the top was a quiet hall, dimly lighted. Many narrow beds were in one straight line down the entire length of the wall. In them lay sleeping brown faces, which peeped just out of the coverings. I was tucked into bed with one of the tall girls, because she talked to me in my mother language and seemed to soothe me.

I had arrived in the wonderful land of rosy skies, but I was not happy, as I had thought I should be. My long travel and the bewildering sights had exhausted me. I fell asleep heaving deep, tired sobs. My tears were left to dry themselves in streaks, because neither my aunt nor my mother was near to wipe them away.

The Cutting of My Long Hair

The first day in the land of apples was a bitter-cold one; for the snow still covered the ground, and the trees were bare. A large bell rang for breakfast, its loud metallic voice crashing through the belfry overhead and into our sensitive ears. The annoying clatter of shoes on bare floors gave us no peace. The constant clash of harsh voices, with an undercurrent of many voices murmuring an unknown tongue, made a bedlam within which I was securely tied. And though my spirit tore itself in struggling for its lost freedom, all was useless.

A paleface woman, with white hair, came up after us. We were placed in a line of girls who were marching into the dining room. These were Indian girls, in stiff shoes and closely clinging dresses. The small girls wore sleeved aprons and shingled hair. As I walked noiselessly in my soft moccasins, I felt like sinking to the floor, for my blanket had been stripped from my shoulders. I looked hard at the Indian girls, who seemed not to care that they were even more immodestly dressed than I, in their tightly fitting clothes. While we marched in, the boys entered at an opposite door. I watched for the three young braves who came in our party. I spied them in the rear ranks, looking as uncomfortable as I felt.

A small bell was tapped and each of the pupils drew a chair from under the table. Supposing this act meant they were to be seated, I pulled out mine and at once slipped into it from one side. But when I turned my head, I saw that I was the only one seated, and all the rest at our table remained standing. Just as I began to rise, looking shyly around to see how chairs were to be used, a second bell was sounded. All were seated at last, and I had to crawl back into my chair again. I heard a man's voice at one end of the hall, and I looked around to see him. But all the others hung their heads over their plates. As I glanced at the long chain of tables, I caught the eyes of a paleface woman upon me. Immediately I dropped my eyes, wondering why I was so keenly watched by the strange woman. The man ceased his mutterings, and then a third bell was tapped. Everyone picked up his fork and knife and began eating. I began crying instead, for by this time I was afraid to venture anything more.

But this eating by formula was not the hardest trial in that first day. Late in the morning, my friend Judéwin gave me a terrible warning. Judéwin knew a few words of English; and she had overheard the paleface woman talk about cutting our long, heavy hair. Our mothers had taught us that only unskilled warriors who were captured had their hair shingled by the enemy. Among our people, short hair was worn by mourners, and shingled hair by cowards!

We discussed our fate some moments, and when Judéwin said, "We have to submit, because they are strong," I rebelled.

"No, I will not submit! I will struggle first!" I answered.

I watched my chance, and when no one noticed I disappeared. I crept up the stairs as quietly as I could in my squeaking shoes—my mocassins had been exchanged for shoes. Along the hall I passed, without knowing whither I was going.

Turning aside to an open door, I found a large room with three white beds in it. The windows were covered with dark green curtains, which made the room very dim. Thankful that no one was there, I directed my steps toward the corner farthest from the door. On my hands and knees I crawled under the bed, and cuddled myself in the dark corner.

From the hiding place I peered out, shuddering with fear whenever I heard footsteps near by. Though in the hall voices were calling my name, and I knew that even Judéwin was searching for me, I did not open my mouth to answer. Then the steps were quickened and the voices became excited. Women and girls entered the room. I held my breath and watched them open closet doors and peep behind large trunks. Someone threw up the curtains, and the room was filled with sudden light. What caused them to stoop and look under the bed I do not know. I remember being dragged out, though I resisted by kicking and scratching wildly. In spite of myself, I was carried downstairs and tied fast in a chair.

I cried aloud, shaking my head all the while until I felt the cold blade of the scissors against my neck, and heard them gnaw off one of my thick braids. Then I lost my spirit. Since the day I was taken from my mother I had suffered extreme indignities. People had stared at me. I had been tossed about in the air like a wooden puppet. And now my long hair was shingled like a coward's! In my anguish I moaned for my mother, but no one came to comfort me. Not a soul reasoned quietly with me, as my mother used to do; for now I was only one of many little animals driven by a herder.

End of excerpted manuscript.

Figure 2.3. At play in the prairie grass.
Illus. by Angel de Cora.

THE WRITER'S LIFE

A Time of Upheaval

The last quarter of the nineteenth century brought profound and rapid change to many American Indian cultures in western North America. During that time, especially in the United States, the last battles were fought, new treaties were made, old—and new—treaties were broken. Some tribes were forcefully relocated to strange lands called reservations, their former homes usurped by an ever-growing number of newcomers. Native people were told, often ordered, to quickly "assimilate" to their new government and society. Yet, in that society, they were not citizens. They could neither vote, nor govern themselves.

Into those chaotic times, on the Yankton Reservation in South Dakota in 1876, Gertrude Simmons was born. Her mother, Tate Iyohinwin (Reaches for the Wind) or Ellen Simmons, raised her in the traditional ways and language of her Nakota people. (Speakers of the Lakota, Dakota, and Nakota dialects comprise the Lakota, or Sioux, tribe.) Gertrude's father, a white man, deserted his family before her birth. As a child, Gertrude (Zitkala-Ša) loved to run through the prairie grass, pushed by the ever-present wind. She listened closely at night to traditional stories, called *ohunkankans*.

In March 1884, Quaker missionaries came to Yankton recruiting children for boarding school at White's Manual Training Institute in Wabash, Indiana. Gertrude's older half-brother, Dawée, had attended White's for three years. Influenced by her friends, Gertrude naively begged Ellen to let her take the "iron horse" to the wonderful "land of the red apples." According to Zitkala-Ša in *American Indian Stories*, Ellen believed that she could best and most lovingly raise her youngest child at home. But, she also understood that Gertrude must become familiar with the American culture, then surrounding and inundating the Nakota world. Ellen reluctantly agreed to let her go.

Zitkala-Ša describes her first days at White's in nightmarish terms. In her writing, she captures the sense of alienation she felt about the place and its regimen, the "paleface" people, their strange language, and their expectations. Her long hair was cropped off. She wore a uniform. Her quick feet were bound in hard shoes, not soft moccasins. Gertrude grieved for her lost freedom and her mother. Though the staff at White's was more respectful of their charges than those at some other boarding schools for American Indians, rapid assimilation for the children was the policy of the U.S. government's Bureau of Indian Affairs (BIA).

Immersed in her new language and school, Gertrude slowly adapted, though not without a few small rebellions. Knowing little English, she and her playmates mistakenly tried to answer for the forbidden act of falling in the snow with a single word—No! On another occasion, while mashing turnips for supper as a punishment, she mashed them well—right through the bottom of the bowl!

Caught Between Two Worlds

To comprehend the negative impacts of forced assimilation on Zitkala-Ša, we need only to read the autobiographical chapters of *American Indian Stories*. She lays them forcefully before us sometimes emotionally, sometimes matter-of-factly. To understand how a young woman caught in the cultural cross fire between Native and non-Native worlds developed expressive powers to speak eloquently to both worlds, we must read between the lines of those chapters. To do that, we must know more of this gifted woman's life and achievements than she describes in her autobiographical writing.

In 1887, after three years at White's Manual Training Institute, Gertrude returned to live with her mother in South Dakota. She no longer felt like a little girl "as free as the wind that blew my hair, and no less spirited than a bounding deer." Though she loved her mother, she found herself uncomfortable with Tate Iyohinwin's traditional ways. Zitkala-Ša describes her adolescent feelings in *American Indian Stories,* page 69: "During this time, I seemed to hang in the heart of chaos, beyond the touch or voice of human aid. . . . My mother had never gone inside of a schoolhouse, and she was not capable of comforting her daughter who could read and write. Even nature seemed to have no place for me. I was neither a wee girl nor a tall one; neither a wild Indian nor a tame one. . . ." She would never feel completely at home in her mother's world again.

For the school year of 1888–89, Gertrude enrolled at the nearby Santee Normal Training School, previously attended by Charles A. Eastman and others. In 1891, her personal turmoil drove her back to White's, from which she graduated in 1894. Gertrude Simmons was growing skilled in many ways—reading, writing, music, and oratory. But her mother wanted her at home, like the other Lakota children who had completed their course in the East. Without Ellen Simmons's approval, Gertrude enrolled at Earlham College, Richmond, Indiana, in the fall of 1895.

Creative Self-Expression

At Earlham, Gertrude studied long and hard, often in lonely isolation. She wrote and delivered her college's winning oratorical speech in the spring of 1896. The adulation of her schoolmates was heartening, although also embarrassing. Soon after, she represented Earlham in the Indiana collegiate oratorical competition. Before the judges announced their decision, some rowdy students from another school unfurled a banner that ridiculed Gertrude and the college represented by a "squaw." When Gertrude received second place, the banner dropped from sight.

After two years at Earlham, Gertrude Simmons took her studies on the violin to the prestigious New England Conservatory of Music in Boston. There, she made friends in the artistic and literary communities. Having recovered from a serious illness that cut short her studies, Gertrude taught at the Carlisle Indian Industrial School in Pennsylvania in 1898 and 1899. Her performances with the Carlisle orchestra as violin soloist and orator received excellent reviews in New York and at the Paris Exposition of 1900.

At about that time, the young Nakota took the name Zitkala-Ša (Red Bird) for herself, perhaps as much as a pen name as a statement of cultural identity. Her writing was receiving considerable attention—both positive and negative. Widely read national magazines published a number of her essays. But, when she criticized the policy and results of forced assimilation of Native American children, newspapers at the Carlisle and Santee schools reacted harshly to her writing. It is likely that Carlisle fired her because of the opinions she expressed.

In addition to her essays, Zitkala-Ša wished to share traditional Nakota stories with the wider world she was coming to know. Drawing on childhood favorites and tales from Lakota storytellers she interviewed, she cleverly retold 14 *ohunkankans* in English. This book, *Old Indian Legends*, was published in 1901, with illustrations by American Indian artist, Angel de Cora.

A Life of Purpose

Gertrude Simmons's marriage to Raymond Bonnin, also an educated Nakota, in 1902, opened a new chapter in her life. The Bonnins moved to the Uintah and Ouray Reservation in Utah, where Raymond worked with the Ute people for the BIA. Their only child, Raymond, or Ohiya ("Winner" in the Nakota dialect), was born in 1903. In addition to motherhood, Gertrude worked in the community organizing among the Utes, teaching for a time and starting a childrens' music program, among other activities.

Ever interested in interpreting Lakota culture to the world, Zitkala-Ša collaborated with composer William Hanson on the opera, Sun Dance, based in her knowledge of traditional musical themes, customs, and ceremonies. Premiering in 1913, the work had several Utah performances. The New York Light Opera Guild put on a revival of *Sun Dance* in 1937, which Zitkala-Ša attended.

During their 14 years in Utah, the Bonnins became increasingly concerned about Indian rights issues. Gertrude corresponded regularly with the journal of the Society of American Indians until 1916, when the Bonnins moved to Washington, D.C. after her election as secretary of the all-Native organization. In 1918 and 1919, she edited the Society's journal. For the next 20 years, Gertrude Simmons Bonnin researched, wrote, and spoke widely on behalf of American Indians. She campaigned for Indian citizenship, reform of the BIA, Indian land rights, and equitable laws for Native peoples. From 1926 until her death in 1938, she was president of the National Council of American Indians. The Council endeavored to assist all American Indians in the struggle to secure their rights and a place in American politics and society. This was a struggle that, from her earliest days, Zitkala-Ša knew by heart.

TEACHING ADVICE FOR ZITKALA-ŠA

Autobiographical Writings

Zitkala-Ša's childhood and young adult autobiography comprises the first 18 chapters and approximately 100 pages of *American Indian Stories* and is the focus of this chapter of Writers of the American West. This chapter also explores her folklore collection, *Old Indian Legends*. Interested students are encouraged to read the additional short stories and essays in *American Indian Stories*.

Age Appropriateness

Though not inappropriate for younger children, students in grades six and higher will use *American Indian Stories* most effectively, due to its writing style and, especially, its content. They may identify with the adolescent anxieties Zitkala-Ša shares. *Old Indian Legends* is appropriate for all ages, children and adults.

36 STORYTELLERS

Meeting the Devil

In *American Indian Stories*, chapter 4, "The School Days of an Indian Girl," Zitkala-Ša has a disquieting first encounter with a graphic portrayal of the Biblical devil.

Lakota, Dakota, Nakota?

The Lakota-oyate, or Sioux, culture is composed of many subgroups, some of which speak different dialects of their language. One tribal member describes the meaning of Lakota-oyate as "many tribes in one nation." Zitkala-Ša's group is the Nakota and she belonged to the Yankton band. Ohiyesa's people (see chapter 1) are the Dakota and sometimes also called the Eastern or Santee, as well as by the name of their individual band, in his case Wahpeton. The final group is the Lakota, which is also the overall name for the culture. The name Sioux, commonly used to refer to the Lakota, was given to them by people outside of the culture.

Native American, American Indian, First People?

In the United States, the appropriate term of reference for Native people may be Native American for some, American Indian, or First American for others. In Canada, First People may be appropriate. Since there is a variety of preferred racial and cultural reference among Native peoples today, this text uses them somewhat interchangeably, for variety's sake, but with respect for all. The most important thing to remember is that groups of people and individuals should be free to refer to themselves in any way they find appropriate and others should respect those preferences.

Zitkala-Ša and Ohiyesa

There is sharp, interesting contrast between Zitkala-Ša's impressionistic, often bitter autobiographical style and the more detailed, affirmative writings of her fellow Lakota and friend, Charles A. Eastman (see chapter 1). What unifies their writings is a mutual desire to sympathetically portray the humanity and value of their native culture to an oppressive, often racist outside world.

Figure 2.4. Storytelling time in a Lakota lodge. Illus. by Angel de Cora.

LEARNING HORIZONS

Literature Aloud Experiences

> *In both Dakotas, North and South, I have often listened to the same story told over again by a new story-teller. While I recognized such a legend without the least difficulty, I found the renderings varying much in little incidents.*
>
> —Zitkala-Ša, from the Preface to *Old Indian Legends*, page v.

❖ ORIGINAL RETELLINGS OF TRADITIONAL TALES

Level: Grades four and higher.

Student Learning Opportunities: Reading; Story selection; Individual and group rehearsal; Memory; Performance.

Background: Individual creativity—it's what separates us humans from parrots. It's what makes storytelling a uniquely individual art form (though nearly all people possess storytelling skills). Different people will tell the same story, even a familiar traditional folk story, with varied conception and style, thanks to their individual creativity. Zitkala-Ša's artful retellings of Lakota folktales in *Old Indian Legends* are a perfect example.

An involving process that blends individual creativity with research, story preparation, and performance is detailed below, in figure 2.5, page 38. The skills developed in Preparing a Story for Telling in **Literature Aloud Experiences** in chapter 1 are a prerequisite.

Extensions: See *Intergenerational Storytelling*, chapter 1.

Teacher Evaluation Opportunities: Story selection; Story rehearsal; Cooperation; Performance.

38 STORYTELLERS

MAKING THE STORY YOUR OWN

1. **Research**

    Locate at least two different versions of a traditional story that you like. (Teachers may provide students with story versions to shorten or simplify the research process.)

    Research Tips—Focus research in the Folklore section of a library (Dewey Decimal System number 398). *The Storyteller's Sourcebook: A Subject, Title, and Motif Index to Folklore Collections for Children* by Margaret Read McDonald (Neal-Schuman) provides an excellent reference for locating story versions. Librarians can be a big help, too.

2. **Story Preparation**

    a. Read each of the story versions several times. Highlight favorite portions of each version's language or story line to include in your version. Jot down any of your own creative ideas you would like to include into the story. Make an outline of the story to organize the plot in your mind.

    b. Referring back to the text versions as needed, begin retelling a simple version of the story in your own words, "blending" the favorite parts together into your version of the story.

    c. Retell your version of the story several more times aloud or on tape. Refer to "Preparing a Story for Telling" in **Literature Aloud Experiences**, chapter 1, for more help in polishing your storytelling.

    d. Swap stories with a sympathetic partner. Provide constructive criticism for each other.

3. **Performance**

    a. When ready, tell your story to a larger audience. Then briefly discuss with them what parts of the story came from the different versions with which you began and which parts came from your own creativity.

    b. If desired for evaluation, teachers can ask students to provide a written text of their version and information about their process for developing it.

Figure 2.5. Preparing a Story for Telling.

Language Arts Experiences

◈ RECOLLECTION

Level: Grades four to eight.

Student Learning Opportunities: Memory; Oral retelling; Written retelling; Narrative writing; Six-Trait Writing—Word Choice, Sentence Fluency, Conventions.

Background: In *American Indian Stories*, Zitkala-Ša delivers a testament to the power and clarity of childhood memories. The same power source, memory, is available for all of us to tap in productive ways, especially as a stimulus for retelling and writing.

Basics:
1. Suggest a topic to stir students' memories. For example: bikes, scars, long trips, holidays, water, pets, favorite people, favorite food, brothers, sisters, cousins, big mistakes. There are countless other evocative prompts to stimulate personal recollection. If individuals are in any way uncomfortable with the first topic, suggest another for them.
2. Give students about 60 seconds to silently revisit the details of the remembered scene. They may close their eyes if it helps with recollection.
3. As a role model, briefly retell a memory of your own on the same topic, if you wish.
4. Connect each student with a partner with whom they can work cooperatively. If necessary, designate which partner is the first storyteller or allow partners to decide who goes first.
5. Have each partner *briefly* retell his or her memory. Allow 60-90 seconds for each recollection. Give a signal halfway through to facilitate the transition of storytellers.
6. To polish the stories, have students form new groups with two to four others for retelling their recollections. Again, allow 60-90 seconds each and give time cues to keep the process moving.
7. Review the steps in the recollection process and solicit discussion about the experience.

Extensions:
1. Have students develop a one- to two-page written version of their recollection. They may add illustrations, if desired.
2. After revision, combine recollections on the same topic into a thematic "book" to share with parents, teachers, and other students and adults.
3. Generate more recollection-powered stories on different topics for retelling and writing.

Teacher Evaluation Opportunities: Cooperation; Oral retellings; Written retellings; Use of Six-Trait Writing techniques.

◆ TRICKSTER TALES, TEACHING TALES

Level: Grades four to eight.

Student Learning Opportunities: Listening; Reading; Text analysis; Narrative and imaginative writing; Six-Trait Writing—Ideas and Organization.

Background: In *Old Indian Legends,* Zitkala-Ša retells many stories of Iktomi, the Lakota spider fairy, the snare weaver, the cunning trickster. Like the West African Anansi, the Polynesian Maui, the Chinese Monkey King, the European Jack, the African and American Brer Rabbit, the American Indian Coyote and many others, Iktomi (Unktomi in Dakota dialect) sometimes does the tricking and sometimes gets tricked. Though all of these characters may be classed as tricksters, each is distinct, coming from widely divergent lands and cultures. These trickster characters provide students with entertaining role models, both positive and negative, through which many lessons in human behavior can be explored.

Basics:
1. Read aloud, or tell the stories to students and have them read a number of examples of trickster tales about Iktomi from *Old Indian Legends* and about other tricksters from a variety of sources.

2. After students become familiar with the trickster characters, discuss the following story elements for each story with them:

    the trickster's mental and physical skills and characteristics

    the trickster's motive(s)

    the trick(s) played

    the reasons for success or failure of the trick(s)

    the behavioral lesson(s) (like the moral of a fable) derived from the story, as identified by students and teacher.

3. As students become familiar with this process, ask them to record their analysis of each story in a section of the **Keeping Track of Tricksters** form, figure 2.6.

Extensions:
1. After students are familiar with the characteristics of trickster tales, have them create their own trickster tales, using their favorite traditional trickster or a main character of their own invention. Prior to writing, they should fill out the Keeping Track of Tricksters form to help organize their trickster tale.

2. Have students prepare traditional or original trickster tales for storytelling. See "Preparing A Story For Telling" in **Literature Aloud Experiences**, chapter 1.

Teacher Evaluation Opportunities: Discussions of characteristics of trickster tales; Keeping Track of Tricksters form; Original trickster tales; Student storytelling; Use of Six-Trait Writing techniques.

KEEPING TRACK OF TRICKSTERS

Story Name_____ Trickster's Name_____

Trickster's Motive_____
_____

Trick(s) Played_____
_____
_____

Reason for Success or Failure of Trick(s)_____
_____
_____

Story's Lesson_____
_____
_____
_____
_____

Story Name_____ Trickster's Name_____

Trickster's Motive_____
_____

Trick(s) Played_____
_____
_____

Reason for Success or Failure of Trick(s)_____
_____
_____

Story's Lesson_____
_____
_____

Figure 2.6. Keeping Track of Tricksters.

42 STORYTELLERS

Social Studies Experiences

❖ *NORTH AMERICAN INDIAN BOARDING SCHOOLS*

Level: Grades six to eight.

Student Learning Opportunities: Historical and literary research; Expository written reporting; Oral reporting; Six-Trait Writing—Ideas, Organization, Word Choice, Sentence Fluency, Conventions.

Background: Boarding schools have played a controversial role in the education of American Indian children in the United States and Canada (and Australia) for more than 100 years. Whether for rapid assimilation, as in the nineteenth century, or for other reasons, children from about the age of eight were routinely removed from family and community to distant locations for long periods of their childhood. As with Zitkala-Ša, this separation had profound and permanent effects. Many individuals view their boarding school experience with distaste and negativity. Others view it positively. A number of residential Indian schools continue to operate today. Boarding schools provide a compelling, if little-known, chapter in North American history for student inquiry.

The topic, Indian boarding schools, suggests many possibilities for student research, reporting, and presentation through text, graphics, audio, video, creative drama, and other media. Some potential information resources for student research are contemporary Native American boarding schools, Indian governmental bodies, historical societies, libraries and librarians, appropriate Internet sites, and knowledgeable individuals in the community. Specific information resources are detailed below. Potential research subjects include:

- The history of American Indian boarding schools in your community, region, state, or province.

- Charles A. Eastman and Zitkala-Ša on Indian boarding schools. Potential information sources—sections of each authors' writings in *From the Deep Woods to Civilization* and *American Indian Stories*, respectively. Also see N. Scott Momaday's childhood autobiography, *The Names* (Tucson: The University of Arizona Press, 1976), for an interesting depiction of a Pueblo day school.

- The lifestyle of a boarding school teacher. Potential information sources—contact with past or present teachers of Indian schools.

- A student-written-and-performed creative drama about events in an Indian boarding school, based on their research, the writings of Eastman or Zitkala-Ša, or other sources.

- The daily life of Indian boarding school students of the past, including both mental and physical tasks performed. (For potential information sources, see North American Indian Boarding School Resources, below.)

- Schools for American Indian students of today. Potential information sources—U.S. Bureau of Indian Affairs, Individual Tribal Governments.

- The traditional play and games of Indian children at home and at boarding school. (For potential information sources, see North American Indian Boarding School Resources, below.)
- The depiction of American Indian schools, students, and teachers in books, fiction and nonfiction. Potential information sources—literature resource guides.

North American Indian Boarding School Resources: Listed below is a sampling of resources on the topic of boarding schools for Native Americans, with suggested reading levels for each literary source:

Text Resources

Adams, David. *Education for Extinction: American Indians and the Boarding School Experience, 1875–1928.* Lawrence, KS: University Press of Kansas, 1995.
 A reference that takes a critical look at boarding schools and the government policy of the era. Adult nonfiction.

DeJong, David H. *Promises of the Past: A History of Indian Education in the United States.* Golden, CO: North American Press, 1993.
 Using excerpts from documents and eyewitness accounts, this resource provides a comprehensive overview of the troubled past of Indian education and suggests options for a more positive future. Adult nonfiction.

Eastman, Elaine Goodale. *Sister to the Sioux.* Lincoln, NE: University of Nebraska Press, 1978.
 The wife of Charles A. Eastman describes her long career as a teacher and advocate for Indian education, as well as her family life. Young adult and adult nonfiction.

Ellis, Clyde. *To Change Them Forever: Indian Education at the Rainy Mountain Boarding School, 1893–1920.* Norman, OK: University of Oklahoma Press, 1996.
 Dealing with education and assimilation among the Kiowa People of Oklahoma, this is one of many recent books telling the stories associated with various boarding schools. Adult nonfiction.

Grutman, Jewel, and Gay Matthaei. *The Ledgerbook of Thomas Blue Eagle.* Illustrated by Adam Cvijanovic. Charlottesville, VA: Thomasson-Grant, 1994.
 A fictional autobiography of a Lakota young man at home on the plains and at Carlisle Indian School. The text presents a sometimes odd mix of realistic fiction and folklore, accompanied by clever illustrations in the style of early day Native student ledger book drawings. Another visually interesting fictional autobiography, the sequel, Julia Singing Bear (Charlottesville, VA: Thomasson-Grant, 1995), replicates an annotated early photo album. Both are juvenile fiction.

Horne, Esther Burnett, and Sally J. McBeth. *Essie's Story: The Life and Legacy of a Shoshone Teacher.* Lincoln, NE: University of Nebraska Press, 1998.
 The story of a longtime educator in Indian boarding schools. Young adult and adult nonfiction.

Qoyawayma, Polingaysi. *No Turning Back.* Albuquerque: University of New Mexico Press, 1964.
 The story of this pioneer educator's life is subtitled, "A True Account of a Hopi Indian Girl's Struggles to Bridge the Gap Between the World of her People and the World of the White Man." Young adult and adult nonfiction.

44 STORYTELLERS

Santiago, Chiori. *Home to Medicine Mountain*. Illustrated by Judith Lowry. San Francisco: Children's Book Press, 1998.

Based on the experiences of the illustrator's father and uncle, two Maidu Indian boys find a way to escape from their California residential school to return home for the summer. Juvenile fiction.

Sterling, Shirley. *My Name Is Seepeetza*. Toronto: Douglas and McIntyre, 1992.

A fictionalized autobiography in the form of a diary, based on the author's experiences in a British Columbia residential school during the 1950s. Young adult fiction.

Video Resources

In the White Man's Image. Christine Lesiak and Mathew Jones. 58 minutes. Alexandria, VA: PBS Video, 1992. From the American Experience Series.

Videocassette that takes a look at students schooled at the Carlisle Indian Industrial School and at its founder Richard Pratt. A Cyberguide for secondary studies based on this video can be found at: http://www.phileadfund.org/grandconverse/E.I.Marcus/eimarcus_nativeam.htm (Accessed June 1, 2000).

Spirit of the Dawn. Heidi Schmidt. 29 minutes. Ho-ho-kus, NJ: New Day Films, 1996.

Videocassette that contrasts boarding schools of the past with a contemporary Crow Reservation school, focusing on the innovative poetry of two sixth-grade boys.

Electronic Resources

Bay Mills Community College Virtual Library, Three Fires Collection. Available: http://www.bmcc.org/vlibrary/special/threefires/tfboardingschools.html (Accessed June 1, 2000).

Provides information on boarding schools and residential schools.

Carlisle Indian Industrial School Website. Available: http://home.epix.net/~landis (Accessed June 1, 2000).

Site features school history and background on students and teachers, including Zitkala-Ša.

First Peoples on Schoolnet. Available: http://schoolnet.ca/aboriginal/cultural_resources-e.html (Accessed June 1, 2000).

A good source for information on contemporary Indian schools in Canada and the U.S.

Feature Articles about Boarding Schools. Available: http://www.canoe.com/CNEWSFeatures9904/28_indians4.html (Accessed June 1, 2000).

Contains information on past problems and current situations in North American Indian schools.

Teacher Evaluation Opportunities: Research and note-taking; Written report; Oral reporting; Other reporting media; Use of Six-Trait Writing techniques.

ZITKALA-ŠA RESOURCES

Zitkala-Ša Books

Zitkala-Ša. American Indian Stories. Lincoln, NE: University of Nebraska Press, 1985 (1921).
  Zitkala-Ša's childhood and young adult autobiography and other essays, with a thorough introduction to the author's life and times by Dexter Fisher.

———. *Old Indian Legends.* Illustrated by Angel de Cora. Lincoln, NE: University of Nebraska Press, 1985 (1901).
  Artful retellings of 14 traditional Lakota stories. The foreword, by Agnes M. Picotte, provides additional information about the author, stories, and customs.

Selected Zitkala-Ša Educational Materials

Rappaport, Doreen. *The Flight of Red Bird: The Life of Zitkala-Ša Re-created from the Writings of Zitkala-Ša and the Research of Doreen Rappaport.* New York: Dial Books, 1997.
  A detailed, 186-page biography, suitable for young adults and adults, which chronicles Zitkala-Ša through her reminiscences, letters, speeches, and stories.

Susag, Dorothea. *Roots and Branches: A Resource of Native American Literature—Themes, Lessons, and Bibliographies.* Urbana, IL: National Council of Teachers of English, 1998.
  Includes a unit for secondary students based in American Indian Stories, with background material on the Lakota, their worldview, and Zitkala-Ša.

Electronic Resources

A Celebration of Women Writers. Available: http://digital.library.upenn.edu/women/ (Accessed June 1, 2000).
  Web site includes information and links on Zitkala-Ša and the complete text of *American Indian Stories* online.

The Internet Public Library. Available: http://www.ipl.org/cgi/ref/native/browse.pl/A91 (Accessed June 1, 2000).
  A brief biography, links, and bibliography are listed.

The Internet School Library Media Center. Available: http://falcon.jmu.edu/~ramseyil/natauth.htm (Accessed June 1, 2000).
  Site provides text links and a teaching unit based on Zitkala-Ša.

The Online Archive of Nineteenth-Century U.S. Women's Writings. Available: http://www.facstaff.bucknell.edu/gcarr/19cUSWW/ZS/rh.html (Accessed June 1, 2000).
  A detailed biography focuses on Zitkala-Ša as a writer, with text links and a further reading list.

University of Virginia Electronic Text Center. Available: http://etext.lib.virginia.edu/etcbin/toccer-new?id=ZitLege&tag=public&images=images/modeng&data=/texts/english/modeng/parsed&part=0 (Accessed June 1, 2000).
  Web site includes the complete text of *Old Indian Legends* online. This text is also available from *Project Gutenberg.* Available: http://www.promo.net/pg/ (Accessed June 1, 2000).

PIONEERING YOUNG PEOPLE

Hal Borland

Julia Archibald Holmes

Ralph Moody

In his book, *Growing up with the Country: Childhood on the Far Western Frontier* (Albuquerque: University of New Mexico Press, 1989), historian Elliott West examines the non-Indian settlement of the western United States. The book claims, quite rightly, that the wandering mountain men, merchants, or cowboys, who are so famous, did not settle the nineteenth- and early-twentieth-century West. It was the lesser-known farming, ranching, town-building families, including the children, who truly settled and transformed it. Yet, even more than the settler parents, the children and young people of this era have been almost completely ignored by historians and popular culture.

Elliott West gives us three very good reasons not to overlook the childrens' history:

◈ Children see the world through different eyes than adults, so their view of the frontier is fresh and distinctive.

◈ Young people play important, and more autonomous, roles in pioneering families and societies, differing from their roles in older, more established communities.

◈ Unlike adults or their city peers, frontier children experience change doubly, because they are growing up personally at the same time that society is "growing up" around them.

48 PIONEERING YOUNG PEOPLE

As with West's, this book tries to highlight, not overlook, the young peoples' remarkable part in the western story. The autobiographers featured in this section, Hal Borland, Julia Archibald Holmes, and Ralph Moody, all embody the distinctive traits of frontier youth that Elliott West identifies. John Muir, Margaret Murie, and even in some ways, Charles A. Eastman, also have pioneering insight that inspired their lives and writing. They all provide excellent models of positive, creative accomplishment, despite of, or even because of, adversity.

If educators and parents can inspire students with the traits of a pioneer childhood—a fresh outlook on life, a sense of independence and involvement, and the ability to cope with change—the young people will certainly benefit. Frontiers are defined by psychological landscapes, not geography or history. No matter in what era children are born, they can see themselves as pioneers ever-approaching new frontiers. As Hal Borland writes at the conclusion of *High, Wide and Lonesome* about what he learned from his childhood on the remote Colorado plains, "I came to know that a frontier is never a place; it is a time and a way of life. I came to know that frontiers pass, but they endure in their people."

The readings and **Learning Horizons** divisions of the chapters in **Pioneering Young People** strive to reinforce for students some positive traits of a frontier childhood. They emphasize personal creativity and point-of-view, autonomous selection of learning tasks, cooperation, a variety of individual and group presentation options, and exploration of social issues and societal change.

HAL BORLAND

CHAPTER 3

Born May 14, 1900 in Sterling, Nebraska. Died February 22, 1978 in Sharon, Connecticut. Childhood and young adult autobiography describes eastern Colorado.

Figure 3.1. Hal Borland, age 16.

AN APPRECIATION OF THE WRITER

By an accident of time and place, I grew up on an American frontier. I was born in 1900, ninety-six years to the day after Lewis and Clark left St. Louis on their expedition across the newly acquired Louisiana Purchase; but my formative years were spent under circumstances not far different from those my great-grandfather knew in western Pennsylvania a century earlier. . . . In that sense, I was born old. I am a kind of bridge between an almost legendary past and a fabulous but often worrisome present. . . . In terms of social history I have lived close to one hundred and fifty years, simply because I grew up on an island of isolation in eastern Colorado.

—Hal Borland from the Foreword of
High, Wide and Lonesome

Hal Borland didn't write for children or young adults. He didn't write just for adults, either. He wrote for all readers. Those of any age who read Hal Borland's books find themselves transported by his direct, evocative style. They find themselves living in the landscapes of his description, living the life that he and his family lived. Like a subtle magician, he brings people and other animals to life with deftly chosen words. These abilities made Borland an expert nature (or in his term, "outdoors") writer. They contribute greatly to his novels and autobiographies.

Will Borland, Hal's father, was a printer and newspaper editor by trade. For his son, he served as an expert writing teacher. He shared the skills of a newspaper office/print shop with Hal, his apprentice. More than just typesetting, the boy learned grammar, syllabication, punctuation, spelling, and graphic layout through firsthand experience. From his apprenticeship he received at least as much as he learned in school. The elder Borland wrote straightforward, forceful prose that was as lean as bone. Hal states that his father gave him the elements of strength and clarity he would need as a writer.

As a reporter, editor and publisher, essayist, editorial writer, novelist, freelancer, scriptwriter and more, Hal Borland made a living with words all of his life. For decades, he wrote regularly for the *New York Sunday Times*. He also authored or edited more than 30 books. Borland's autobiographies of childhood experience, *High, Wide and Lonesome* (1956) and *Country Editor's Boy* (1970), examine homesteading and small-town life on the plains of eastern Colorado. His best-known novel, *When the Legends Die* (1963), presents a dramatic character study of a young Ute Indian coming to terms with himself and American culture. It remains a staple of literature classes from middle school to college, as well as with adult readers. Among many awards, Hal Borland received the John Burroughs Medal for distinguished nature writing in 1968.

Figure 3.2. Sunflowers growing on the site of the Borland homestead cabin, looking east into Ketchem Hollow, Washington County, Colorado. Photo by John Stansfield.

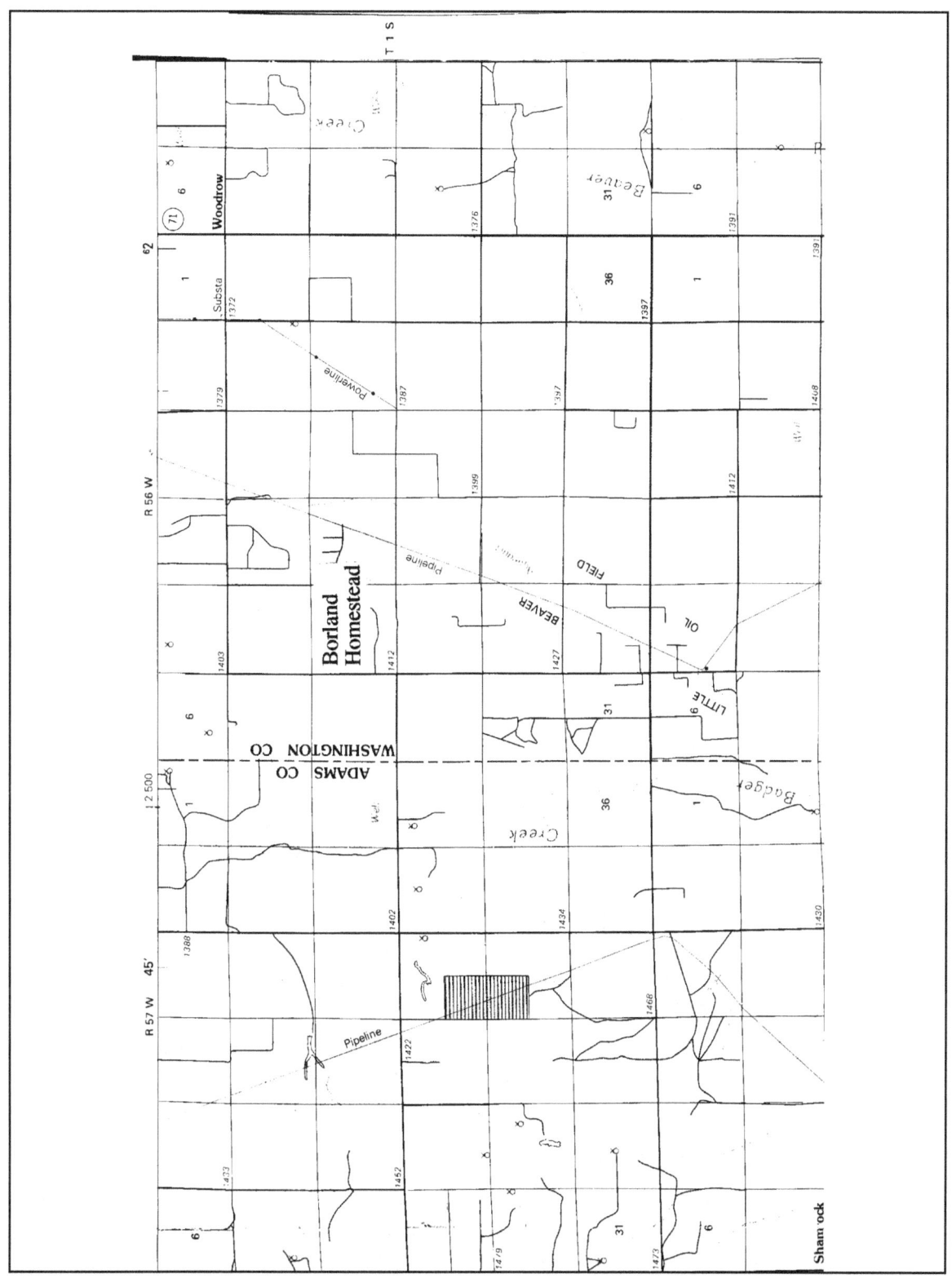

Figure 3.3. Contemporary map of Borland homestead area. Public Domain, courtesy of U.S. Bureau of Land Management.

IN HIS OWN WORDS

Will Borland, Hal's father, suffered through a life-threatening bout with typhoid fever in the fall of 1912. Before Christmas he went to work at the print shop in Brush, Colorado, to earn money for his medical bills, leaving Hal and his mother, Sarah, alone at the homestead to tend the house and the stock. In chapter 16 of *High, Wide and Lonesome,* Hal Borland describes their trials during the arduous first week of January 1913.

Note: The following is excerpted as punctuated and spelled in the original manuscript.

I wanted winter to be exciting. I wanted some real storms. . . . I wanted a real rip-tearing blizzard.

I got it.

The Saturday when we were all set to try to get to Gary (the nearest store and post office) in the buggy it began to snow in midmorning. It was just a slow, quiet snowfall with hardly any wind, but Mother said we'd better not set out in it. I thought she was being too cautious, but by the middle of the afternoon I knew she was right. The wind came up and it really started to blizzard.

[I] said, "We've got a *real* storm this time!"

Mother said, "I'm afraid so. We'd better bring in some extra sheep chips for the night."

. . . She wasn't afraid of wind or weather. She tied a scarf over her head and took a fuel pail and we started for the barn. We barely got around the corner of the house when the wind hit her. It blew her skirts against her legs and knocked her feet right out from under her. When I ran to help her, both our pails blew away . . . I had to chase those pails halfway up the slope on the far side of the draw. When I started back the air was so full of snow the light in the window at the house was only a faint distant glow. . . .

I helped her back to the house (with the chips), then finished the barn chores. By then it was drifting so much that I had to wade waist deep in snow to get to the door, and I stopped and got a shovel to take in the house. If this kept up we might have to dig out by morning.

While we ate supper the wind sifted snow in around every window. . . . We hung old quilts over the windows to break the gusts of fine snow and we stuffed a towel under the door. Mother put the hot flatirons in our beds and I tried to read for a while, sitting with my feet in the oven. But the fire died, sucked right up the chimney, and I went to bed. . . .

It snowed and blew all night. When I awakened the next morning there was a little drift of snow on the edge of my bed, and when I stepped down I went into a drift a foot deep on the floor. . . . When I opened the house door I found a solid wall of snow. The drift there was six feet deep.

We knew it was still blowing. We could hear it. But we didn't know it was still snowing until I tunneled through that drift at the door. . . . It took me an hour to get clear. . . . It was eleven o'clock when I reached the barn and got the door open there.

Everything was all right at the barn. The snow had banked it and the animal heat made it almost as warm as the house. I did the milking and rationed out the extra hay I had got in the day before and started back to the house. I had to dig out every path because they'd all drifted full again. Before I got to the house, the milk was full of slush, half frozen though it had been warm when I left the barn.

The wind eased off somewhat that evening, but the snow continued. The second day I had to dig out all over again. And that day I had to water the stock. They couldn't go any longer without it. Mother said she was going to help. She'd learned what wind could do to her skirts, so she put on a pair of Father's overalls, belted them at the waist, tied them at the ankles, and put on overshoes, coat and scarf. She carried kettles of boiling water and thawed the pump while I got on [our horse] Mack and broke trail from the barn to the well. When we had a trail opened through the shallower drifts, Daisy and the calves followed to the well, drank, and were very happy to get back in the barn. And that afternoon I had to find some way to get hay. The only way was to dig a path to the stacks, carve off a big slice of one stack with the hay knife, and carry it into the barn.

Before I got the hay into the barn I began to wonder if I really wanted a blizzard. My arms ached, my ears stung, I was sweating like a horse and when I stopped to catch my breath the sweat seemed to turn to icicles in my armpits. But I got the hay in, and I did the evening chores, and I shoveled my way back to the house, where the big bowl of pinto beans was worth all the sweating. . . .

That was our pattern for four days, wind and snow and shoveling, and pumping and milking and carrying sheep chips. . . . The snow probably stopped on the third day, though we couldn't tell. There were flashes of sunlight, but the air was still full of snow, undoubtedly blown from the hilltops. . . . But at last the wind eased away and the plains lay white and silent. And new—white, gleaming, pristine new. . . .

For ten days the snow lay crusted. Then we wakened one morning to the bawling of cattle. I went outside and saw a thin and wavering band of a dozen steers working their way slowly toward the house from Ketchem Hollow. They would walk a little way through the crusted drifts, then stop and bawl, and the snow behind them was dark with the blood from their ice-gashed legs. . . .

As they came closer to the house Fritz and I worked our way toward them. I shouting, Fritz barking, trying to turn them back. But by then they had smelled the hay. . . . If they got [to] the stack yards, starving as they were, no fence could hold them. . . . One taste of [hay] and they would go mad; they would stay till they finished the last of it.

I ran back to the house for the buggy whip. Mother was up and ready to help. She took the whip and I got a pitch fork. We went back and lashed and jabbed and clubbed the steers till they milled in a big hollow in the snow. But they wouldn't turn and go back the way they came. . . .

We fought them for half an hour, a losing fight. Then Mother ran to the house and came back with the .25.20 rifle. She stood on a drift and aimed at a big red steer. The steer stood staring at her, a perfect target. Then she lowered the rifle and asked, "Where do you shoot a steer to kill it, the head or the heart?"

"The head," I said. "I'll do it." I reached for the rifle.

"No!"

Again she aimed. Again I held my breath, waiting for the shot. It didn't come. Again she lowered the rifle. She closed her eyes and shook her head and whispered, "I can't. I can't!"

"Here!" I reached for the gun again.

"No!" And she turned and fired a shot, at last. Over the heads of the steers.

The steers snorted, turned and lunged away. Mother fired another shot. Those nearest us crowded the others into the path they had made up the hollow. Fritz was at their heels, yelping and snapping. I was shouting. One more shot and they were trotting down their bloody path, away from the house and the hay. I ran along the drifts, shouting encouragement to Fritz. Together we kept them going all the way down into Ketchem Hollow. There they turned north, down the big valley, no longer even bawling. They were still going, still crowding through those ice-edged drifts, when we turned back to the house.

End of excerpted manuscript.

THE WRITER'S LIFE

In the Foreword to *High, Wide and Lonesome*, Hal Borland remarks, "Looking back from this age of atomic power, our life on the homestead seems almost as strange as life in Medieval England." Strange, but true. In his writing, Borland maintains a historian's perspective on the rapid changes of the twentieth century and a clear-eyed view to the events of his childhood.

Will Borland, Hal's father, was the son of a son of a frontiersman, the family ever-moving westward since coming from Scotland before the Revolutionary War. Hal's mother, Sarah Clinaburg Borland, came from pioneer stock, as well. Both parents were raised in southeastern Nebraska. From the age of 14, Will was a printer and, later, a newspaper editor by trade.

At 32, Will Borland got the westering urge to homestead on the high, dry plains of Colorado. This prairie stood mostly undisturbed, passed by waves of earlier settlement. Gone were the Native Americans, driven into relocation on reservations. Gone were the great herds of bison and other large animals that amazed Lewis and Clark. But the land remained. In the late winter of 1910, Will located and filed claim to a treeless, 320-acre homestead about 30 miles south of the South Platte River community of Brush, Colorado. Sarah and Hal, their preparations completed in Nebraska, followed him in April. In *High, Wide and Lonesome*, Hal tells of the family experience with that land.

The Homestead

"When father and I started out, that late April [1910] morning, it was like the dawn of creation . . . all spring and new beginnings." Bound for their homestead on a wagon full of building supplies, Hal had his first views of the wide-open country that was to be his home for the next five years. The grassy world brimmed with promise for a boy, almost 10—and for his father.

On their first morning in Ketchem Hollow, Washington County, Colorado, Will and Hal located their house on the south-facing slope of the valley. Built of lumber, it measured 14 feet by 20 feet. It was wooden-walled and roofed with an exterior, insulating layer of native sod blocks. The front door faced east, toward Nebraska and the rising sun. With a hand auger, Will drilled a well at the foot of the slope that produced "good soft water" at a depth of 17 feet. With their new home taking shape, Will and Hal returned to Brush for Sarah and more supplies.

When the three Borlands headed south from Brush, the wagon was heaped with windows, a door, a well pump, a stove, furniture, a barrel of dishes, two crates of chickens tied on top, and two balky cows trailing behind. Most important, Sarah rode in the wagon with them this time. Sarah liked the rough skeleton of their house. To her it was big enough for living and not too big to care for.

Soon a sod chicken house and a sod-walled wooden barn kept company with the house. Hal planted "sod corn" in furrows Will plowed, each row separated by strips of grass to hold the moisture of the soil. They cut, raked, and stacked nutritious bluestem grass hay from the valley bottom for winter animal feed. Then they fenced the haystacks to keep their cows out. But it was someone else's cattle that taught the new homesteaders a valuable lesson.

A large herd of open-range cattle invaded their land one night. The Borlands drove them away from their haystacks, but the greening cornfield was badly damaged. The next morning a cowboy, Jack Clothier from the Lazy Four ranch, stopped by. With his apology for the cornfield, he delivered bad news, "When land is not under fence it's technically open range. You should have fenced your corn, mister." The era of free grazing for ranchers' stock on public lands was not yet over. (In much of the West, the laws still stand—fence out or suffer the consequences.)

In the years that followed, despite their rocky first meeting, Jack Clothier and the Borlands became friends. Living few and far between on the land, the hard-working homesteaders appreciated the occasional companionship, mutual aid, and help in emergencies provided by neighbors. Bachelor Jake Farley, a lifelong farmer and great storyteller whose homestead was two miles east, was the Borlands' nearest neighbor. Nearest, except in summer, when Louie, the eccentric sheepherder, and 1,000 or more of rancher John Gerrity's sheep inhabited Ketchem Hollow and surrounding open range. Louie gave Hal a clever pup, which he named Fritz.

Other homesteaders, for a great variety of reasons, took up their pieces of the prairie. Some lasted the five years it took to patent a homestead claim. Many did not. Emily Woods, a former teacher with only one leg, built her own house on top of a hill. Lanky George Grant, dying of tuberculosis, chose a hilltop, too, on which he could sit and watch the clouds and sky. Emily and George grew close, for "in both of them was an acceptance of what life had done to them." The Bromleys, former Chicagoans inexperienced at farming, loaned Hal books of classic literature, which he read voraciously. John Kraus died violently, trampled to death by the horses he physically abused. Vagabond Jim Walker sent his wild children out to rob the neighbors, who banded together and threatened the Walkers into moving on. All of these neighbors and more, Hal Borland describes in deft character sketches, scattered throughout *High, Wide and Lonesome*.

As deftly drawn are Borland's descriptions of his discoveries in the natural world of the prairie. The boundaries of his boyhood were the distant lines of the horizon. Awaiting discovery within that expanse were badgers, beetles, burrowing owls, rattlesnakes, prairie chickens, hawks, and prairie dog towns. There were lots of jackrabbits to be hunted with Fritz. Hal found buffalo skulls and bones near arrowheads and spear points, all remnants of the recent past. He watched sunrises from the wagon seat on trips to town and sunsets from his favorite perch on a haystack behind the house. And the wind most always blew.

After a dry, "open" winter of 1911, hot winds of spring and summer brought a drought. Crops were poor. The Borlands lost their two horses and a cow from eating death camas, a poisonous plant. Worst of all, during the fall of 1912, Will nearly died after contracting typhoid fever while working a short stint on a newspaper in the mountains. After his six weeks in the tiny Brush hospital, the family's debt was substantial. But, Sarah gamely stated that they had never starved yet. Two weeks later Will found work at the print shop in Brush. Hal and Sarah fought that winter's heavy blizzards alone, burning sheep chips to stay warm. By the time the sod corn was planted in May, the Borlands were free of debt—and the worry that comes with it.

For four years, until a one-room school was built nearby in 1914, Hal Borland's schooling came from his parents, his work and play experiences on the homestead, the natural world around him, and some borrowed books and magazines. During his frontier boyhood, he learned firsthand one of the primary lessons that the North American West can teach. As he states at the conclusion of *High, Wide and Lonesome*, "I came to know that a frontier is never a place; it is a time and a way of life. I came to know that frontiers pass, but they endure in their people."

Figure 3.4. Flagler, Colorado, celebrates its famous son. Photo by John Stansfield.

The Prairie Town

The time had come, Hal's parents knew, for Hal to have more formal education. It was time, too, for Will to look for a town that needed a newspaper editor; time for them all to have a better life.

In *Country Editor's Boy*, Hal Borland presents a straightforward depiction of his life from 1915 to 1918 and that of his family and that town—Flagler, Colorado. Absent are some of the poetic descriptions and character sketches found in *High, Wide and Lonesome*. However, both books deliver autobiography with clean, muscular narrative style.

In the summer of 1915, Will Borland "proved up" on his homestead claim and received the land patent. He bought a newspaper in Flagler, Colorado, *The News*. It was just what the editor was looking for—an opportunity to build a business in a small, but growing eastern Colorado town. It also provided the opportunity to teach Hal the skills of a printer, so he would always have a trade to fall back on. Hal's apprenticeship began the day after he and Sarah arrived in Flagler. (As of this writing, the newspaper is still being published.)

Like his father before him, Hal began as printer's devil, each day cleaning the basement office and the inky presses. Learning typesetting was his next task. He arranged the backward, movable metal type by hand and became adept at proofreading it upside down. Next came the skill and timing involved in feeding single paper sheets into the printing press. Most of all that summer, Hal learned the art of composition, of using words well, a skill that sustained him all his life. For the next four years, most days after school and during summers, he worked at the ink trade, becoming a journeyman printer.

Time off from *The News* meant time to explore the prairie country around Flagler on foot and bicycle with new friends, Little Doc Williams and Spider Miner. In September, Hal entered high school as a freshman, a year behind his friends of the same age due to his lack of formal schooling on the homestead. The principal, grudgingly at first, allowed him to take six classes for two years to catch up, instead of the usual four. With hard work, Borland finished high school in three years, and was valedictorian for his graduating class of 11.

Figure 3.5. Hal Borland in his later years.

Hal Borland studied at the University of Colorado for two years and graduated from the Columbia University School of Journalism in 1923, with a stint as associate editor of the *Flagler News* in between. He worked as a journeyman newspaperman in Colorado and Philadelphia, before becoming a staff writer for the *New York Times* in 1937. He began freelance writing editorials, articles and books in 1943 and continued for the rest of his life. Hal Borland may have inherited technical skills as a newsman from his father, but his perspectives as a writer are all his own.

Writing of his boyhood in *High, Wide and Lonesome*, chapter 2, Borland makes a statement that may be profoundly true of the western childhoods of many of the men and women featured in this book, when he says, "The boundaries of boyhood, as I knew them for a time, were that thin, distant line of the horizon; and even that did not bound the dreams and the imagination. . . . Those who live with a far horizon in their boyhood are never again bound to a narrow area of life. They may bind themselves, but that is a different matter."

TEACHING ADVICE FOR HAL BORLAND

Autobiographical Writings

Hal Borland's two autobiographies of childhood are *High, Wide and Lonesome* (1956), about his family's struggles with a dry-land homestead from 1910 to 1915, and *Country Editor's Boy* (1970), which deals with his adolescent years in the eastern Colorado town of Flagler. Interested students are encouraged to read additional works by Borland, including the true-life *This Hill, This Valley* (1957) and *The Dog Who Came to Stay* (1961); the brief seasonal folklore work, *The Youngest Shepherd* (1962); and *When the Legends Die* (1963), a novel.

Age Appropriateness

All of Borland's works read well aloud for listeners of any age. Good readers in fourth and fifth grade should have no problem mastering his narrative due to its clarity of style. If length is a problem for less able fourth or fifth graders, appropriate episodes can be excerpted easily from the mostly chronological texts of the autobiographies. *High, Wide and Lonesome* presents the most appropriate content for study by students in grades four to eight.

Borland and Moody

Hal Borland and Ralph Moody (chapter 5) came to eastern Colorado at almost the same time. They shared many similar experiences with horses, injury, severe weather, and outdoor discovery. Yet, they possess quite different personalities, perspectives, and writing styles. In becoming familiar with both, students may learn much from comparing and contrasting the lives of these two well-known western writers.

Touchy Terminology

Chapter 20 of *High, Wide and Lonesome* includes mild profanity and brief mentions of rape and human castration. At various points in *Country Editor's Boy*, there is mild profanity in the dialogue. In chapter 15, strong profanity and sexual reference appear in the dialogue, along with descriptions of violent acts inflicted upon wildlife.

Out of Print

At the time of this writing, both *High, Wide and Lonesome* and *Country Editor's Boy* are out of print. Until some intelligent publisher reissues them, the texts, especially *High, Wide and Lonesome*, are still readily available from school and public libraries.

LEARNING HORIZONS

Literature Aloud Experiences

◈ *PREPARING AND PRESENTING A CLASSROOM CHAUTAUQUA*

Level: Grades four and higher.

Student Learning Opportunities: Selection of art form and content; Rehearsal; Staging; Cooperation; Performance.

Background: In the summer of 1917, a traveling series of Chautauqua (shuh-TAW-kwa) programs came to Flagler, largely at the suggestion of Will Borland in the *Flagler News*. Begun to stimulate both soul and intellect at the summer resort of Chautauqua Lake, New York in 1874, these literature and performing arts–centered programs soon spread to communities across North America, and were presented in all seasons. Like many of the latter-day traveling series, the Standard Chautauqua that came to Flagler offered culture and entertainment, two programs a day for five days. The series included a musical quartet, serious and humorous lectures, a small operetta company, games and activities for young people, and more.

Chautauquas provided high-quality cultural enrichment for many isolated western communities in the days before television and radio. Unlike electronic media, they educated and entertained people of all ages in a powerful way—in person. Chautauquas of various kinds are still popular in a number of western states and provinces. Students, teachers, and others from the school and community can work together to put on their own classroom Chautauqua, drawing upon their varied interests and abilities.

Orientation: Teachers can introduce students to the concept of Chautauquas by reading aloud chapter 19 of *Country Editor's Boy* or other material (such as encyclopedia entries) about Chautauqua and its history. Remind them that a Chautauqua is more than a talent show or series of skits. It is a performing arts festival, involving music, dance, theater, and the spoken word. It should be entertaining *and* educational.

Selection: Have all Chautauqua participants decide which form of presentation they want to make. Do they want to perform alone or in a group? Possibilities are nearly endless, limited only by the bounds of entertainment and/or education, appropriateness of content, and good taste. To assure quality, teachers or a student–teacher committee can review and suggest revisions for each presentation at the outset. Some classroom Chautauqua options include:

- Musical performance—solo or ensemble; instrumental, vocal, or both
- Short operetta—ensemble
- One-act play—ensemble
- Poetry reading or recitation—solo or ensemble
- A choreographed dance piece—solo or ensemble
- Speech—an original oration or a famous speech from the past read aloud or recited
- Humorous monologue—solo
- Dramatic interpretation of literature—solo or ensemble
- Choral reading—ensemble
- Reenactment of a significant event from history—solo or ensemble
- An Autobiography Alive characterization—see **Literature Alive Experiences**, chapter 6
- Storytelling—solo or tandem; see **Literature Alive Experiences**, chapter 1 and chapter 2

Every community contains performers and presenters, skilled in various interests, professions, and art forms, who might help coach performers and/or participate in a classroom Chautauqua. If required, determine funding sources to pay them for their contribution to the event.

Preparation: Adequate rehearsal time is essential to quality performances. If possible, recruit and orient teen or adult volunteers to work with each student or group throughout rehearsals. Encourage students to rehearse at home, not just at school.

Staging for the Chautauqua should be simple and functional. This puts emphasis on the art form and content of the performances, rather than on props and technology. Simple staging facilitates quick transition from one performance to another and ease of movement to different performance venues, when necessary.

Performance: In the tradition of the Chautauqua series, spread the performances over several days or nights, if possible. In program planning, be conscious of the attention span of your audience, as well as your performers. Present an interesting variety of art forms at each performance. Integrating adult performers into the event provides for excellent role modeling, as well.

Extensions: If feasible, take your Chautauquans "on the road," into the community at large, enhancing both the performers' skills and community goodwill.

Teacher Evaluation Opportunities: Selection of art form and content; Thoroughness of rehearsal and staging; Cooperation; Performance.

Chautauqua Resources: Listed below is a sampling of resources on the topic of Chatauquas, with suggested reading levels for each literary source:

Text Resources

Simpson, Jeffrey. *Chautauqua: An American Utopia.* Photos by Paul Solomon. New York: Harry N. Abrams in association with the Chautauqua Institution, 1999.

A concise history of the Chautauqua Institution of New York State, the "home base" of the Chautauqua movement since 1874. The 128-page text is illustrated with contemporary and archival photographs. Most appropriate as a reference for grades seven to adult.

Tapia, John E. *Circuit Chautauqua: From Rural Education to Popular Entertainment in Early Twentieth Century America.* New York: McFarland, 1997.

Tracing the history of the Chautauqua Movement from its roots in nineteenth-century lyceum programs through the rise and fall of circuit Chautauqua, this book also provides details about the performers and presenters who made it a reality. For adults.

Electronic Resources

The Chautauqua Institution Online. Available: http://www.chautauqua-inst.org (Accessed November 20, 2000).

The Chautauqua Institution in New York State is alive and well with a nine-week session each summer, attended by more than 140,000 people. The Web site includes a brief history, information about summer programs in the performing arts and lectures, descriptions of arts schools and workshops for children and adults, and details on year-round programs.

Language Arts Experiences

❖ TALL TALE–MAKING

Level: Grades four to eight.

Student Learning Opportunities: Reading; Understanding tall-tale story forms; Imaginative writing; Six-Trait Writing—Ideas, Word Choice, Voice.

Background: One of the most popular story types in western North America in the past 150 years is the form of folklore called the tall tale. Perhaps the grand scale of the western landscape, itself, encourages such exaggerated stories, also known as "whoppers," "stretchers," "big windys," and "just plain lies." Although western tall tales are often associated with real or imaginary characters, such as Pecos Bill, Slewfoot Sue, Paul Bunyan, or Annie Oakley, some of the best are first-person narratives that sneak up on listeners with humor and hyperbole. Young people can deepen their involvement with things western by becoming skilled in the tall-tale story form.

Basics:
1. Read aloud or have students read Hal Borland's description of neighbor Jake Farley's tall-tale telling in chapter 8 of *High, Wide and Lonesome.* Explore a number of other western tall tales through storytelling, reading aloud, or individual reading. Good sources are the Pecos Bill stories and books by B. A. Botkin, Sid Fleischman, Glen Rounds, and Roger Welsch.

2. Discuss and identify the characteristics of tall tales, particularly that they:

   - begin with common, everyday situations
   - are rooted in earthly reality, not science fiction or fairytale (For example, Babe, the blue ox, is big, but still an ox, not an alien. What occurs happens through exaggeration, not magic.)
   - stretch the truth well beyond the normal
   - have a humorous, not derogatory, intent
   - use folksy, colloquial language
   - use first-person or third-person narration

3. In a small-group or whole-group setting, have the teacher and students *briefly* retell their own version of a "short tall tale," a favorite tall tale from among those recently read or heard.

4. Have students prepare a written version of their "short tall tale" in a maximum of one to two pages.

Extensions:
1. Using their knowledge of tall-tale story form, have students write an original tall tale.
2. When revision is complete, have students share their stories aloud with the class and other audiences.

Teacher Evaluation Opportunities: Participation in discussion; Written traditional tall tale; Written original tall tale; Performance of tall tale; Use of Six-Trait Writing techniques.

Social Studies Experiences

◆ *A QUICK CLASSROOM HISTORY EXHIBIT*

Level: Grades four to eight.

Student Learning Opportunities: Reading; Research; Expository writing for interpretation; Six-Trait Writing—Organization, Word Choice, Sentence Fluency.

Background: What separates an educationally effective history exhibit from a collection of junk is the way it is interpreted. Interpretation involves telling a story, through words and pictures, that helps people understand a particular person, place, time period, or thing. Putting objects into context, presenting an appropriate story or clear information about them, is the job of the interpreter. Whether it is an artifact made by a human or a natural object, an interpreter, young or old, can make it meaningful to others. All that is needed is a special something to interpret and the ability to express the object's importance.

Basics:

1. Read aloud the interpretation Hal Borland does in describing his flint and arrowhead discoveries, near the beginning of chapter 5 of *High, Wide and Lonesome*. Ask students to share their recollections of interpretive programs they have experienced at zoos, museums, parks, or other locales.

2. Ask students to identify an interesting object with connections to their personal or family history, similar to the way the arrow points and buffalo skull are connected to Hal. It should be something that, with a little research, they can interpret through background information or a story. For example, the object might be a silver dollar or a military relic.

3. Have students develop text, with a *maximum* of 60 words, and graphics or illustrations, if desired, that interpret their object. Don't forget the exhibitor/interpreter's name. When completed, text and graphics must fit attractively on one 8½-x-11-inch, cardboard-backed placard. (Professional interpreters often face word and size limitations in their work, too.) Most important, interpreters must explain the significance of the object clearly and simply. For example, in story format, explain how the silver dollar was handed down in the family; in information format, describe where and when the dollar was minted and how it was made.

4. To avoid loss, breakage, and other trauma, bring objects to school only when the interpretive placards are complete, on the day of the exhibit. Photocopies, videos, or photographs can be substituted for items too fragile, valuable, or large to transport.

5. Place the historical objects and placards on display. Interpreters should be prepared to answer questions and provide additional oral information about their objects when requested.

Extensions:

1. Judging of interpretive placards is an option. Give each exhibit visitor three or more small pieces of colored paper to place beside their favorite placards during viewing. Recognition can be given to those receiving the most colored pieces.

2. Have students develop a longer interpretive presentation on their historical objects. This can be done in written and/or illustrated form, audio or video tape recording, storytelling, play, or reader's theater, choreographed dance, or other creative means. The sky's the limit, as long as interest lasts among students and teachers.

Teacher Evaluation Opportunities: Thoroughness of research; Clarity and presentation of text (and graphics, if used) in interpretive placard; Expanded interpretive presentation; Use of Six-Trait Writing techniques.

Multidisciplinary Language Arts and Social Studies Experiences

◈ THE PUBLIC DOMAIN—PART 1: HOMESTEADING — "OH, GIVE ME A HOME..."

Level: Grades four to eight.

Student Learning Opportunities: Historical and literary research skills; Descriptive and expository written reporting; Oral reporting; Creative dramatics; Six-Trait Writing —Ideas and Organization.

Background: When President Thomas Jefferson masterminded the purchase of the Louisiana Territory from France in 1803, it greatly expanded the public domain of the United States. First recognized by the Continental Congress in 1779, the revolutionary concept of public domain meant that all the lands west of the 13 original colonies to the Mississippi River belonged to the nation's people. No king, emperor, or powerful individual or family controlled the lands, as in other parts of the world. Many historians claim that creation of the public domain was second in national importance only to the Constitution and the Bill of Rights.

The Lewis and Clark expedition to the Pacific Ocean via the Missouri and Columbia rivers (1804–1806) was in the preparation stage at the time the Louisiana Purchase occurred. It soon provided the young nation with valuable information about the West's geography, economic potential, and Native peoples. Settlers and land speculators rapidly followed in the explorers' footsteps, despite recommendations by Jefferson and Meriwether Lewis that western lands be reserved for Natives, fur trappers, and traders. The Native American tribal claims to the lands were largely ignored. They were not yet citizens with the right to purchase or preempt (homestead) land from the public domain.

Hal Borland's family homestead claim was probably filed under the Enlarged Homestead Act of 1909. One of the last of numerous U.S. homestead laws, the Act addressed "dry-farming" lands not suitable for irrigation. Although the Borlands and many others successfully patented their land claims from the public domain during a relatively wet period of years, the drought and dust bowl of the 1920s and 1930s proved the error of encouraging "sod-busting" for dryland farming on the plains west of the 100th Meridian and showed the ecological value of intact native grasslands.

Basics: The topics, homesteading and the public domain, suggest many possibilities for student research and reporting through text, graphics, audio, video, creative dramatics, vocal performance, and other media. Some potential information resources for student research are historical societies, museums, libraries and librarians, appropriate Internet sites, videos, history textbooks, and knowledgeable individuals in the community. More specific information resources are detailed below. Potential research subjects include:

- The history of public lands and settlement in your family, community, region, state, or province. Potential information sources—family histories, public library, local history collections, historical societies, and museums.

- The remarkable story of the Lewis and Clark expedition. Potential information sources—*The Journals of Lewis and Clark* (New York: Dover) and other books about the expedition.

- Native American views of settlement in the West. Potential information sources—Indian governmental bodies, tribal museums, and historical societies.

- Everyday life on a pioneer homestead in western North America. Potential information sources—contact with past or present homesteaders.

- A student-written-and-performed creative drama about homesteads or homesteading, based on their research, the writings of Hal Borland or Laura Ingalls Wilder, or other source material.

- The depiction of homesteading children and adults in various books, fiction and non-fiction. Potential information sources—literature resource guides such as various editions of *Adventuring with Books* (Urbana, IL: National Council of Teachers of English).

- The songs of the emigrant and homestead era (including "Sweet Betsy from Pike," "Starving to Death on a Government Claim," "Home on the Range," and many others). Potential information sources—contact with folk musicians and folk music societies in the United States and Canada.

- The play and games of homesteading children, including re-creating the games.

- Mapping and analyzing the routes used by American Indians, Spanish explorers, Lewis and Clark, the Oregon, California, Mormon, Santa Fe and other western trails, and railroad rights-of-way across western North America.

Teacher Evaluation Opportunities: Opportunities for formal and informal evaluation vary greatly depending on the homesteading-related project selected by individuals or groups of students.

❖ THE PUBLIC DOMAIN—PART 2: PUBLIC LANDS— "WHERE THE BUFFALO ROAM AND THE DEER AND THE ANTELOPE PLAY"

Level: Grades four to eight.

Student Learning Opportunities: Map skills; Narrative, expository, and imaginative written reporting; Oral reporting; Six-Trait Writing —Word Choice and Voice.

Background: In the final chapter of *High, Wide and Lonesome*, Hal Borland describes the location of his family's homestead as the north half of section 17 in Township one south of Range 56 west, containing 320 acres. Based on a cadastral (real estate) survey, a rectangular system of township, range, and section (T-R-S) was used to define and quantify almost all of the vast public domain of the United States.

In the T-R-S system, each township is composed of 36 square miles arranged in a six-by-six grid, with each one-mile-square section containing 640 acres. (So, the Borland's north half of section 17 was 320 acres.) The numbered Townships define the north-to-south axis of the grid, while the Ranges number the grid's east-to-west dimensions. Smaller parts of each Section are identified by halves and quarters. This system for defining land is still in use today, especially on public lands. T-R-S creates a "language" for "reading" the landscape.

66 PIONEERING YOUNG PEOPLE

About one-third of the United States still remains in public ownership. This is primarily the result of the conservation and preservation movements and laws of the late nineteenth and twentieth centuries, which recognized that, in the long term, disposal of all of the public domain would not benefit the American people or the environment. The laws established agencies to manage portions of the public lands and resources for the people: the U.S. Forest Service (USFS) to manage national forests; the National Park Service (NPS) for national parks, monuments, and historic and cultural sites; the U.S. Fish and Wildlife Service (USFWS) to manage wildlife and their habitat; and, the Bureau of Land Management (BLM) to manage the rest of the public domain. The U.S. system of public land protection has been emulated, with many variations, by many other nations, including Canada. These public lands are a substantial legacy for present and future generations worldwide.

Students can come to know and feel at home with their lands in the public domain by learning to navigate and to "read" the Township, Range and Section system.

Basics:
1. Acquire multiple copies of one USFS or BLM map using the T-R-S coordinate system for use as reference by individual students or small groups. Maps of areas near home are especially good. (See **Map Resources**, below, for guidance in obtaining maps.)

2. Have students take time to familiarize themselves with the various elements of the map: compass directions, scale, key symbols, color system, familiar locations (if any), landmarks listed, township and range grid markings at the map edges, and the section lines and numbers within the map. Point out to students the section numbering system—section numbers arranged both from right to left and left to right, from 1 to 36 starting in the upper right (northeast) corner.

3. To help students become more familiar with the T-R-S system, distribute copies of the T-R-S worksheet, figure 3.6, page 68, with 36 blank square boxes, arranged in a six-by-six grid. Ask students to number the center of each box from 1 to 36, as on the map.

4. Locate a variety of landmarks and their T-R-S coordinates on the public land map. Have students play the Coordinate Quiz by finding landmarks when given the T-R-S numbers. Also, ask them to determine the T-R-S numbers for given landmarks. Play until they are comfortable locating map details using the grid system. For example, "I'm looking for the name of a creek in Township 13 south, Range 68 west, Section 32," or "I'm looking at Lake George near the top edge of the map. Has everyone found it? OK, tell me in what township and range it is located. In what sections is it located?" This activity can be done orally, in writing, or both.

5. Assign each student one township of their own on the public land map. Ask them to copy the number for that township on the right (east) edge of the section grid on the T-R-S worksheet. Copy the corresponding range number on the top (north) edge of the section grid. Finally, ask students to make a map of their township by transferring details from the public land map to the corresponding location on the worksheet, using the section numbers and lines for guidance. Add color to student maps, if desired. If a large blank wall is available, display the student maps in correct T-R-S relation to each other.

Extensions:

1. Provide students with a T-R-S map showing more detail than the USFS or BLM map, such as a U.S. Geologic Service topographic map. (A map in the "7.5 minute series" is best. See **Map Resources**, below, for guidance in obtaining maps.) Prepare a brief Coordinate Quiz for this map. After taking time for students to become acquainted with this map, present the Coordinate Quiz, as in **Basics**, step 4.

2. Ask students to create a 10-question Coordinate Quiz of their own, offering landmarks and T-R-S coordinates for their classmates to locate, as in **Basics**, step 4.

3. Have students select a real locale in western North America where they would have liked to homestead, if they had lived in Will and Sarah Borland's day. After researching the geography of that locale, they can write a letter to an imaginary friend elsewhere describing how they make a living, their lifestyle, the landscape, natural resources, and other details of their "homestead." Share letters aloud.

4. Have students create their own map of an imaginary township and a key for it, using a blank T-R-S worksheet and symbols from their public lands map key plus additional ones they want to invent. (See Appendix, page 249, for map symbols.)

5. Provide students with maps, like the *National Geographic Trails Illustrated* series, which are based in other geographic systems (such as degrees, minutes, and seconds of latitude and longitude). (See **Map Resources**, below, for guidance in obtaining maps.) After familiarization time, give students a Coordinate Quiz, as in **Basics**, step 4, reinforcing their ability to locate information in the new "language" of that system.

6. If possible in your locale, take students on a hike and have them apply their map skills to help navigate by using a detailed T-R-S (or other system) map.

Teacher Evaluation Opportunities: Cooperation and participation in group activities; T-R-S worksheet; Letter to an imaginary friend; Imaginary township map; Informal observation of concept mastery; Post-test Coordinate Quiz or other test format using the T-R-S system as formal evaluation of concept mastery; Use of Six-Trait Writing techniques.

Map Resources: USFS, BLM, and USGS maps are available from: USGS Information Services, Box 25286, Federal Center, Denver, CO 80225, 1-888-ASK-USGS. State-by-state USGS map lists are online at: http://mapping.usgs.gov/mac/maplists (Accessed November 20, 2000). Many outdoor equipment retailers, including Recreational Equipment Incorporated (REI) stores throughout North America, stock a variety of maps and map software programs suitable for use in this activity.

68 PIONEERING YOUNG PEOPLE

T-R-S WORKSHEET

Figure 3.6. T-R-S worksheet.

HAL BORLAND RESOURCES

Selected Borland Books

Borland, Hal. *Country Editor's Boy.* Philadelphia and New York: J. B. Lippincott, 1970.

    Moving from the homestead to Flagler, a small town on the Colorado plains, Borland continues the autobiography of his youth, recounting his high-school years, his induction into the printer's trade, his family life, and the development of his community, as he saw it, from 1915 to 1918.

———. *High, Wide and Lonesome.* Boston: G. K. Hall, 1984 (1956).

    Borland eloquently describes his experience with the land, animals, and people while growing up on a frontier homestead in eastern Colorado from 1910 to 1915.

———. *When the Legends Die.* New York: Bantam Books, 1984 (1963).

    A dramatic character study of a young Ute Indian coming to terms with himself and American culture, this book is a must-read for young adults and adults interested in the fiction of the North American West.

Audio Resources

High, Wide and Lonesome. Read by Robert Gorman. Prince Frederick, MD: Recorded Books, 1988. Book on audiocassette.

When the Legends Die. Read by Norman Dietz. Prince Frederick, MD: Recorded Books, 1991. Book on audiocassette.

JULIA ARCHIBALD HOLMES

CHAPTER 4

Born February 15, 1838 in Noel, Nova Scotia. Died January 19, 1887 in Washington, D.C. Young adult autobiography describes Kansas and Colorado.

Figure 4.1. Julia Archibald Holmes at work on her writing. Used by permission of Denver Public Library, Western History Collection.

AN APPRECIATION OF THE WRITER

Pike's Peak, Aug. 5, 1858

I have accomplished the task which I marked out for myself, and now I am amply repaid for all my toil and fatigue. Nearly every one tried to discourage me from attempting it, but I believed that I should succeed; and now, here I am, and I feel that I would not have missed this glorious sight for anything at all. In all probability I am the first woman who has ever stood upon the summit of this mountain and gazed upon this wondrous scene, which my eyes now behold.

—From a letter by Julia Archibald Holmes

When Julia Archibald Holmes set out in a wagon train for Pikes Peak in June 1858, she was just 20 years old, married only eight months, and "young, handsome, and intelligent," as one of her traveling companions described her. Every meaning of the word pioneer applied to her. She was also a fine writer.

By the age of 20, Julia Holmes had mastered not only Pikes Peak, but also a variety of written forms—journal, formal and informal letter, travel narrative, newspaper article, and scientific description. She knew how to credibly slant her written content for various audiences. Her writing expressed a clear and interesting point of view and, sometimes, a strongly held opinion.

Unlike many of those included in this book, Julia Holmes never made much of her living as a writer for the general public. What is known of her work is limited in quantity. But the quality of her writing remains vibrant in the depiction of her experiences and ideas. Holmes wrote letters to her family and to a women's rights magazine during her sojourn to Pikes Peak. She kept a daily journal on the trek and possibly afterward. Except for a few segments transcribed into letters, the journal has been lost. As a correspondent to the *New York Herald Tribune*, Holmes reported on events from New Mexico during the Civil War. Later, she worked as a clerk and translator for the U.S. government. In spite of Julia's relative obscurity, her poetry and public speaking were noted by a number of sources.

The story of Julia Archibald Holmes's life is also not well known. It is most completely recorded in *A Bloomer Girl on Pikes Peak—1858*, a well-documented book published as a limited edition in 1949 and edited by Agnes Wright Spring for the Western History Department of the Denver Public Library. Much of the information here is drawn from that book. To make them available to a younger and wider audience, large portions of Julia's rare and remarkable letters are reprinted in this chapter's **In Her Own Words** section.

We are fortunate to have Holmes's writings, sparse though they are, because she presents a vital and personal picture of a critical time in American history. Without her written works we would never know of Julia Archibald Holmes's adventures in the West or the pioneering spirit that shines so brightly through her words.

IN HER OWN WORDS

As gathered together by editor Agnes Wright Spring, in *A Bloomer Girl on Pike's Peak—1858*, Julia Archibald Holmes's letters paint a vivid portrait of her life with the Lawrence party. Because they are historically significant, yet seldom seen, large sections of her letters from the Santa Fe Trail and Pikes Peak region are reprinted here. They offer educators a variety of teaching opportunities in a number of subject areas, including history, geography, geology, and language arts.

Julia Holmes was a clever writer. The events described in the longest letter, sent to Lydia Sayer Hasbrouck of *The Sibyl* magazine in New York State and published in two parts, are written with a fresh perspective, as if they had just occurred. In fact, Julia took five months, until late January 1859, to edit them. In voice and content, these letters target *The Sibyl* readers, participants in the women's rights movement of that time. Because of Julia's writing skill, they also speak effectively to interested readers of any time, (despite her doubts about men expressed in the first paragraph). The two letters written to her family are effective, too, but have very different voice and content. Beginning on page 73, the family letters are interspersed with the letters to *The Sibyl* to provide a clear, chronological picture of Julia's experience for the reader.

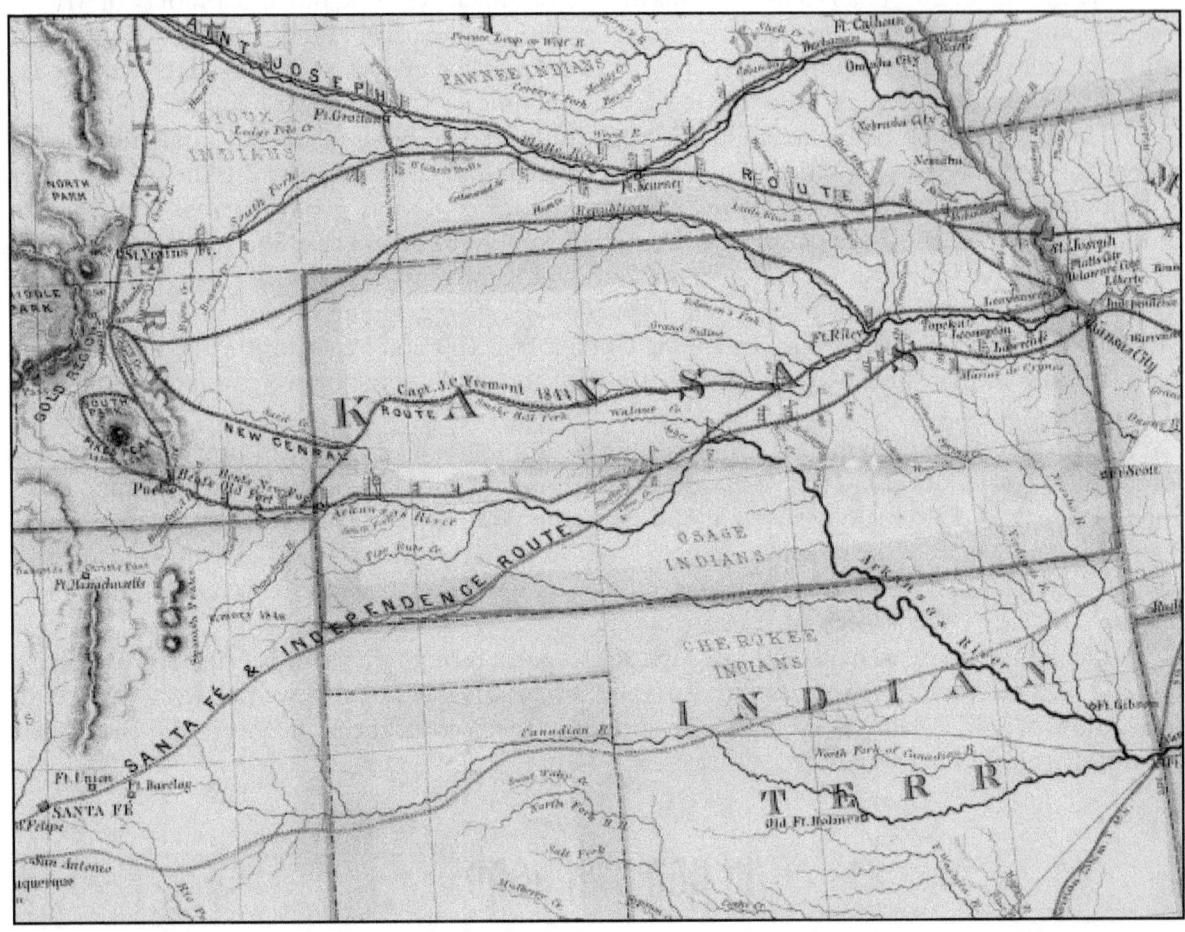

Figure 4.2. Detail from an 1859 map of the United States, showing the Santa Fe Trail, Pikes Peak and nearby "gold regions," and other locales mentioned in Julia Archibald Holmes's letters. Public Domain, courtesy of the Library of Congress.

Note: The following is excerpted as punctuated and spelled in the original manuscript.

A Journey to Pike's Peak and New Mexico—Part I

Fort Union, New Mexico, Jan. 25th, 1859

Sister Sayer—

I think an account of my recent trip will be received by my sisters in reform, the readers of *The Sibyl*—if not by the rest of mankind—since I am, perhaps, the first woman who has worn the "American Costume" across that prairie sea which divides the great frontier of the states from the Rocky Mountains. In company with my husband, James H. Holmes, and my brother, I traveled in an ox wagon and on foot upwards of eleven hundred miles during the last three summer months.

We were on our farm on the Neosho River, in Kansas, when news reached us that a company was fitting out in Lawrence for a gold adventure to Pike's Peak. Animated more by a desire to cross the plains and behold the great mountain chain of North America, than by any expectation of realizing the floating gold stories, we hastily laid a supply of provisions in the covered wagon, and two days thereafter, the 2nd of last June, were on the road to join the Lawrence company. The next morning we reached the great Santa Fe Road, and passed the last frontier Post Office, Council Grove. Here we mailed our last adieus, and felt somewhat sad that we should hear no more from our friends for so long a time—a period of six months, it afterward proved, we were to be imprisoned from the world and friends. Here we learned that the train we were to join had passed the day before, and we drove as rapidly as staid cattle could travel for the next fifty miles to overtake it. Several millions of dollars' worth of merchandise is transported annually over this road from the Missouri River to New Mexico, entirely in wagons, and we now met many trains from that Territory, coming to Independence for loads. These teams are composed of from five to seven pairs of cattle, attached to huge wagons, capable of carrying seventy to ninety hundred pounds of freight each. Many Americans follow freighting for a living, and have made large fortunes. The price of freight from Independence to Santa Fe is ten cents per pound, so that a good team will earn $800 a load. One freighter, an American, residing in this Territory (New Mexico), realized last year from a single trip with eighteen wagons, from Kansas City, Mo. to Salt Lake, the sum of $12,000.

But I am digressing from the subject of my trip. We reached the Cottonwood Creek, crossing the 5th of June, where we found the train encamped. We were now fairly launched on the waving prairie. A person who has beheld neither the ocean nor the great, silent, uninhabited plains, will find it impossible to form any adequate idea of the grandeur of the scene. With the blue sky overhead, the endless variety of flowers underfoot, it seemed that the ocean's solitude had united with all the landscape beauties. In such a scene there is a peculiar charm for some minds, which is impossible for me to describe; but it made my heart leap for joy.

Finding that we were to have all day to rest, we took our large cooking stove out of the wagon and cooked up provisions for two or three days.

Nearly all the men were entire strangers to me, and as I was cooking our dinner some of them crowded around our wagon, gazing sometimes at the stove, which, with its smoke pipe, looked quite as much out of place as will perhaps the first engine which travels as far away from civilization; but oftener on my dress, which did not surprise me, for, I presume, some of them had never seen just such a costume before. I wore a calico dress, reaching a little below the knee, pants of the same, Indian moccasins on my feet, and on my head a hat. However much of it lacked in taste, I found it to be beyond value in comfort and convenience, as it gave me freedom to roam at pleasure in search of flowers and other curiosities, while the cattle continued their slow and measured pace.

I was much pleased to learn on my arrival, that the company contained a lady, and rejoiced at the prospect of having a female companion on such a long journey. But my hopes were disappointed. I soon found that there could be no congeniality between us. She proved to be a woman unable to appreciate freedom or reform, affected that her sphere denied her the liberty to rove at pleasure, and confined herself the long days to feminine impotence in the hot covered wagon. After we had become somewhat acquainted, she in great kindness gave me her advice.

"If you have a long dress with you, do put it on for the rest of the trip, the men talk so much about you."

"What do they say?" I inquired.

"Oh, nothing, only you look so queer with that dress on."

"I cannot afford to please their taste," I replied. "I could not positively enjoy a moment's happiness with long skirts on to confine me to the wagon."

I then endeavored to explain to her the many advantages which the reform dress possesses over the fashionable one but failed to make her appreciate my views. She had never found her dress to be the least inconvenient, she said; she could walk as much in her dress as she wanted to, or as was proper for a woman among so many men. I rejoiced that I was independent of such little views of propriety, and felt that I possessed an ownership in all that was good or beautiful in nature, and an interest in any curiosities we might find on the journey as much as if I had been one of the favored lords of creation.

The next day we moved on, and everyone was looking out for buffalo. Every solitary wolf or mound of earth in the distance, was transformed by some of our most anxious and imaginative hunters into a buffalo. A few short pursuits of these delusive objects served to render our braves more cautious, and towards the close of the day the cry, "a buffalo! a buffalo!" became less frequent.

After the merits of several camping grounds had been vigorously discussed by our several leading men, one was finally selected; and the corral made by driving the teams so that the wagons formed a circle enclosing a yard large enough to contain the cattle belonging to the train. The cattle were allowed to feed until dark, and then driven into the corral for safe keeping, and guarded until morning. This was the course pursued throughout the journey. The next morning the camp was aroused at daylight by a chorus of mingled yelling and screeching—music wild and thrilling as only a band of prairie wolves can make.

When camped on the Little Arkansas River, as I was searching for different flowers, a few rods from the camp, I cast my eyes across the river, and there within forty yards of me stood a venerable buffalo bull, his eyes in seeming wonder fixed upon me. He had approached me unobserved, behind the trees which lined the bank. His gaze was returned with equal astonishment and earnestness. Much as I had heard and read of the buffalo, I had never formed an adequate idea of their huge appearance. He was larger and heavier than a large ox; his head and shoulders being so disproportionate, he seemed far larger than he really was. He looked the impersonation of a prairie god—the grand emperor of the plain. His countenance expressed terrible majesty and fierceness, and on his chin he wore hair sufficient for the faces of a dozen French emperors. His presence soon became known in the camp, and in a few seconds he was coursing westward with our fleetest horses in pursuit. He was overtaken and shot within three or four miles. Buffalo now began to be a common object.

One evening we neglected the precaution to cross the stream before camping. During the night a heavy rain came swelling the creek to a depth of twelve or fifteen feet, and flooding the camp, which was pitched on low ground, with several inches of water. The men were thus driven from the tents to the wagons or a more uncomfortable upright position. In consequence of this neglect, we were detained three days. During this time my husband went out buffalo hunting and returned bringing with him a buffalo calf apparently but a week old. It was a great curiosity to all; and, in the fullness of my compassion for the little thing, I mixed up a mess of flour and water, which I hoped to make it drink. I approached it with these charitable intentions, when the savage little animal advanced toward me and gave me such a blow with its head as to destroy the center of gravity. His hair was wooly in texture, and of an iron grey color. Unlike the young of our domestic cows, he seldom cried, and when he did only made a faint noise. The buffalo cow as well as the bull is naturally a very timid animal, save when wounded or driven to bay. I learned that the mother of the captured calf made a heroic stand, and presented a beautiful illustration of the triumph of maternal feelings over fear. She was in a herd of many hundred buffaloes, fleeing wildly over the plain before the hunter. After a few miles chase the calf gave signs of fatigue. At its faint cry she would turn and come to the calf, but at sight of the hunter bounded off to the herd. This she did two or three times in a chase of as many miles, the calf falling behind more and more, and his mother wavering between fear for his life and her own, at last her decision was made, and she determined to defend her offspring alone on the prairie. She died in his defence.

I commenced the journey with a firm determination to learn to walk. At first I could not walk over three or four miles without feeling quite weary, but by persevering and walking as far as I could every day, my capacity increased gradually, and in the course of a few weeks I could walk ten miles in the most sultry weather without being exhausted. Believing, as I do, in the right of woman to equal privileges with man, I think that when it is in our power we should, in order to promote our own independence, at least, be willing to share the hardships which commonly fall to the lot of man. Accordingly, I signified to the Guardmaster that I desired to take my turn with the others in the duty of guarding the camp, and requested to have my watch assigned with my husband. The captain of the guard was a gentleman formerly from Virginia, who prided himself much upon his chivalry, (and who, to use his own expression, was "conservative up to the eyes,") was of the opinion that it would be a disgrace to the gentlemen of the company for them to permit a woman to stand on guard. He would vote against the question of universal franchise, were it to be submitted to the people, although he was a hero in the struggles of Kansas, and must have witnessed the heroic exertions of many of the women of that Territory to secure for their brothers the boon of freedom. He believes that woman is an angel (without any sense) needing the legislation of her brothers to keep her in her place; that restraint removed, she would immediately usurp his position, and then not only be an angel but unwomanly.

After reaching the Great Bend of the Arkansas River, we camped on Walnut Creek, where we found many new varieties of flowers, some of them of exceeding beauty.

Yours,

J. Annie Archibald

A Journey to Pike's Peak and New Mexico—Part II

We passed on the 14th of June, a large number of Cheyenne and Arrapahoe Indians. Fifty men armed with Sharp's rifles and revolvers were afraid to allow the Indians to know that the company contained any women, in consequence of something which the carriers of the Santa Fe mail told them when they passed a few days previous. I was, therefore, confined to the wagon, while we passed many places of interest which I wished very much to visit. Notwithstanding this care to be unobserved, my presence became known. At one time, by opening the front of the wagon for ventilation, at another by leaping from it to see something curious which two or three Indians had brought, not knowing, as afterwards proved true, that we were very near a village. I soon discovered my mistake, and though I did not myself feel there was any cause for alarm, I was sorry I had been seen on account of the feeling existing in the train. It was of no use to hide now, for every Indian within a mile knew of my whereabouts. Though there was not a shadow of danger in such a company as ours, as many of us well knew at the time and as many experienced men have since informed us, it is very true that the red men have an unaccountable fancy for white women. My husband received several flattering offers for me. One Indian wanted to trade two squaws, who could probably perform four times the physical labor I could. Others, not quite so timid, approaching the wagon made signs for me to jump behind them on their ponies, but I declined the honor in the most respectful language I knew of their dialect—a decided shake of the head.

We now had a stretch of land to pass over, of forty or fifty miles, on which there was ordinarily no water, no wood, nor any good grass. We started an hour or so before sundown, and traveled until midnight without resting. Here we halted a half hour, and made some coffee over a fire made of wood we had brought from our camp the day before. Resuming our journey, we continued traveling until after sunrise in the morning, when we arrived at Coon Creek, which we were glad enough to find was not dry as it generally is. Here we camped, having traveled thirty miles or more.

Touching on the Arkansas again, we found many new varieties of flowers, some of them of very delicate tint and color. As the train passed the Arkansas crossing, James and I went to the river to see some Santa Fe wagons cross. The river was here perhaps a mile wide, and the bottom one broad bed of sand, with here and there a channel nearly as deep as the cattle's backs. After unloading a part of their freight, and placing perishable articles above where the water would enter the wagons, they attached twelve or more yoke of cattle and entered the swift running river. It was indeed an amusing scene. Twenty Mexicans with sharp sticks punching the cattle, shouting and tumbling in the water, the leading cattle continually endeavoring to turn back, the wagon master on horseback, swearing in Mexican, now at the cattle and then at the men—creating a wonderful confusion. There were in the wagon a number of barrels of whiskey standing on end. When in the middle of the stream, as the wagon ascended out of the channel one of these tipped out, together with some of the Mexicans' coats. After a deal of excitement to the Mexicans, and diversion to those on the bank, the whiskey and clothing were saved.

The Arkansas River is very beautiful. Dotted as it is with many little islands, the banks in all cases adorned with flowers, and in many places lined with trees and shrubs. But the current is so swift that it is very unpleasant bathing—that delightful and greatful recreation of the dusty traveler. A number of large rattlesnakes were killed along this river. They were formerly very numerous, but have been killed off to a great extent by the California emigrants and others.

On the 28th we reached Bent's fort—a large stone structure built by Mr. Bent for the purpose of trading for robes with the prairie Indians, and the Cheyennes in particular. The price paid for a buffalo robe at present is ten cups of sugar, about eight pounds. They were formerly bought for from one to four cups of sugar or coffee. Many of the men were so enthusiastic in their admiration of the fort that they took the liberty of getting very drunk by way of compliment, perhaps to it and the very gentlemanly man who did the honors of the house in Mr. Bent's absence. After tarrying an hour or so, the merry men continued their journey, but went only three miles further that day. Up to this time our company had been remarkably healthy. This afternoon, however, several were taken very ill.

After leaving Bent's fort we began to look anxiously for a glimpse of Pike's Peak. On the evening of July 3rd, after camping, a sudden rain and hail storm came upon us, penetrating more or less every wagon cover, and blowing down most of the tents. The next morning we bid farewell to the Arkansas River, whose company we had kept three hundred miles. Traveling but fifteen miles, the train camped early this evening, in order to celebrate the "glorious fourth." This was done by consuming what little whiskey remained among the members. This day we obtained the first view of the summit of the Peak, now some seventy miles away. As all expected to find precious treasure near this wonderful Peak, it is not strange that our eyes were often strained by gazing on it. The summit appeared majestic in the distance, crowned with glistening white.

78 PIONEERING YOUNG PEOPLE

> We were passing over an uneven road today, and getting a mile or two in advance of the wagons; we came upon a pair of antelope grazing. Immediately dropping upon the ground that we might not frighten them, we had a fine opportunity to examine their beautiful form and motion. They advanced towards us until they were scarcely ten rods off, with eyes riveted upon us, perhaps a minute, when sudden as lightning they started and bounded away as like the wind. Their smooth form, with slender, tapering legs, glossy hair, bright, large eyes, their graceful, lofty and intelligent motion, left a deep impress of their beauty.
>
> Proceeding up the Boiling-Spring River [Fountain Creek], we arrived on the 8th as near as wagons could approach the mountains.
>
> From this time until the tenth of August, with the exception of two days, the train remained encamped in this locality.

Figure 4.3. Contemporary view of Pikes Peak, with the Garden of the Gods (foreground), near the 1858 campsite of the Lawrence party. Photo by John Stansfield.

(NOTE: Julia's first letter to her family is inserted here. The people who carried this letter east were members of the larger Cherokee or Green Russell party of gold seekers, who preceded the Lawrence party up the Santa Fe Trail by a few weeks, prospecting and laying out town sites to the north of Pikes Peak where Denver sits today.)

From near Pikes Peak											July 12th 1858

Dear Mother and Father and all the loved ones

    Greetings to you from across the plains in sight of the Rocky Mountains. About 3 days ago we arrived at Pikes Peak, or as near there as the wagons can go. The search for gold hitherto has been unsuccessful. Some are discouraged and talk of going home along with the company which has just overtaken us and with whom this is to be sent. The first opportunity we have had of writing to you since we left the Walnut. And this must be very hurried as they will not wait long. About the prospect I do not feel at all discouraged yet for we have not looked much at all. Some of the company are going to Oregon if we do not find gold here. Some to California and some back to Lawrence. Among this number we will probably be included, but we won't go back until we are very sure there is no gold to be found. We have been very well indeed and enjoyed the journey very much. No danger on the road, the Indians all very friendly, but awful beggars.
    We may start for home in the course of two weeks that is, if we are obliged to go empty. I wish we were not obliged to go at all, this fall, I would like to travel through to the Pacific.
    There is about 47 men in the company, the most of them very pleasant all of them very respectful to me—much superior to the neighbors I left behind.
    The mountains are very beautiful. Pikes Peak looks sublime. I have seen a great deal of beautiful scenery, have not been lonesome and the journey has not seemed very tedious. I am forgetting how to spell right. My love to all the dear ones Allie, Jane, Freddy, Clara, Nancy, Ebenezer. Albert is very well, he would probably write but this is his turn to guard the cattle. He sends his love. The next time we write I think you will have some better news. The cattle stand it very well as yet; some of them have been a little sore footed, ours have not. I cannot write much more at present, you shall hear from us at every opportunity which occurs. My love to all inquiring friends. I have seen Buffaloe, Antelope, Deer, wolves and prairie dogs. We like the meat of the Antelope best to eat, we have some every day or so. I wish Allie could see a couple of young fawns which we have here, they are very beautiful.

    In haste your affectionate daughter

    Excuse all mistakes in writing & spelling.						Julia

(NOTE: The letter to *The Sibyl* now continues.)

> For one who has not experience to aid his efforts, it will be quite impossible to imagine the disgusting inactivity, and monotony of camp life. Occasionally the routine would be interrupted by alarms of Indians trying to stampede the cattle. Sometimes, too, a few of the men would wake up and start out for a trip of three or four days, perhaps in search of gold; for the summit of the mountain; or as was more frequently the case to hunt deer, antelope, bears, etc. On these hunting expeditions they always started in fine spirits, but returned generally quite serious, without game, reporting having seen thousands of deer and antelope, but the timid animals would not permit them near enough to kill them. For a description of our visit to the summit of Pike's Peak, I take the following extract from my journal.
>
> Aug. 1st, 1858—After an early breakfast this morning, my husband and I adjusted our packs to our backs and started for the ascent of Pike's Peak. My own pack weighed 17 pounds; nine of which were bread, the remainder a quilt and clothing. James' pack weighed 35 pounds, and was composed as follows—ten pounds bread, one pound hog meat, three fourths pound coffee, one pound sugar, a tin plate, knife and fork, half gallon canteen, half gallon tin pail and a tin pint cup, five quilts, clothing, a volume of Emerson's Essays, and writing material made up the remainder. We calculate on this amount of food to subsist six days. A walk of a mile brought us to the crossing of the Boiling spring river. It is an impetuous, ice cold stream at this point, about twelve feet wide, knee deep, with a cobble stone bottom. Undressing our feet we attempted it several times before we could cross, the water was so intensely cold we were ready to drop down with pain on reaching the opposite bank. Three miles further we reached the wonderful Boiling springs, which Fremont has made known to the world in his expeditions. There are but three which we noticed. The strong carbonated waters mingled with bubbles of carbonic acid gas, boil continually in the rocky fountains within which they are set by nature better than they could be by art. We drank deep from these Saratogas of the wilderness, and leaving them, in another mile were vigorously attacking the mountain. The first mile or so was sandy and extremely steep, over which we toiled slowly, as we frequently lost all we gained. But by persevering and every rod laying, or rather falling on our backs to rest, we at last reached the timber where we could obtain better footing. We neglected to fill our canteens and now began to feel the want of water. The questions was should we descend that terrible canyon only to ascend again, or proceed on our journey not knowing when we should reach water? Our longing for water triumphed and down we rushed with such eagerness as is only inspired by suffering. We are camped here until tomorrow. It is now ten o'clock in the evening, and I am reclining before some blazing pine logs beside a torrent in a mountain canyon several hundred feet deep. The straight, slender, tapering pines that stand around so beautiful in their death, smooth, white and sound, having been stripped of their bark by fire, calmly point to a sky more serene, and to stars far brighter than usual. The trees and the sky almost seem to strive together in preserving a deeper silence. But there is music from the foaming stream, sounds from a dozen little cascades near and far blend together—a thundering sound, a rushing sound, a rippling sound, and tinkling sounds there are; and a thousands shades of sound to fill up between them. The burning pine crackles and snaps, showering sparks, cinders and even coals

around and all over the sheet I am writing on, as if to mock the tame thoughts they light me to write.

(NOTE: An excerpt from Julia's second letter to her family is inserted here.)

Snowdell

Aug. 2d, 1858

Dear Mother: I write this to you sitting in our little house among the rocks, about one hour's walk from the summit of Pike's Peak. . . .

Two days of very hard climbing has brought me here—if you could only know how hard, you would be surprised that I have been able to accomplish it. My strength and capacity for enduring fatigue have been very much increased by constant exercise in the open air since leaving home, or I never could have succeeded in climbing the rugged sides of this mountain. There were some steep climbing the first day, and I would sometimes find it almost impossible to proceed. I was often obliged to use my hands—catching, now at some propitious twig which happened to be within reach, and now trusting to some projecting stone. But fortunately for me, this did not last more than a mile or so. . . .

But I shall not write any more now, for I mean to finish this on the top of the mountain. . .

(NOTE: The letter to *The Sibyl* now continues.)

Snowdell, Aug. 4th—We have given this name to a little nook we are making our home in for a few days. It is situated about four or five rods above the highest spring which gushes from the side of the Peak. On the cold moss overhung by two huge rocks, forming a right angle, we have made a nest of spruce twigs. This we call our home. Eastward, we can look on a landscape of Kansas plains, our view hemmed only by the blue haze of the atmosphere, and extending perhaps two hundred miles. The beauty of this great picture is beyond my powers of description. Down at the base of the mountain the corral of fifteen wagons, and as many tents scattered around it, form a white speck, which we can occasionally distinguish. We think our location grandly romantic. We are on the east side of the Peak, whose summit looming above our heads at an angle of forty-five degrees, is yet two miles away—towards the sky. Today we remain at home resting, writing, and admiring the mocking landscape. For with beauty and deep truth does Emerson remark "the landscape must always appear mocking until it has human figures as good as itself.". . .

Aug. 5—We left Snowdell early this morning for the summit, taking with us nothing but our writing materials and Emerson. Arriving within a few hundred yards of the top the surface changed into a huge pile of loose angular stones, so steep we found much difficulty in clambering up them. Passing to the right of a drift of snow some three or four hundred yards long, which sun and wind had turned into coarse ice, we stood upon a platform of near one hundred acres of feldspathic granite rock and boulders. Occasionally a little cranny among the rocks might be found in which had collected some coarse soil from the disintegration of the granite, where in one or two instances we found a green tuft about the size of a teacup from which sprung dozens of tiny blue flowers most bewitchingly beautiful. It was cold and rather cloudy, with squalls of snow, consequently our view was not so extensive as we had anticipated. A portion only of the whitened back-bone ridge of the Rocky Mountains which forms the boundary line of so many territories could be seen, fifty miles to the west. We were now nearly fourteen thousand feet above the sea level. But we could not spend long in contemplating the grandeur for it was exceedingly cold, and leaving our names on a large rock, we commenced letters to some of our friends, using a broad flat rock as a writing desk.

(NOTE: The conclusion of Julia's second letter to her family, finished at the top of Pikes Peak, is inserted here.)

Pike's Peak, Aug. 5, 1858

I have accomplished the task which I marked out for myself, and now I am amply repaid for all my toil and fatigue. Nearly every one tried to discourage me from attempting it, but I believed that I should succeed; and now, here I am, and I feel that I would not have missed this glorious sight for anything at all. In all probability I am the first woman who has ever stood upon the summit of this mountain and gazed upon this wondrous scene, which my eyes now behold. How I sigh for the poet's power of description, so that I might give you some faint idea of the grandeur and beauty of this scene. Extending as far as the eye can reach, lie the great level plains, stretched out in all their verdure and beauty, while the winding of the great Arkansas is visible for many miles. We can also see distinctly where many of the smaller tributaries unite with it Then the rugged rocks all around, and the almost endless succession of mountains and rocks below, the broad blue sky over our heads, and seemingly so very near; all, and everything, on which the eye can rest, fills the mind with infinitude, and sends the soul to God.

(NOTE: The letter to *The Sibyl* now continues.)

When we were ready to return I read aloud the lines from Emerson.

"A ruddy drop of manly blood,
The surging sea outweighs;
The world uncertain comes and goes,
The looser rooted stays."

Leaving this cloud capped bleak region, we were soon in Snowdell, where we remained long enough to make up our packs. Before we were ready to say 'good bye' the snow was falling quite fast, and we left our pretty home as we first saw it, in a snowstorm. We pursued our journey in all possible haste, anxious to find a good camp for the night before dark. At last when I thought I could not go a rod further, we found a capital place, a real bears den it seemed, though large enough for half dozen. And here we are enclosed on every side by huge boulders, with two or three large spruce trees stretching their protecting arms over our heads.

The next day near noon we arrived at camp, where we found some excitement existing regarding an attempt which the Indians had made the night before, to drive away the cattle belonging to the train.

I must now close this letter, which has already grown too long, though I have omitted many things equally interesting as those I have recorded. In accordance with a decision of a previous meeting, the camp broke up on the 10th and moved toward New Mexico. We arrived in the Sangro Christi [Sangre de Cristo] Pass, N.M., on the 18th, and after remaining there a few days, decided, so far as our wagon was concerned, to abandon camp life and spend the winter in New Mexico. When we last saw the gold seekers most of them were engaged in fishing for trout in the creek of the Sangro de Cristi [Sangre de Cristo].

Yours truly,

J. A. Archibald

End of excerpted manuscript.

Figure 4.4. Julia Archibald Holmes in later years. Used by permission of the Denver Public Library, Western History Collection.

THE WRITER'S LIFE

Kansas Emigrants

In July 1854, 16-year-old Julia Archibald stood with her family in the Boston railway station. In harmony with many others leaving Massachusetts that day, they sang a newly written hymn:

> *We cross the prairie as of old*
> *The pilgrims crossed the sea,*
> *To make the West, as they the East,*
> *The homestead of the free!*
>
> *We go to rear a wall of men*
> *On Freedom's southern line,*
> *And plant beside the cotton-tree*
> *The rugged Northern pine!*
>
> *We're flowing from our native hills*
> *As our free rivers flow;*
> *The blessing of our Motherland*
> *Is on us as we go.*
>
> *We go to plant her common schools*
> *On distant prairie swells,*
> *And give the Sabbaths of the wild*
> *The music of her bells.*
> *We'll tread the prairie as of old*
> *Our fathers sailed the sea,*
> *And make the West, as they the East,*
> *The homestead of the free!*

The singers, like the hymn, were called "The Kansas Emigrants." The hymn was written in their honor by the famed poet and abolitionist John Greenleaf Whittier.

With the singing finished, Julia helped her parents and seven sisters and brothers board the train heading west. They were emigrating to the brand new Kansas Territory.

The Archibalds and other Kansas emigrants were pioneers with a purpose. For soon a vote would be taken—would the Territory be slave or free? Should slavery be legal in Kansas? Julia, her parents, and the other members of the New England Emigrant Aid Company believed strongly that slavery was morally wrong and should be illegal, in Kansas and everywhere. They were abolitionists, also called Free-Staters. They hoped to make the West "the homestead of the free." Supporters of slavery poured across the border from Missouri to be part of the vote, as well.

The only member of the family eligible to vote was Julia's father, John. Her mother, Jane, was not free to cast a ballot against slavery, although she may have wanted to desperately. Women did not have voting rights, also known as suffrage or universal franchise, in most places at that time. Government officials threw out the results of the first vote on Kansas slavery. Too many nonresidents, especially pro-slavery Missourians, had voted. Kansas became a free territory and, in 1861, a free state.

The Archibalds helped found Lawrence, Kansas. Their home became a meeting place for abolitionists and a "station" on the Underground Railway for slaves escaping from the South. Battles were fought in "bloody Kansas" between those for and against slavery. In December 1854, pro-slavery militias besieged Lawrence for a short time. For Julia they were exciting and dangerous times, quite different from her earlier life in the East.

Born on February 15, 1838 in Noel, Nova Scotia, Canada, Julia Anna Archibald was the second oldest of eight children. Her brothers and sisters were Ebenezer, the oldest, Albert, Nancy, Clara, Frederick, Caleb, and Alice, the youngest and only child born in the United States. In 1848 the Archibald family emigrated to Worcester in central Massachusetts. They became neighbors of Eli Thayer, an abolitionist organizer. When Congress passed the Kansas–Nebraska Act on May 30, 1854, creating the Kansas Territory, John and Jane decided to put their principles to the test and move again. The Emigrant Aid Company, chartered by the State of Massachusetts, assisted in their relocation.

In addition to her abolitionist principles, Jane Archibald had an ardent interest in rights for women, especially suffrage. Susan B. Anthony, the women's rights movement leader with family ties to Kansas, was her friend. Jane held office in a Kansas woman's suffrage organization. In 1869, she addressed the first woman's suffrage convention held in Washington, D.C., on the same program with her daughter Julia.

From her parents Julia learned much, including the importance of freedom and equality for all, both men and women, regardless of race. She also learned the importance of acting responsibly upon her beliefs, in spite of obstacles.

In 1856, at her parents' house, Julia met James Henry Holmes, recently arrived from New York State. As a member of the radical Free-State militia organized by John Brown and his sons, Holmes quickly won a reputation as a bold, even reckless fighter. Upon Brown's resignation, Captain Holmes succeeded him as militia commander. Brown became nationally famous as leader of the 1859 abolitionist raid on the federal arsenal at Harpers Ferry, Virginia, which ultimately cost him his life.

As the slavery-related "border war" subsided, James Holmes settled on a homestead on the Neosho River near Emporia, early in 1857. On October 9, Julia Anna Archibald married James H. Holmes. The couple spent the winter at the homestead.

Headed West

But the free-spirited newlyweds did not long let the prairie grass grow under their feet. With the coming of spring, 1858, word came from Lawrence that a wagon train was forming to travel west on the Santa Fe Trail. Rumors of gold discoveries near Pikes Peak were trickling back from the western end of Kansas Territory. Julia and James decided to join the amateur gold seekers. After two days of preparation, a team of oxen pulled their wagon up the Neosho River toward the Santa Fe Trail, at Council Grove. They soon overtook the Lawrence party, as historians refer to it. Accompanying them was Julia's 18-year-old brother, Albert. The Holmes's journey of adventure and discovery had begun.

It took the Lawrence party five weeks to travel 500 miles, a feat now easily accomplished in one day in an automobile. Wagon train travel on the Santa Fe Trail or any other western route was slow at best. Making 20 miles was a good day's trek. In hot weather, parties often drove early, stopped to "noon it" during the heat of the day, and continued on in the cool of the evening. The wagons usually rolled on through rainy weather, but in mud they often stopped—and stuck—until extra teams of oxen or mules pulled them out. There were no bridges over streams on that part of the Santa Fe Trail in 1858. Waiting a day or more for creek water to drop was common. Fresh food, firewood, and clean water were often scarce. Wagons broke. Animals ran off. Patience was required of all the travelers.

The Lawrence company was made up of 12 wagons with almost 50 men, two women, and one child. As evidenced by her writing, Julia's first meeting with the other woman, Mrs. Robert Middleton, resulted in a disagreement. Julia could be impetuous and strong-willed. At issue were Holmes's controversial values versus Middleton's more conventional ones. Julia's dress, longer than knee-length with pants beneath, was a prime concern. The clothes she wore, so practical to her and so curious and radical to others, were called the "reform dress," "American costume," or "bloomer." For Julia and many other women of her time, the reform dress was a symbol of independence and ability, in a time when society credited women with neither. Though Mrs. Middleton preferred a dress that reached her toes and included petticoats beneath, it "denied her the liberty to rove at pleasure, and confined her the long days to feminine impotence in the hot covered wagon," as Julia states.

Climbing around in wagons with jagged corners, walking over rough terrain, crossing streams, working daily around campfires on the windy prairie—all are hazards for wearers of long dresses. Putting the fashions and conventions of their times aside, Julia's dress certainly seems more sensible for the strenuous life of a wagon train woman.

As the company entered the shortgrass prairie of central Kansas, they encountered great numbers of bison. Close to the bison herds lived bands of American Indians, particularly the Cheyenne and Arapahoe peoples. Although a number of Santa Fe Trail wagon parties came into conflict with the Natives over the years, the Lawrence party experienced little, if any, trouble. In her writings, Julia Holmes seems to view her encounters with the Native people with a slightly wary, but real interest, mixed with a dose of humor. (The humor springing, in part, from the offers James received to exchange wives!) Julia is in no way an informed observer of Plains Indian people. She appears willing to take them as they were, to live and let live, expressing few of the prejudices about them common in her time.

The gold seekers reached William Bent's trading post at Big Timbers on the Arkansas River on June 28. It was the first permanent building they had seen for many miles. The post, near the present Lamar, Colorado, was Bent's "new fort," established primarily for trade with the Plains Indians. It succeeded Bent's Old Fort, destroyed in 1849, farther up river (and now rebuilt as Bent's Old Fort National Historic Site by the U.S. National Park Service).

When Julia Holmes received her long-awaited first view of Pikes Peak on Independence Day, 1858, she could not know that her life story and the history of that great mountain would soon be entwined forever. On July 8, the company arrived at the foot of Pikes Peak. From the place they camped, near the spectacular rock formations of the Garden of the Gods in today's Colorado Springs, the mountain rapidly rises more than 8,000 vertical feet to an elevation of 14,110 feet at its summit.

To make the arduous climb of Pikes Peak, as Julia, James, and other members of the Lawrence party did, means ascending through five distinct zones of vegetation from semi-desert grasslands through foothills scrub, then montane and subalpine forests and meadows, to alpine tundra. The climate and vegetation changes seen in the 16-mile Pikes Peak ascent are equivalent to those seen by traveling 1,600 miles north, from Colorado Springs far into Canada.

On July 9, three members of the Lawrence company, Augustus Voorhees, F. M. Cobb, and John D. Miller, set out to climb Pikes Peak, while the rest of the men hunted game and prospected for gold. The following day they reached the rock-strewn summit. The climbers added stones to a small pile, built as a summit marker at the time of Pikes Peak's first recorded ascent by Dr. Edwin James in 1820. American Indian climbers probably ascended the peak before that date, but they left no record of their achievement.

The climbers' stories upon their return to camp and the sights of the magnificent peak before them awakened the mountaineering spirit in Julia and James. With John D. Miller as their guide, they began the ascent on August 1. Four days later, Julia Archibald Holmes became the first woman known to have reached Pikes Peak's summit. She also recorded the first ascent by a woman on any 14,000-foot peak in North America, a major mountaineering milestone. In the 1850s, her climbing feat on Pikes Peak was a substantial achievement, akin to the first woman to climb Mt. Everest, in our time. Given Julia's pioneering spirit, it seems fitting that she was first.

Without finding much gold in the Pikes Peak region, the Lawrence party broke up in August. Three wagons headed east on the Santa Fe Trail. The rest turned southwest to acquire supplies at trading posts in the San Luis Valley. From there most returned north again to investigate the Cherry Creek gold fields and to help lay out towns, which became the cities of Denver, Pueblo, Cañon City, and Colorado Springs. James, Julia, and Albert left the company in the San Luis Valley, traveling south to Taos, New Mexico. Albert found work with wealthy land grant owner and trader, Lucien Maxwell. A few years later, along with older brother Ebenezer Archibald, Albert helped settle the city of Trinidad, Colorado, which became his home.

Julia, and possibly James, taught the children of wealthy merchants at Taos and, in 1859, at Barclay's Fort, close to Fort Union, the military post near the southern end of the Santa Fe Trail. At Fort Union, the first of their four children, Ernest Julio, was born. Only Ernest Julio and his sister Phoebe survived childhood. The family moved to the territorial capital of Santa Fe in 1860.

Headed East

In April 1861, Julia was with James in Washington, D.C., where he, along with other Kansas volunteers, helped defend Abraham Lincoln and the White House for two weeks at the outset of the Civil War. James subsequently lobbied for and received the position of Secretary of New Mexico Territory, appointed by President Lincoln. He held the office for one year. During that time, Julia served as a correspondent for the *New York Herald Tribune*. Her fluency with languages (English, Spanish, and French) helped her gather news from the mostly Spanish-speaking population.

The Holmes family led a nomadic life during the rest of the Civil War years. They traveled in both the North and the South. In 1863, James helped recruit two regiments of African American troops for the Union army in Tennessee. Near the end of the war, the Holmes family settled in Washington, D.C. The uncertainty of the war, the frequent and extensive traveling, the loss of two children, their forceful and independent personalities—all were undoubtedly hard on the relationship of James and Julia. They divorced shortly after arriving in Washington.

Until her death on January 19, 1887, Julia Archibald Holmes continued her pioneering ways. She wrote poetry. She wrote and delivered speeches in favor of women's rights, including one before a committee of Congress. Julia also faced the challenges of the working single mother. As one of the first female employees of the U.S. government, she worked for the Department of the Interior and the Bureau of Education from 1870 to 1887, often using her Spanish-language skills.

In 1893 New Englander Katherine Lee Bates stood admiring the view from Pikes Peaks's summit. Just like Julia 35 years before, Bates was moved to write by the spectacular panorama .

> *O beautiful for spacious skies,*
> *For amber waves of grain,*
> *For purple mountain majesties*
> *Above the fruited plain.*
> *America! America!*
> *God shed his grace on thee,*
> *And crown thy good with brotherhood*
> *From sea to shining sea!*

Although Julia Archibald Holmes never read Bates's now-famous poem, they are words she would most certainly have appreciated.

TEACHING ADVICE FOR JULIA ARCHIBALD HOLMES

Autobiographical Writings

Because access to Julia Archibald Holmes's writings is limited today, lengthy segments of her rare and remarkable letters are reprinted in this chapter's **In Her Own Words** section. After reading what Julia wrote, at the age of only 20 and not yet considered an adult in her time, we can only wish that she had written more for the public throughout her life. Humor, irony, geographic and biologic description, voice, organization, interesting vocabulary, and word choice—she uses all of these writing tools and more with skill in telling her story. Julia's brash and willful tone in parts of the letter to *The Sibyl* may be excused, not just by her youth, but by the fact that she "walked her talk," she lived out her beliefs, and, when allowed, accomplished what she determined to do.

Age Appropriateness

Like poetry, Holmes's letters really come to life when read aloud. Even with those endless, phrase-filled sentences, strung together with commas and semicolons, the sense of her narrative is most always clear and powerful. The best way to introduce young people, especially fourth and fifth graders, to her letters is through oral reading by an adult. This enables the adult to interpret, when necessary, what might be puzzling historical content or vocabulary. Reading **The Writer's Life** as an introduction to the letters will help place them in context.

Women's Rights Then and Now

In many ways, Julia Archibald Holmes was a woman ahead of her time. She might have been as at home in the women's rights movement of the 1960s and later as she was in the woman's suffrage movement of the 1860s. (Note: The adjective *woman's* was used to modify suffrage and rights in the nineteenth century.) Julia would certainly be proud to participate in the constitutionally guaranteed rights women currently possess in the United States, Canada, and in many parts of the world. She would also realize that "universal franchise" for women is still not universal. Women—and men—are still denied voting rights in a number of countries. Many of the issues with which Holmes struggled, including gender bias, discrimination, male chauvinism, and being a working single mother, are still women's concerns today.

Notable Names

As with Ohiyesa and Zitkala-Ša (see chapters 1 and 2), Julia Anna Archibald Holmes's names and how and when they were used were very important to her. The name, Julia, she used formally. Annie was the name used within her family. Archibald, she used even after marriage to express her independent identity as a person. (Note that she signs the letter to *The Sibyl* with her maiden name or initials.) Holmes, the name she took in marriage, she used regularly, even after her divorce.

The mountain's name, Pikes Peak, is the conventional spelling today. In Julia's day it was Pike's Peak, and so it appears in her letters.

Slavery

Human bondage was not just a black and white issue in western North America during the nineteenth century and before. People of every color, especially women and children, were kidnapped, bought, sold, and traded by people of every color. The practice of slavery in the West diminished slowly in the years following Emancipation and the end of the Civil War.

Touchy Terminology

Julia Holmes uses the term squaws, meaning the wives of American Indians, once in her letter to *The Sibyl*. As is evident from an incident in Zitkala-Ša's life, the word squaw also had a more derogatory meaning in the late nineteenth century, as it does today. Whether Holmes intended to use "squaws" in a demeaning sense is not clear from the context.

LEARNING HORIZONS

Literature Aloud Experiences

◆ *HISTORYTELLING CONNECTIONS*

Level: Grades four and higher.

Student Learning Opportunities: Research; Story preparation; Rehearsal; Staging; Cooperation; Performance.

Background: Historytelling means bringing history and storytelling together. This medium re-creates real people, animals, settings, and events of the past through research and the power of the imagination. Historytelling is an entertaining and instructive activity for teachers and other adults. It is also highly beneficial for young people to take on the role of the historyteller. Students are especially effective in this role after they reach the "age of history"—which is found somewhere between the "age of reason" and the "age of puberty." After reaching this milestone, young people begin to have a perspective on time and events and can mentally journey beyond their own lifetimes and experiences. They are capable of exploring various time periods and encountering characters, creatures, events, and eras recorded in history. From those journeys, children and adults can bring back invaluable treasures—stories waiting to be retold. **Putting the Pieces Together**, below, gives an example of the historytelling process detailed here.

Basics: Find a Story. The process for finding and preparing a story for retelling is not difficult. The good news is that there is no shortage of stories from which to draw.

1. Start by identifying an interesting topic related to the past—family members, historical figures, events, inventions, eras, and more, all are possibilities.

2. Research the topic. Research is the key to finding the right material. Information can be found at school, libraries, museums, on the Internet, or with family members or neighbors. If necessary, start with secondary source materials, such as books, after-the-fact news articles, historical photos or films, and other items about the topic. Even better and often more accurate, find primary source materials, which include autobiographies, firsthand accounts of events, oral histories, and interviews.

Basics: Prepare a Story

1. After becoming familiar with source materials and selecting a topic, determine what focus your story should have. Ask yourself: What is most interesting about this topic? What part of my subject should I emphasize to create a short, tellable story out of all this material?

2. Next, decide what style of presentation to use. Options for a style of presentation are numerous and reflect your personality, interests, and abilities:

    - Personal experience or family story (see **Language Arts Experiences, Recollection,** chapter 2)

- First-person narrative depicting an event or character (see **Literature Aloud Experiences**, chapter 7)
- Third-person narrative, re-creating real events and characters
- Creative visualization, verbally re-creating people, places, or events as if you were there
- Story in spoken or sung verse (ballad), such as Longfellow's *Paul Revere's Ride*
- Story with historically accurate costume and/or props
- Historical reader's theater (see **Literature Aloud Experiences**, chapter 10)
- Audience participation techniques appropriate to the tale and audience
- Retelling an original historical fiction story developed from factual sources
- A blend of several presentation styles

3. If direct quotations from copyrighted materials are used in the historytelling, determine if copyright (or personal) permission is needed to develop the story. Contact publishers or authors for information. If an original script for historical storytelling is being developed from a variety of information sources, no permission is usually necessary. Even though educators and students have limited permission to use direct quotations from most materials under the fair use provision of the copyright law, it's still a good idea to acknowledge sources in some way. Acknowledging sources could inspire listeners to research and tell stories of their own. Permission is especially important if the historytelling is planned for performance, recording, and/or broadcast beyond the school community.

4. Finally, develop the story for telling. (For guidelines, see **Literature Aloud Experiences**, chapters 1 and 2.) Historytelling is more demanding than other types of telling in several ways. Beyond the importance of appealing to the five senses, a historical tale must re-create an accurate sense of place, the setting where real events occurred. It must have a sense of story that shapes an interesting tale from beginning to end, while recounting the history accurately. Historytellers must also develop a sense of character so that the real lives in actual events are believable in the retelling. If desired, develop costumes, props, photos, drawings, and maps to help develop these senses. Finally, the names, dates, and other facts in historical tales require upkeep—maintenance that keeps the story accurate.

Putting the Pieces Together: Here is an example of the historytelling process, using Julia Archibald Holmes as an example:

Finding a Story, Secondary Source. You come upon a one-page description of Julia that interests you in *Colorado's Colorful Characters* by Gladys Bueler (Boulder, CO: Pruett, 1981).

Finding a Story, Primary Source. Wanting to know more, you read and take notes from Julia's letters in *A Bloomer Girl on Pike's Peak—1858*, edited by Agnes Wright Spring (Denver: The Denver Public Library, 1949).

Preparing a Story, Focus. You decide to begin with the start of her journey on the Santa Fe Trail and end with her climb of Pikes Peak.

Preparing a Story, Style of Presentation. If you are female, you might decide to tell the story in the first person using Julia's own words and wearing bloomers. If a male, you could tell it in the third person as narrator using props and a map. Or, you might combine the first and third person in tandem performance. (See **Learning Horizons, Personal History for Two Voices** or **Western History for Two Voices,** below.)

Preparing a Story, Permission. You contact the Western History Department of the Denver Public Library and learn that they hold the copyright to *A Bloomer Girl on Pike's Peak—1858*. They grant you permission for free, because they want Julia's story retold as much as you do.

5. Rehearse stories at home and in pairs or small groups at school prior to classroom performance. If possible, perform stories for school and family audiences at a day or evening Historytelling Festival.

Extensions: Present the past to audiences as far and wide as possible in the community. Local history organizations and museums may be glad to host your student and adult historytellers at a special event.

Teacher Evaluation Opportunities: Selection of story topic; Quality of research; Development of story content; Thoroughness of rehearsal and, if used, costume and props; Cooperation; Performance.

Language Arts Experiences

◆ *PERSONAL HISTORY FOR TWO VOICES*

Level: Grades four to eight.

Student Learning Opportunities: Reading; Journal or diary writing; Third-person expository writing; Six-Trait Writing—Ideas, Organization, Voice, Word Choice, Sentence Fluency, Conventions.

Background: As with the writings of Julia Archibald Holmes, journal or diary entries and letters provide a fascinating look at personal history, but they sometimes don't tell the whole story. They leave out historical facts and background information necessary for a reader or listener to understand the context in which the entries or letters were written. Students can use their first-person writing, accompanied by third-person expository passages, to develop dramatic tandem presentations. (This experience can be done independently or in preparation for **Western History for Two Voices,** below.)

Basics:

1. If students are already keeping a journal or diary, have them select an entry that tells an interesting story that they do not mind sharing in public and is from one to three pages in length. If they are not journaling, have them create a one- to three-page rendition of an interesting personal event in journal or letter form.

2. Have students, with teacher assistance, review the entry or letter, locate places where additional information or explanation is required and can be written in third-person exposition, and mark those places with a "+" (plus sign). For example, an entry begins, "I don't believe it. My brother did it again! He listened in on my phone call with Maria this afternoon.+..." A plus sign could be put by "this afternoon," indicating that there we need more information, written in the third-person, about the brother—his name, age, why he listens in, or what happened at other times when he listened in. Or include this information in an introduction to the entry. For example, "There lives in a certain unnamed house, a 10-year-old named Daniel, who needs to get a life of his own! He is incredibly nosy. An entry from the diary of Daniel's sister, also unnamed, reveals more of the story...."

3. Have students write short (one sentence to one paragraph) third-person expository passages for each plus sign marked, giving background information on the entry or letter and, at the same time, creating a script for a narrator.

4. After text revision, students pair up with other classmates with whom they can work cooperatively. Have students rehearse oral presentations of their writing, with one classmate reading the narration accompanying the other's first-person reading of his/her entry or letter. When ready, have students present the tandem readings to others.

Extensions:

1. Discuss the similarities and differences between the first-person and third-person styles of presentation for both reader and audience. List effective characteristics of both styles as seen in students' tandem presentations. Retain the list for future reference in **Western History for Two Voices**, below.

Teacher Evaluation Opportunities: Journal entry or letter; Third-person writing; Use of Six-Trait Writing techniques; Rehearsal and performance of tandem personal history.

◈ WESTERN HISTORY FOR TWO VOICES

Level: Grades four to eight.

Student Learning Opportunities: Reading; Historical research; Writing historical commentary; Six-Trait Writing—Ideas, Organization, Voice, Word Choice, Sentence Fluency, Conventions.

Background: With experience in writing expository passages to complement journals, diaries, or letters from **Personal History for Two Voices**, students emulate professional writers and historians by researching and writing third-person commentary on excerpts from real historical journals or letters from western North America. Length and detail of historical commentaries can vary with age, experience, and abilities of students.

Basics:
1. **Option One.** Have students select a passage from the letters of Julia Archibald Holmes. Ask them to mark with a "+" (plus sign) the places in the passage that need background information Holmes does not provide. Using data from **The Writer's Life** in this chapter and from other research, have students write historical commentary, in the third-person, to interpret the passage.

   Option Two. Read and discuss with the students the organization of "Pioneering Spirit: The Story of Julia Archibald Holmes," a chapter from *Many Voices: True Tales from America's Past* (Jonesborough, TN: The National Storytelling Press, 1995) as an example for students of the process of historical commentary.

2. Make available a number of journals and letters of western experience from which students select a favorite passage on which to base their commentary. Excellent sources, all of which are in print and available in modern editions, are listed below:

Bird, Isabella. *A Lady's Life in the Rocky Mountains*. Norman, OK: University of Oklahoma Press, 1999 (1879).
   Letters of an English traveler in Colorado in 1873. Includes details about a 250-mile solo horseback trip.

Drumm, Stella M., ed. *Down the Santa Fe Trail and into Mexico: The Diary of Susan Shelby Magoffin, 1846–1847*. Lincoln, NE: University of Nebraska Press, 1982 (1926).
   Perceptive observations of a teenage bride traveling in the midst of the U.S.–Mexico War.

Garrard, Lewis H. *Wah-to-yah and the Taos Trail*. Norman, OK: University of Oklahoma Press, 1955 (1850).
   The adventures of a seventeen-year-old on the Santa Fe and Taos trails in 1846 and 1847.

Holmes, Kenneth L., ed. *Covered Wagon Women: Diaries and Letters from the Western Trails*. Glendale, CA: The Arthur H. Clark Company, various publication dates.
   There are numerous volumes in this series, with a brief historical background on each writer.

Lewis, Meriwether and William Clark. *The Journals of Lewis and Clark*. New York: Dover Books, 1964 (1814).
   A classic of western discovery, this edition includes historical background on their journey.

Parkman, Francis, Jr. *The Oregon Trail*. New York: Penguin Books, 1985 (1849).
   Autobiography of a young explorer in 1846, includes details about a side trip to Bent's Old Fort.

Powell, John Wesley. *The Exploration of the Colorado River and Its Canyons*. New York: Dover Publications, 1961 (1895).
   A classic narrative of western discovery and adventure.

Schlissel, Lillian. *Women's Diaries of the Westward Journey*. New York: Schocken Books, 1982.
   A history of western migration as told through women's diaries.

Stewart, Elinore Pruitt. *Letters of a Woman Homesteader*. Lincoln, NE: University of Nebraska Press, 1990 (1914).
   In her letters to a friend, Stewart describes the joys and hardships of establishing her own ranch in remote Wyoming in the early twentieth century.

———. *Letters on an Elk Hunt*. Lincoln, NE: University of Nebraska Press, 1979 (1915).
   Stewart continues her lively observations of people and places, begun in *Letters of a Woman Homesteader*.

3. Have students, with teacher assistance, review their selected entry or letter and locate places where additional information or explanation is required that can be written in third-person exposition. Mark those places with a "+" (plus sign).

4. Ask students to research and take notes about the writer and the era in which he or she lived.

5. Have students write short (one sentence to one paragraph) third-person expository passages for each plus sign marked, giving background information on the entry or letter and, at the same time, creating a script for a narrator. If available, refer students to the list of effective characteristics for first- and third-person writing, as developed in the **Extensions** section of **Personal History for Two Voices**, above. Each historical commentary should include, at least:

- An introduction giving the name and some biographical information about the writer.
- The time and location(s) in which the entry or letter was written.
- The writer's motive(s) for and means of travel, if appropriate.
- General information about the era in which the writer lived, especially that pertinent to the selected entry or letter.
- Closing comments briefly describing what became of the writer after the conclusion of the selected entry or letter.

Extensions:

1. Have students pair up with other classmates with whom they can work cooperatively. Ask them to rehearse oral presentations of their commentary and entry or letter, with one partner as narrator accompanying the other's reading of the entry or letter. When ready, have them present the tandem readings to classmates.

2. Organize a number of tandem presentations into a thematic program for performance in school and community. Examples of program themes are: Covered Wagon Men, Covered Wagon Women, Letters from the West, Written on the Trail, and 100 Years of Discovery.

Teacher Evaluation Opportunities: Selection and markup of journal entry or letter; Research and note-taking; Third-person historical commentary; Use of Six-Trait Writing techniques; Rehearsal and performance of tandem western history.

Social Studies Experiences

❖ *CLOTHES MAKE A STATEMENT*

Level: Grades four to eight.

Student Learning Opportunities: Discussion; Reading; Historical research; Illustration; Captioning; Expository writing; Persuasive writing; Six-Trait Writing—Ideas, Organization, Voice, Word Choice, Sentence Fluency, Conventions.

Background: When Julia Archibald Holmes wore the reform dress, also known as the "American Costume" or the bloomer, she did so to make a statement to others about her beliefs, and for other practical reasons, as well. Clothes have a great variety of practical and social uses. The history of clothing is also fascinating. Students can explore this history and their own relationships with clothes and the statements clothes can make.

Basics:
1. Read aloud or have students read Julia Holmes's description of her attire and her discussion about it with Mrs. Middleton from Part I of **In Her Own Words**, this chapter.

2. Discuss and then list what teacher and students think are the practical uses of Julia's bloomers. For example, warmth, sun protection, ease of walking, and so on. Do the same thing for Mrs. Middleton's attire. Next, list the social statements that students and teachers think both women's clothes made. For example, Julia—expressing independence, different from the normal, solidarity with the women's rights movement, and so on.

3. On a single sheet, have students illustrate their perception of Julia and Mrs. Middleton's attire. Ask them to caption the drawings to clarify the illustrations. Next, show students illustrations of the "American Costume" from encyclopedias and the **Reform Dress Resources,** below. In discussion, compare and contrast these illustrations with student drawings and perceptions.

4. Students individually list the practical uses they perceive for their own favorite style(s) of clothing. Next, they list social statements they think their clothes make. Discuss their responses.

5. Discuss these questions: Have there been times when students or teachers have been criticized for their attire? Have they had a difference of opinion with anyone about appropriate attire?

6. Have students illustrate themselves (or an imaginary character) in clothing appropriate for a long journey in a car, bus, train, plane, or on foot, bike, or horseback. Ask them to caption this drawing with a detailed description of the traveling clothes. Then, have them illustrate themselves in clothing designed to make a certain social statement. Ask them to caption this drawing with their reason(s) for selecting this clothing style.

Extensions:
1. Have students research the historical significance of the reform dress, aka bloomers, Julia Archibald Holmes's "American Costume," clothes that definitely made a statement in their day. Then, have them develop a one- to two-page report on the reform dress, accompanied by their illustration of Julia and Mrs. Middleton, along with one more related illustration of their own creation. Possible information sources—Internet, encyclopedia, books on the history of clothing, especially *Bloomers!* and *You Forgot Your Skirt, Amelia Bloomer: a Very Improper Story* (below), both short histories of the bloomer, suitable for young people. The best topic heading for research is "Amelia Jenks Bloomer," for whom the reform dress is named.

2. Have students research and report on other revolutionary clothing style changes from throughout history. Some examples are hippie styles from the 1960s and cowboy/cowgirl styles from the nineteenth and twentieth centuries.

3. Have each student write and illustrate a letter to the editor defending a clothing style that made a strong social statement in its time or one that makes a statement today.

Teacher Evaluation Opportunities: Participation in discussion; Practical and social uses lists; Illustrations and captions; "American Costume" reports; Letter to the editor; Use of Six-Trait Writing techniques.

Reform Dress Resources: Listed below is a sampling of resources on the topic of reform dress, with suggested reading levels for each literary source, and add reading levels to entries as in other chapters.

Blumberg, Rhoda. *Bloomers!* Illustrated by Mary Morgan. New York: Bradbury Press, 1993. Juvenile nonfiction.

Corey, Shana. *You Forgot Your Skirt, Amelia Bloomer: a Very Improper Story.* Illustrated by Chesley McLaren. New York: Scholastic Press, 2000. Juvenile nonfiction.

◈ HISTORY CONNECTIONS

Level: Grades four to eight.

Student Learning Opportunities: Discussion; Reading; Historical research and note-taking; Six-Trait Writing—Ideas, Organization, Voice, Word Choice, Sentence Fluency, Conventions.

Background: Julia Archibald Holmes and her family were deeply involved in many of the most significant national issues in the nineteenth-century United States. Some are still issues in the twenty-first century. Students can learn much about their own time and nation by becoming knowledgeable about the era in which Julia lived.

Basics:
1. Use the **History Connections** sheet, figure 4.6, page 100, in discussion with students, to identify at least four primary issues or events with which Julia Archibald Holmes and her family were involved during her life. Among others, possible primary issues or events are slavery, the abolition movement, women's rights, westward migration, Kansas, the Civil War. See the **History Connections Teacher's Page**, figure 4.5, page 99, for guidance in organizing the History Connections sheet.

2. With students, discuss and identify at least four other related issues for each primary one. For example, connected to the primary issue, the abolition movement, are the related issues of abolition movement history, abolition leaders, John Brown and sons, John Greenleaf Whittier, abolitionists in Kansas, and more. See the **History Connections Teacher's Page**, figure 4.5, for examples of other related issues. Complete the **History Connections** sheet, figure 4.6, with students.

3. Have each student select a topic from among the 20 primary and related issues displayed on the class **History Connections** sheet, figure 4.7, for individual research and note-taking. Possible information sources—libraries, the Internet, encyclopedias, U.S. history texts, topical books, museums.

4. Students can develop their research results in a variety of creative formats. These include: a written report with illustrations or copies of historic photographs; a newspaper article, laid out with historic photographs; a radio talk-show interview script, recorded on audiotape; a television newscast script with visuals, recorded on video; a Web site homepage on computer, recorded on floppy disk or CD-ROM; or a picture-book format, laid out with interrelated text and illustrations or historic photographs.

5. Have students deliver their research to the teacher and classmates orally or via the technology appropriate for the format of their presentation.

Extensions:
1. For maximum educational effectiveness, group presentations according to their relationship with each other on the History Connections sheet. That is, begin with a report on a primary issue, followed by reports on issues related to it.

2. Set up a History Connections learning center, in the public or school library, museum, or other secure public space. Here present or display the students' research projects a few at a time for the educational benefit of children and adults in the community. Rotate the projects frequently.

Teacher Evaluation Opportunities: Participation in discussion; Research and note-taking; Research results format; Research results presentation; Use of Six-Trait Writing techniques.

HISTORY CONNECTIONS TEACHER'S PAGE

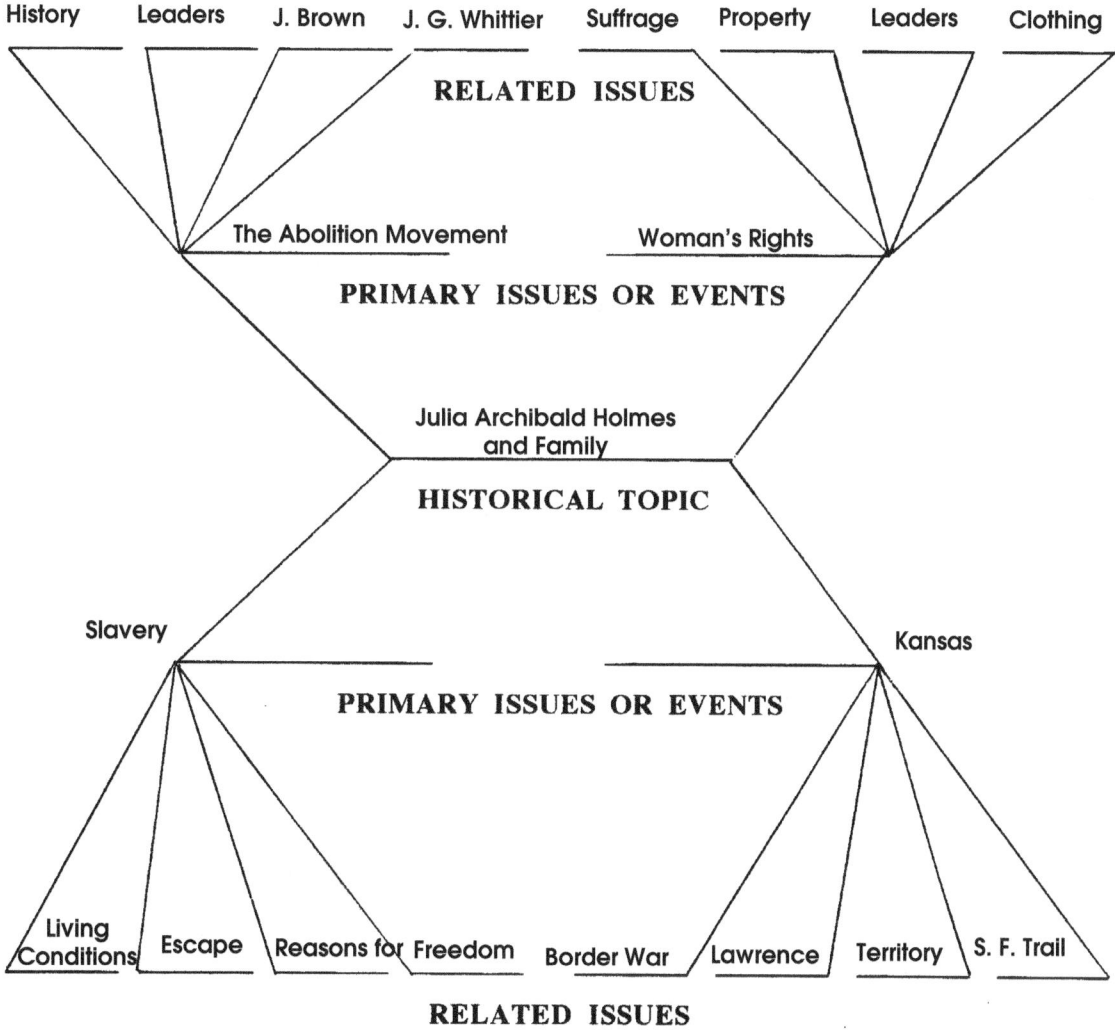

Figure 4.5. History Connections Teacher's Page.

100 PIONEERING YOUNG PEOPLE

HISTORY CONNECTIONS

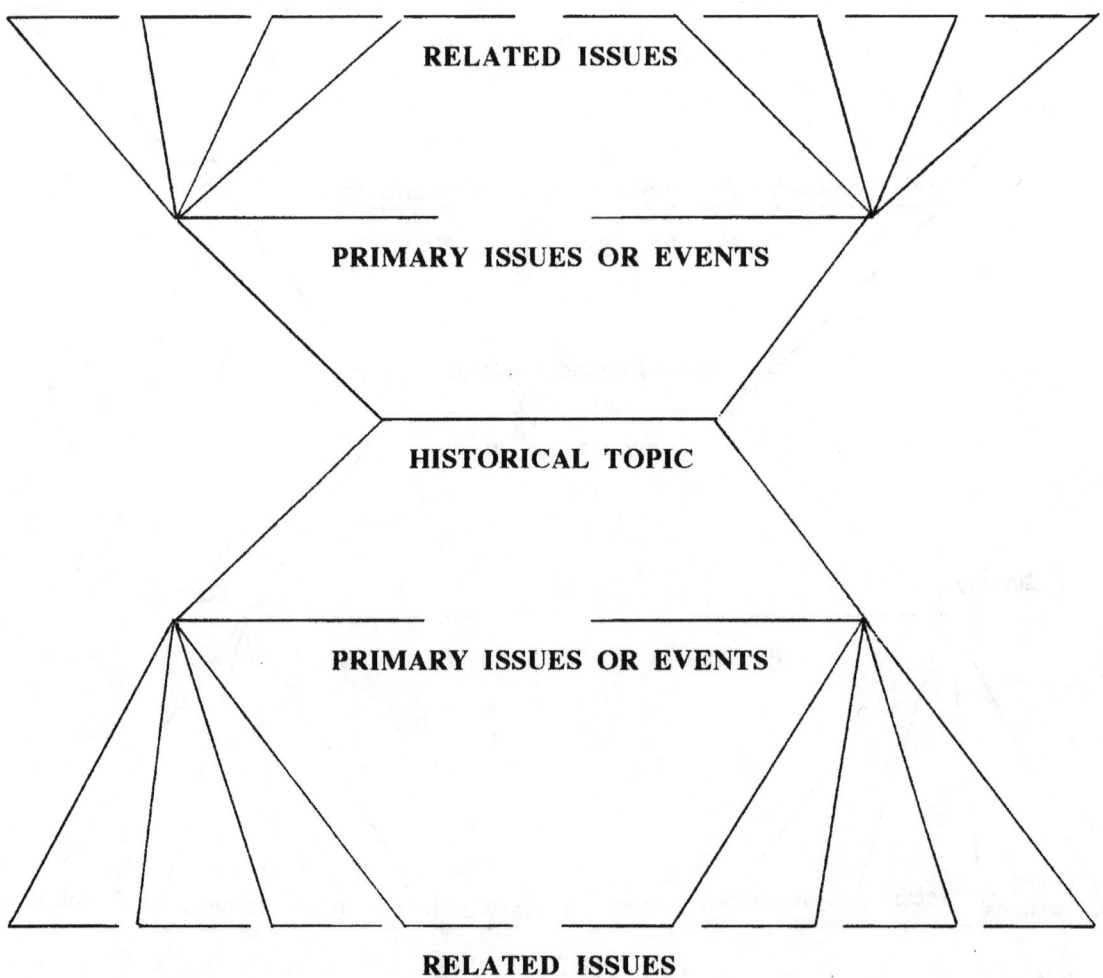

Figure 4.6. History Connections.

JULIA ARCHIBALD HOLMES RESOURCES

Selected Holmes Biographies

Holmes, Kenneth L., ed. *Covered Wagon Women: Diaries and Letters from the Western Trails, 1840–1890.* Volume VII. Glendale, CA: Arthur H. Clark Company, 1988.

Holmes's letter to *The Sibyl* magazine is reproduced, as part of this remarkable series of books dedicated to the writings of westering women. A brief biographical introduction to Holmes begins this chapter.

O'Brien, Mary Barmeyer. *Heart of the Trail: The Story of Eight Wagon Train Women.* Helena, MO: Falcon, 1997.

A well-researched chapter of seven pages describes Holmes's 1858 journey to Pikes Peak and is appropriate for readers, fourth grade and up. Also in this 81-page volume is a chapter on Colorado African American pioneer Aunt Clara Brown.

Robertson, Janet. *The Magnificent Mountain Women: Adventures in the Colorado Rockies.* Lincoln, NE: University of Nebraska Press, 1990.

This excellent history of female mountaineers in Colorado begins its first chapter with a five-page description of Holmes and her Pikes Peak ascent before detailing the accomplishments of many other women in 220 pages. In this book, which is suitable reading for young adults and older, Robertson states that Julia was the first woman known to climb a mountain in Colorado.

Spring, Agnes Wright, ed. *A Bloomer Girl on Pike's Peak—1858.* Denver: Denver Public Library Western History Department, 1949.

The definitive book on Julia Archibald Holmes, it includes most of her existing letters and some of those of her husband, James, and the Archibald family. It is extremely well documented with Spring's detailed historical commentary, footnotes, and a bibliography. At 66 pages, it is easily accessible to young people and adults—if you can find a copy of this rare book.

Weaver, Mary C., ed. *Many Voices: True Tales from America's Past.* Jonesborough, TN: The National Storytelling Press, 1995.

This 206-page anthology of both famous and not-so-famous North Americans features memorable stories from 36 historical storytellers. The nine-page chapter on Julia Archibald Holmes, authored by John Stansfield, presents biographical commentary interspersed with excerpts from her letters. A number of other westerners are also featured in the book, which is fine for readers in fourth grade and up. A separate Teacher's Guide offers activities with reproducible pages for each story.

Audio Resources

Song of the Mountains Song of the Plains. Produced by Brad Bowles, 60 minutes. Monument, CO: Storytelling by John Stansfield, 1989. Audiocassette.

A collection of true tales and ballads from the West performed by storyteller John Stansfield and interspersed with traditional music. The tape, appropriate for ages eight to adult, features an 11-minute version of the story of Julia Archibald Holmes, told in tandem with actress Nancy Harris. Available for $10 postpaid from John Stansfield, P.O. Box 588, Monument, CO 80132. Telephone: 800-484-6963, PIN 8253 or 303-660-5849.

Electronic Resources

Colorado Artists Showcase Website. Available: http://bcn.boulder.co.us/arts/schoolprograms (Accessed December 6, 2000).

Visit storyteller John Stansfield's homepage at the Colorado Artists Showcase site for program and workshop information. Featured are workshops on historical storytelling and historical writing for young adults and adults. Also offered is a storytelling program about Julia Archibald Holmes, from the special perspective of a local historian and mountaineer very familiar with the Santa Fe Trail and the Pikes Peak region.

Lawrence, Kansas Historical Timeline. Available: http://www.umkc.edu/imc/lawrence.htm (Accessed December 6, 2000).

This site provides brief historical notes on Lawrence, especially its early days as the center of Kansas abolitionism.

Pikes Peak Cam Website. Available: http://www.pikespeakcam.com (Accessed December 6, 2000).

See live pictures of Pikes Peak today, much as Julia Archibald Holmes saw it in 1858. Also available at this site are a brief human history of the mountain, current weather conditions, and scenic and time-lapse photos of "America's Mountain."

Ride into History Website. Available: http://rrnet.com/~plains/ ride/index.htm (Accessed December 6, 2000).

Julia Archibald Holmes is one of several historical characters reenacted, with costume, props (and, sometimes, even a horse!) by American History scholar Ann Birney. Birney's other character portrayals are aviator Amelia Earhart and suffragist Elizabeth Hampstead.

RALPH MOODY

CHAPTER 5

Born December 16, 1898 in East Rochester, New Hampshire. Died June 22, 1982 in Shirley, Massachusetts. Childhood and young adult autobiography describes Colorado, Massachusetts, Maine, Arizona, New Mexico, Nebraska, and Kansas.

Figure 5.1. Ralph Moody, in 1958, at the Colorado ranch described in his book, *Little Britches*. Used by permission of Littleton Historical Museum.

AN APPRECIATION OF THE WRITER

My goal in writing is to leave a record of the rural way of life in this country during the early part of the twentieth century, and to point up the values of the era which I feel that we, as a people, are letting slip away from us.

Ralph Moody on his reasons for writing autobiography

With the notable exception of Laura Ingalls Wilder, no writer has written more extensively about his childhood experiences in the West than Ralph Moody. Moving from New Hampshire to Colorado at age eight permanently changed Ralph's perspective on the world. Except for a few adolescent years spent in New England, Moody was a westerner for his entire life.

103

Moody is best known for his eight autobiographical works, which trace his life from 1906 to 1921. He also wrote 11 other books, all western history and biography for children and young adults. Though prolific, Moody did not begin his writing career until he was past age 50. An instructor in a beginner's short story class encouraged him to expand a short character sketch about his father into a book, which became *Little Britches*, published in 1950. That book sold more than 25 million copies. Walt Disney Productions turned it into a feature film, *The Wild Country*. The National Little Britches Rodeo Association, sponsor of rodeo events for young people, chose its name to honor Moody, both as a young rodeo performer and as a person of value.

Each of Moody's autobiographies presents a distinctly separate segment of his growing up. *Little Britches*, *Man of the Family*, and *The Home Ranch* deal with his family's trials and adventures in Colorado. His adolescent hiatus in New England is covered in *Mary Emma and Company* and *The Fields of Home*. *Shaking the Nickel Bush*, *The Dry Divide*, and *Horse of a Different Color: Reminiscences of a Kansas Drover* present Ralph as a young adult, back in the West, ambitiously making his own way with hard work, humor, and creativity in an often hostile world.

IN HIS OWN WORDS

Ralph Moody lived at the end of an era in Colorado. The open cattle range of the late 1800s was being fenced. Communities were rapidly growing where there once had been nothing but grass. But large herds of cattle still needed to move to summer and winter ranges and to market.

With the death of his father, Ralph saw a way to raise money for his cash-strapped family—acting as a "drover" to guide cattle drives through his town of Littleton. Besides, it gave him a chance to ride a horse, his favorite occupation, even though his family could no longer afford to keep one. Ralph heard that a large herd of cattle was approaching Littleton from the south. He rented a horse, "Pinto," from classmate Eva Snow, enlisted friends and his dog, "King," to help, and rode out to make a deal with the trail boss. With the Denver & Rio Grande mail train expected soon, Ralph saw the cattle straying through downed fences into a place where railroad tracks cut through a steep hill. He knew he would have to act quickly.

(An advisory before reading: In this excerpt from chapter 5 of *Man of the Family* by Ralph Moody, there is mild profanity in the dialogue of the trail boss.)

Note: The following is excerpted as punctuated and spelled in the original manuscript.

Ever since I'd seen the cattle in the cut and thought about the mail train being due, I'd been trying to think what Hi [Beckman, his cowboy friend] or Father would do if they had cattle in that kind of fix. By the time I rode up to the trail boss, I knew; so I hollered, "Don't try to turn these back, and never mind the other track. Send your men over the hill to cut 'em off at that end, then drive 'em out this way."

He started bellowing like a bull in a cattle chute, and waving his arm for the men to follow him up over the hill. I didn't go with them, but rode Pinto up onto the track where King and I could head the cattle down off the grade as they came through the cut. One breachy old heifer dodged past us and went galloping along right between the rails, but I didn't have time to go after her. Less than two minutes after the drivers brought the last cattle out of the cut, I saw the mail train coming. I would have had time to ride Pinto to the end of the grade, but I was a bit scared I wouldn't and slid him down the cinder bank. After I saw the train I forgot all about the old cow that had dodged past me, so I didn't see when it hit her. It must have knocked her twenty rods; about all we ever found was hoofs and horns.

Figure 5.2. A close call. Illus. by Edward Shenton from *Man of the Family* by Ralph Moody, used by permission of the University of Nebraska Press.

While the train was going by I rode over to the trail boss. He looked as if he'd just come through a dip tank. He had his head down, and sweat was pouring off both him and his horse. Pinto wasn't acting up so much, either. He was getting a little more used to me, and he was probably a bit tired, too. All of us must have looked sort of beaten up. I didn't know it then, but the side of my face got a little bit skinned when Pinto tossed me off in the schoolyard, and some blood had run down my neck and onto the collar of my blue shirt.

I thought I'd better make my deal right away, before the boss got busy with the cattle again, so I said, "I think you'll have a lot more trouble when you get this herd into Littleton. . . ."

That's as far as I got for two or three minutes, but I don't think it would be right to put down what he said about those cattle, or fences, or the railroad, or Littleton. I waited till he'd cooled off some, then I told him about having ten boys on horseback, and that we'd see his herd safe through town for ten dollars.

"It's a holdup," he hollered. Then he grinned at me, and said, "You didn't bust down that fence so's to get me into this mess, did you?"

"I never broke down any fence," I said. "You come back with me and I'll show you where all the posts are rotted off at the ground. There are a lot more holes between here and Littleton." When I told him there were more holes he began to laugh to beat the band. He slapped his leg with his hand, and howled, "Damned if you ain't a salesman. Sure there ain't no bridges out between here and town?"

"No," I said, "there's only one bridge, but you'll have to look out for the loose planks near Lenheart's end of it. Some of them are pretty bad."

He waved to his men to start moving the cattle out of the C & S cut, then he said to me, "I reckon I already got ten dollars' worth of good outa you, but you ain't going to get it till your outfit sees me from here clean on through town."

I was already pulling Pinto around toward Littleton, but I hollered back to him, "Will I get it then?"

"You'll get it," he called, and I rode after the boys.

We had a dickens of a time. Some of the boys didn't know you have to move cattle easy, and wanted to play cowboy. And some of them just wanted to play. I had stopped by home and put Lady's bridle on Pinto so I could hold him, but he still didn't like me to ride him. He spooked and crow-hopped every chance he got, and sometimes I had about all I could do to stay on him. And he didn't know any more about heading off an angry steer than a billy goat. Ace Alexander gave me more trouble than any breachy old cow in the herd. He had borrowed a horse from one of the girls, and couldn't even ride it at a trot. But he didn't care. He'd grab hold of the saddle horn with both hands and war-whoop. He wouldn't even let me fire him.

We never did have any lunch. By the time Dutch and I got back there with the boys, there were cattle spread from Dan to Beersheba. They were scattered along the highroad for a couple of miles, and had broken fences in a dozen different places. Some of them had even climbed up on top of the hill by the railroad cuts. It was almost three o'clock before we had them rounded up and headed into town. And I was scared half silly.

By that time the cattle were drier than road dust. The river was only a quarter of a mile from the highroad and I knew what dry cattle would do when they smelled water. If they'd stampeded for the river before we hit town, it wouldn't have been my fault, but I'd promised to see them safe through Littleton. It was my first chance to be a drover and I wanted to do a good job.

After we crossed Lenheart's bridge, we boys rode ahead, so I could put the best ones on the river side of the highroad. Just as we came into town, school let out. I saw the kids come boiling out of the schoolyard, and sent Dutch kiting down there to tell the little ones to get back from the highroad, and the bigger ones to get on the river side and help us. The girls were the best of all. I guess those cattle had never seen girls before, and they were afraid of them. All the girls had to do to head them off was to flap their skirts—and they did a good job of flapping. There were over nine hundred cattle in that herd, and not one of them got away from us on the river side of the highroad. By six o'clock we had them all through town and headed west on the River Road.

The drive boss was waiting for me at the corner by the gristmill. I asked him if we'd done all right, and I told him I was sorry about some of the boys running his cattle, and about Ace whooping like an Indian.

The sheriff was there, too, and he started saying that Ace was full of the devil and that his father was a judge and some more things, but I don't think the drive boss heard him. He stuck his hand out to shake hands with me. There was something hard in it, and he said, "You done all right. Some of them boys ain't worth a damn by at least a dollar and a half, but some of em's goin' to make cow hands." Then he winked at me and said, "Them girls is all right, too. Bein' you, I'd see they got a treat. Same deal for you and me in October?"

I said, "Yes, sir." And when I took my hand away there was a ten-dollar gold piece in it.

End of excerpted manuscript.

Figure 5.3. A successful business deal completed. Illus. by Edward Shenton from *Man of the Family* by Ralph Moody, used by permission of the University of Nebraska Press.

Figure 5.4. Bear Creek today, much as Ralph Moody knew it, near the site of the his family's farm. Photo by John Stansfield.

THE WRITER'S LIFE

The first assignment in the night school writing course was, "State your reason for wanting to be a writer." Student Ralph Moody, a successful businessman over 50, wrote, "I want to preserve for posterity a record of the rural way of life in these United States before World War I." His instructor's comment, scrawled across the page, read, "No, you don't either. You want to stir the emotions of your reader." Ultimately, Ralph Moody achieved both his and his instructor's goals through his personal narratives.

Little Britches: Father and I Were Ranchers

The story that grew from that writing course eventually became *Little Britches*. It begins when eight-year-old Ralph Owen Moody and his family arrive in Colorado in December 1906. Charles Moody's lungs could no longer stand the stress of his work in a New Hampshire woolen mill. Doctors advised a cure in the dry air of Colorado. So, Charles and Mary Emma Moody moved their five children to a small farm and ranch near Bear Creek, southwest of Denver. The tasks before them were great—fix and expand a ramshackle house, build a barn, fence the land, plow, plant, and harvest. Work was endless; money was scarce.

As the oldest boy of the family, Ralph was a willing—often impetuous—helper for his soft-spoken, resourceful father and earnest, hardworking mother. He eagerly helped with carpentry, cleaning, hauling supplies, and caring for animals, particularly anything to do with horses. After Ralph was caught lying to his mother about having permission to haul firewood home with their horse, his parents feared for his safety, but, even more, for his character. Charles told him that a person's character is like his house. If he rips boards from the house and burns them to stay warm and comfortable, the house is soon ruined. If the person tells lies, his character will also soon be ruined. From then on, the image of the character–house became a constant, if not always effective, caution for the rambunctious boy.

Ralph and older sister, Grace, attended the one-room Lake School with grades from one through eight. Being the "new kid on the block," he was picked on and beaten up, forced to ride (and was tossed off) bucking horses, and given the distasteful nickname, Molly. Later, a cowboy friend, Hi Beckman, gave the boy lessons in horsemanship and a more desirable nickname, Little Britches.

Because Ralph found creative ways to earn extra money for his cash-strapped family, his father made him a partner in the ranch. During the summer of 1909, Ralph worked as a water boy at the nearby Y-B Ranch, with foreman Hi Beckman, for the considerable wage of $20 a month. There, Hi tutored him even more in horsemanship. Together, they developed riding tricks, which won them first prize at the Littleton Roundup.

In their three years on the ranch, the Moodys encountered a destructive windstorm, a tornado, a flood, broken bones, an economic recession, no water for their crops, and having their house shot up by hoodlums. Eventually, they learned the arid West's hardest lesson—water means survival. Their ranch was at the bottom end of an irrigation ditch with greedy and contentious water users upstream.

The Moodys moved to the nearby town of Littleton that winter. Not long after, Charles, hurt in a horse–automobile accident, developed pneumonia. He died soon after, in March 1910.

Man of the Family

"Ralph, you are my man now; I shall depend on you," Mary Moody told her son. It was a role he took very seriously. He had to, because immediately after Charles's funeral, Mary contracted blood poisoning from contact with her husband's wounds. Hospitalized for a month, she parceled out the children to kind neighbors and friends in Littleton. She resisted suggestions to send them to relatives in New England. Mary wanted her family intact.

Ralph thought that being the man of the family meant leaving school and finding a job. When Mary was better, she put a quick end to that idea. She wanted her son to have as much formal education as possible—something Charles Moody never had. (In fact, Ralph Moody had only eight years of schooling, supplemented by night school courses later in life and his innate intelligence, drive, and creativity. As an adult, he became a partner in a successful retail food business in Kansas City and, later, in the San Francisco area. He and his wife, Edna, raised three children.)

To help support his family, Ralph undertook an impressive array of jobs before and after school, and during weekends and summers, including:

> weeding lawns and cultivating farmer's fields;
>
> organizing boys and girls to help move spring and fall cattle drives through Littleton's streets;
>
> picking cherries and strawberries with Grace and younger siblings, Muriel and Phillip;
>
> taking orders and making deliveries for Mary's cookery business and a milk route;
>
> training and riding horses in races at the Littleton Roundup and in private "match races," where betting took place (which he tried to keep secret from his mother);
>
> breeding and selling rabbits; and
>
> inventing a machine to enable Mary and Grace to begin cleaning and repairing lace curtains for Denver's Brown Palace Hotel.

Figure 5.5. A church now stands at the site of the Moody farm, as described in *Little Britches*. Photo by John Stansfield.

During the summer of 1910, Grace and Ralph worried over their mother's seeming ill health. Mary agreed to take a few days to rest in her room. Then, she presented the children with a little surprise—a baby girl she named Elizabeth—conceived before Charles's accident. Even the oldest children, who knew a lot about where colts and rabbit babies came from, were shocked.

With the new baby and with severe cases of measles affecting all but Mary and Elizabeth that fall, the Moodys benefited from much "neighborly affection," as Ralph later called it. The sheriff did Ralph's chores, the grocery and drugstore extended credit, and two doctors made numerous house calls. When the bills were paid, the Moodys had only $1 left in the bank. But, with her children healthy, a steady stream of curtains from the Brown Palace enabled Mary to give up her arduous cookery business.

The Home Ranch

Two job offers came Ralph's way for summer in 1911. One, from the Y-B Ranch west of Littleton, would allow him to work with Hi Beckman again. But the other offer, from a Littleton cattle trader named Batschelet (whom Ralph calls Mr. Batchlett in his books), was even more lucrative. It was for $1 a day for 100 days, a grown man's wage for a 72-pound cowhand. Hi advised Little Britches to take Batschelet's offer for the extra money and the opportunity to learn an occupation—cattle trading—at the hands of a master. But Ralph knew that his mother had to make the final decision.

"A twelve-year-old boy is too young for such an undertaking," Mary told her son. "But I do realize that circumstances have given you a great deal more experience than most boys your age. And I am sure that you are enough like your father that you will not be influenced by the roughness of the men you will be with, so I have told Mr. Batchlett you may go." So began the 100 days of struggle and adventure, which Moody describes in the pages of *The Home Ranch*.

In the early days of January 1912, the Moody family slipped secretly out of Littleton and fled to Boston. Their mysterious departure involved an unsolved crime, an impending trial, and Mary's unwillingness to testify against an innocent man she knew might be sentenced to hang.

Figure 5.6. The quiet wagon road that passed the Moody house in 1908 has become busy Hampden Avenue, U.S. Highway 285, near Denver. Photo by John Stansfield.

Mary Emma and Company

As the saying goes, you can take the boy out of the country, but you can't take the country out of the boy. So it was with Ralph in the confines of Boston. He missed the freedom, autonomy and, especially, the horses of the West. Gone was the support of small-town friends and neighbors. Despite diligent efforts as a family breadwinner, Ralph got into occasional, often innocent, scrapes involving the law.

The Fields of Home

To avoid further trouble, Mary sent Ralph to live with her father on his farm in Maine. Building an understanding with his irascible grandfather presented more problems than the hardships of farming; problems they ultimately worked out together.

112 PIONEERING YOUNG PEOPLE

Commenting on his first book, Ralph Moody said, "I had to write *Little Britches* from a boy's point-of-view, because I lacked the fancy grammar to do the book from the grown-up viewpoint." For his readers, this is a benefit, not a liability. The child and young adult that was Ralph speaks clearly to the reader through the adult he became. Moody varies his narrative voice to match both his intended audience and the phase of his life about which he writes. His voice sounds more adult in *Shaking the Nickel Bush*, *The Dry Divide*, and *Horse of a Different Color: Reminiscences of a Kansas Drover*—the books dealing with Moody's return to the West as a young man. But, it is no less honest and direct than in his earlier autobiographies.

Ralph Moody had a gift for capturing the essence of his other characters through their dialogue. Clever uses of dialect, colloquialisms, regional patterns of speech, correct and incorrect grammar—all boldly bring the people he knew to life. Perhaps it was the many hours spent listening to his mother read aloud and interpret good literature that helped him develop his remarkable "ear" for language.

On June 28, 1982, Ralph Moody died at the age of 83 at the Shirley, Massachusetts, home of his youngest sister, Elizabeth. He was the first of his long-lived siblings to die. Mary Emma Moody lived past the age of 100.

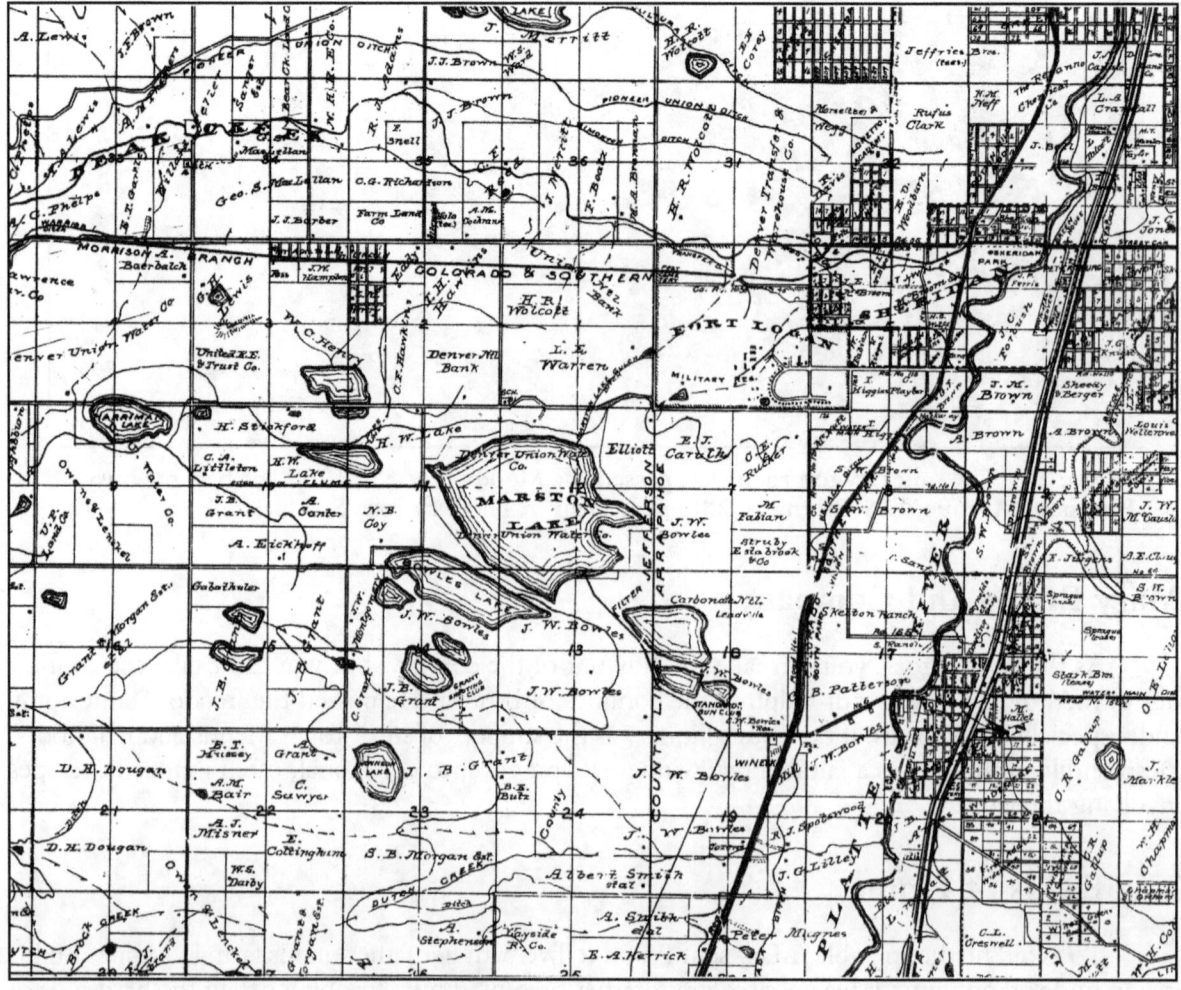

Figure 5.7. Detail from an 1899 farm map showing the area of the Moody farm and Littleton. Courtesy of the Denver Public Library, Western History Collection.

TEACHING ADVICE FOR RALPH MOODY

Autobiographical Writings

Each of Ralph Moody's personal histories stands alone, content-wise. But, as with any books written in a series, readers should start at the beginning, with *Little Britches* and *Man of the Family*, for the richest and most meaningful experience.

Age Appropriateness

All of Moody's books are appropriate (in fact, intended) for children ages 8 and up.

Literary License

The author has taken a few liberties with characters in his works. For example, Moody changed some real names to fictitious ones and made a few characters into composites of several actual people.

Borland and Moody

Hal Borland (chapter 3) and Ralph Moody came to eastern Colorado at almost the same time. They shared many similar experiences with horses, injury, severe weather, and outdoor discovery. Yet, they possess quite different personalities, perspectives, and writing styles. In becoming familiar with both, students may learn much from comparing and contrasting the lives of these two well-known western writers.

Touchy Terminology

As in the excerpt included in this chapter, there is occasional mild profanity in the dialogue of all of Moody's autobiographies. In reading *Little Britches* aloud, I pronounce, Nig, the horse's name, as Nij (as in the name, Nigel). This avoids the appearance of a possible racial epithet, for which there is no connection in the context of the book.

114 PIONEERING YOUNG PEOPLE

LEARNING HORIZONS

Literature Aloud Experiences

> *I'd been a constant reader since childhood, led into it by my mother reading aloud to the family. And strangely, I found that I'd learned to write from reading.*
>
> Ralph Moody, 1967

◈ READING ALOUD

Level: Grades four and higher.

Student Learning Opportunities: Selection and evaluation of read-aloud material; Preparation of material; Read-aloud presentation.

Background: Despite her hectic life, Mary Emma Moody regularly found time to read to her children from the day they were born. She sometimes read for hours on end during picnics and on holidays. Her favorites were literary classics—Shakespeare's plays; *A Christmas Carol*; *The Call of the Wild*; *Ramona*; *Ben Hur*; and, always, the Bible—with which she held her family in rapt attention. As Ralph Moody learned at an early age, reading aloud, like storytelling, fosters a variety of language and literary skills and motivations in young readers and listeners. For more information on techniques and appropriate books for reading aloud, see titles by Jim Trelease, especially *The New Read-Aloud Handbook* (New York: Penguin Books, 1995 [1982]).

Basics:
1. Educators and students prepare material to be read aloud, using figure 5.8 as a checklist for preparation and presentation.
2. After teachers model reading aloud a variety of fiction and nonfiction forms, students prepare and present a read-aloud of their choice, at least 10 minutes in length.

Extensions:
1. Either on a voluntary basis or as an assignment, ask a different student each day to prepare and present a chapter from an autobiography or novel being read aloud to the class.
2. Students can provide a read-aloud community service project to other classes, preschools, senior citizen residences or day programs, and other community institutions.

Teacher Evaluation Opportunities: Material selection and evaluation; Preparation; Read-aloud presentation.

PREPARING TO READ ALOUD

Choose a story you feel comfortable reading and that you like.

Look for books in which the author's voice is active and interesting.

Consider the intended audience for the read-aloud book. Read it before presenting it aloud. As you do, evaluate a book's appropriateness as to:

— Length
— Content
— Vocabulary
— Simplicity or complexity of writing style
— Length of descriptive passages
— Amount of dialogue

Decide if you want to use any of the following techniques to expressively interpret the book:

— Vocal characterizations and dialect(s)
— Sound effects
— Varied reading paces
— Exhibiting real objects that are mentioned in the text
— Explanations of concepts or vocabulary unfamiliar to your audience
— Discussions of important ideas in the text

Prepare a comfortable, quiet location for your reading, with listeners arranged as you want them. Remember that listening skills for people of any age are not automatic. They must be taught and learned.

A Timely Tip—reading aloud juvenile and young adult literature, either fiction or nonfiction, usually takes from two to three minutes per page of text.

PRESENTING BOOKS AS READ ALOUDS

In chapter 7 of *Little Britches*, Ralph Moody suggests several presentation skills learned from his mother:

— Talk the book. Read as if you were telling a story.
— Set limits. Make appropriate behavior clear to listeners.
— Set high expectations. Don't be afraid to challenge listeners with high quality literature.
— Be aware of the point when you or your listeners have had enough. Then quit.

Figure 5.8. Preparing a Story for Telling.

Language Arts Experiences

◆ WORDS TO CAPTURE THE WIND

Level: Grades four to eight.

Student Learning Opportunities: Textual analysis for simile; Descriptive writing; Six-Trait Writing—Ideas, Organization, Voice, Word Choice, Sentence Fluency, Conventions.

Background: Sometimes writing effective descriptions is as hard as trying to capture the wind. Using potent similes and metaphors helps. Numerous examples of similes are found in the portion of chapter 5, "The Big Wind," in *Little Britches* by Ralph Moody, in which Ralph and his family experience a powerful windstorm, called a Chinook.

Basics:
1. Review with students that simile is a comparison of two dissimilar things, often using like, as, or another comparative. Discuss how simile can enliven descriptive speech and writing.

2. Give common examples of similes, such as: "Horses galloped like the wind" and "In the dark I felt blind as a bat." Ask students to suggest more similes of their own.

3. Read aloud "The Big Wind" segment. Ask students to silently listen for similes in the text.

4. Provide students with the text of "The Big Wind" segment and a copy of figure 5.9, **Similes—Words to Capture the Wind**. Review the format of this handout with them. Ask them to silently read the segment, find the similes, and write at least 10 of them on the handout. There are 14 similes in the segment. If desired, use this form to analyze other literary pieces containing similes.

Extensions:
1. Ask the young wordsmiths to imagine being caught in a rainstorm. Have them create two similes to describe the experience. For example, "water poured from the sky like a faucet" and "wet as a hound with no home." Have them choose one of their similes to incorporate into a short descriptive paragraph about a rainstorm. Ask volunteers to share their paragraphs aloud.

2. Incorporating that descriptive paragraph, the students can create a story of four or five paragraphs about the rainstorm, using a simile in each paragraph. Don't forget to use detail, too.

Teacher Evaluation Opportunities: Similes sheet; Written paragraph; Written story; Use of Six-Trait Writing techniques.

Similes—Words to Capture the Wind

Title of Source_____

Page Number(s)_____

Simile 1: _____
_____

Simile 2: _____
_____

Simile 3: _____
_____

Simile 4: _____
_____

Simile 5: _____
_____

Simile 6: _____
_____

Simile 7: _____
_____

Simile 8: _____
_____

Simile 9: _____
_____

Simile 10: _____
_____

Figure 5.9. Finding Similes.

◆ COWHAND LINGO

Level: Grades four to eight.

Student Learning Opportunities: Colloquial language; Writing dialogue; Six-Trait Writing—Word Choice, Sentence Fluency, Conventions.

Background: Ralph Moody develops his characters through their distinctive patterns of speech, adding rich, interesting language to the text. In the dialogue of Hiram (Hi) Beckman, Moody's mentor and foreman of the Y-B Ranch, we "hear" his Texas roots and his cowboy occupation ring through.

Basics:
1. Explore with students the language of Hi Beckman's character by matching phrases from his colloquial speech with conventional phrases, in figure 5.10, **Hi's Cowhand Lingo**. Draw lines to connect the phrases of equivalent meaning. (The answer key on page 120, will assist in the evaluation of this activity.) If desired, read aloud the full sentence in which the phrase appears, as students proceed through the activity. Chapter numbers for *Little Britches* and *Man of the Family* are listed. (Page numbers differ among editions of the books.)

Extensions:
1. Using Hi's phrase list from figure 5.10, ask students to create new sentences of dialogue for Hi's character, spontaneously or in writing. Have them share their sentences orally with the whole group. For example, "Burn some trail" could become, "That hand and his cayuse sure know how ta burn some trail."

2. With students in groups of two, ask them to prepare a short conversation between two cowboys or cowgirls, each using at least *five of Hi's phrases*. Have each partner write down the whole conversation with proper conventions. After rehearsing it together, have them present their cowhand lingo conversations orally to the group.

Teacher Evaluation Opportunities: Cowhand lingo sheet; Cowhand lingo sentences; Cowhand lingo conversation; Use of Six-Trait Writing techniques.

Hi's Cowhand Lingo

Your Task: Draw a line between one of Hi's phrases and the conventional phrase that has a similar meaning. Chapter numbers are from *Little Britches* (LB) and *Man of the Family* (MOTF).

Hi's Phrase	Conventional Phrase
burn some trail (Chapter 2, LB)	climb off
old cayuse (Chapter 7, LB)	only in a serious emergency
stick like a louse (Chapter 24, LB)	shoot a bullet
top-hand cow poke (Chapter 25, LB)	sit on a bucking horse
light down (Chapter 25, LB)	hurt you in some way
hightail on up the canyon (Chapter 26, LB)	stay on securely
nothin' less than prairie fire Chapter 26, LB)	ride quickly
drier'n a burnt boot (Chapter 27, LB)	to go unseen
throw a slug (Chapter 27, LB)	climb quickly up a valley
keep his foot in (Chapter 9, MOTF)	to stay ready
straddle a bronc (Chapter 9, MOTF)	horse
right as rain (Chapter 9, MOTF)	herded cattle
done you some dirt (Chapter 10, MOTF)	correct
never see hide nor hair (Chapter 10, MOTF)	head cowboy
punched longhorns (Chapter 10, MOTF)	extremely dry

Figure 5.10. Cowhand Lingo.

120 PIONEERING YOUNG PEOPLE

Answer Key for Hi's Cowhand Lingo, figure 5.10:

burn some trail (Chapter 2, LB)	ride quickly
old cayuse (Chapter 7, LB)	horse
stick like a louse (Chapter 24, LB)	stay on securely
top-hand cow poke (Chapter 25, LB)	head cowboy
light down (Chapter 25, LB)	climb off
hightail on up the canyon (Chapter 26, LB)	climb quickly up a valley
nothin' less than prairie fire Chapter 26, LB)	only in a serious emergency
drier'n a burnt boot (Chapter 27, LB)	extremely dry
throw a slug (Chapter 27, LB)	shoot a bullet
keep his foot in (Chapter 9, MOTF)	to stay ready
straddle a bronc (Chapter 9, MOTF)	sit on a bucking horse
right as rain (Chapter 9, MOTF)	correct
done you some dirt (Chapter 10, MOTF)	hurt you in some way
never see hide nor hair (Chapter 10, MOTF)	to go unseen
punched longhorns (chapter 10, MOTF)	herded cattle

Social Studies Experiences

◆ ONE-ROOM SCHOOLS

Level: Grades four to eight.

Student Learning Opportunities: Historical and literary research; Expository written reporting; Oral reporting; Creative dramatics; Six-Trait Writing—Ideas, Organization Voice, Word Choice, Sentence Fluency, Conventions.

Background: One-room public schools, like the grade-one-to-eight Lake School attended by Grace, Ralph, and Muriel Moody, provided education for many children in North America for more than 200 years. Today, most, but not all, are gone. Yet, the historical and contemporary saga of one-room schools (or one-teacher schools, as they are sometimes called) continues to be told. For example:

- The rise of home-schooling creates a new generation of "one-room schools" everywhere.

- Ray E. Kilmer Elementary School, east of Monument, Colorado, moved a historic one-room school next to their modern building, restored it, and made it a place for education again.

- Storyteller and teacher Jewell Wolk, of Cutbank, Montana, constructed a quilt depicting the one-room school where generations of her family learned and taught, which she interprets in her performances.

- Guidebooks for locating and learning about existing one-room schools are available for several western states and provinces.

Basics: The topic, one-room schools, suggests many possibilities for student research and reporting through text, graphics, audio, video, creative dramatics, and other media. Some potential information resources for student research are school districts, state or provincial and education departments, historical societies, libraries and librarians, appropriate Internet sites, knowledgeable individuals in the community. Specific information resources are detailed below. Options for student research projects include:

- The history of one-room schools in your school district, community, region, state, or province.

- Laura Ingalls Wilder and one-room schools. Potential information sources—books by and about Wilder.

- The lifestyle of a one-room school teacher. Potential information source—contact with past or present teachers of one-room schools.

- A student-written-and-performed creative drama about events in a one-room school, based on their research, the writings of Moody or Wilder, or other source material.

- The subject matter taught to one-room school students and their ways of learning, possibly including cooperative learning with students of different ages. Potential information source—contact with remote schools in the United States and Canada.

- The play and games of one-room school students. Potential information source—contact with remote schools in the United States and Canada.

- The depiction of one-room schools, students, and teachers in various books, fiction and nonfiction. Potential information source—literature resource guides. Resources on one-room schools: Listed below is a sampling of resources on the topic of one-room schools, with suggested reading levels for each literary source:

Text:

Bial, Raymond. *One-room School.* Boston: Houghton-Mifflin, 1999.
    Presents a brief history of the one-room schools in the United States from the 1700s to the 1950s. Juvenile nonfiction.

Fuller, Wayne E. *One-room Schools of the Middle West: An Illustrated History.* Lawrence, KS: University Press of Kansas, 1994.
    Illustrations help present-day students understand the life style of children in one-room schools. Juvenile, adult nonfiction.

Kalman, Bobbie. *A One-room School.* New York: Crabtree, 1994.
    A brief history of one-room schools in frontier communities. Juvenile nonfiction.

Lenski, Lois. *Prairie School.* Philadelphia: J. B. Lippincott, 1951.
    Inspired by letters from students, Lenski creates text and illustrations describing a school year in a one-room school in South Dakota. Juvenile fiction.

Pringle, Laurence P. *One Room School.* Honesdale, PA: Caroline House, Boyds Mill Press, 1998.
    Relates the author's experience as a boy in a one-room school. Juvenile nonfiction.

Stephens, Donna M. *One Room School: Teaching in 1930s Western Oklahoma.* Norman, OK: University of Oklahoma Press. 1990.
    Historical biographies of women teaching in one-room schools. Adult, nonfiction.

122 PIONEERING YOUNG PEOPLE

Wilder, Laura Ingalls. *School Days*. New York: HarperCollins. 1997.
    Easy-reading collection of school experiences from Wilder's books. Juvenile fiction.

RALPH MOODY RESOURCES

Selected Books by Moody

Moody, Ralph. *Little Britches: Father and I Were Ranchers*. Illustrated by Edward Shenton. Lincoln, NE: Bison Books, University of Nebraska Press, 1991 (1950).
    Moody recollection of his family's struggle to make a living and of his eventful childhood on a small Colorado ranch from 1906 to 1909.

——— . *Man of the Family*. Illustrated by Edward Shenton. Lincoln, NE: Bison Books, University of Nebraska Press, 1993 (1951).
    With their father dead, Moody and his sisters and brothers find creative, though often arduous, ways to help their mother keep the family together.

——— . *The Home Ranch*. Illustrated by Tran Mawicke. Lincoln, NE: Bison Books, University of Nebraska Press, 1994 (1956).
    The story of Moody's adventures working on a ranch and on the trail trading cattle in southern Colorado during the summer of 1910.

——— . *Mary Emma and Company*. Illustrated by Tran Mawicke. Lincoln, NE: Bison Books, University of Nebraska Press, 1994 (1961).
    Back in their native New England, the Moodys test their resourcefulness in the city of Boston.

——— . *The Fields of Home*. Illustrated by Edward Shenton. Lincoln, NE: Bison Books, University of Nebraska Press, 1993 (1953).
    Ralph finds that establishing good relations with his grandfather is the hardest chore of all on a Maine farm.

Moody's later autobiographies, *Shaking the Nickel Bush*, *The Dry Divide*, and *Horse of a Different Color: Reminiscences of a Kansas Drover*, are also available from Bison Books, University of Nebraska Press.

Electronic Resources

Ralph Moody Biography, Littleton Historical Museum Website. Available: http://www.Littleton.org/LCN/governme/Museum/lhistory/PM19.htm (Accessed December 13, 1999).
    In addition to the Web biography, the museum has a detailed brochure and other information on Moody. Contact the Littleton Historical Museum, 6028 S. Gallup St., Littleton, Colorado 80120. 303-795-3950. Fax 303-730-9818.

Rodeo Resources—Text

Tinkleman, Murray. *Little Britches Rodeo*. With additional photos by Ronni and Susan B. Tinkleman. New York: Greenwillow Books, 1985.
    Depicts contestants in Little Britches Rodeo in words and pictures for juvenile readers.

Rodeo Resources—Electronic

National Little Britches Rodeo Association Website. Available: http://www.nlbra.org (Accessed December 13, 1999).
 Reach NLBRA at: 1045 W. Rio Grande St., Colorado Springs, CO 80906. 1-800-763-3694.

REACh—Rodeo Education and Children Website. Available: http://www.reachkids.com (Accessed December 13, 1999).
 Recommended by the National Little Britches Rodeo Association, REACh provides rodeo and western lifestyle education programs and materials for school-age students. Contact them regarding availability, logistics and fees at: HC6 Box 1420, Payson, AZ 85541. 520-472-7492.

YOUNG NATURALISTS

John Muir

Margaret Murie

The title, naturalist, is wonderfully general. Like being a storyteller, people don't need a special degree to be a naturalist. The dictionary defines a naturalist as a student of plants and animals. We all fit the title in many ways. When we differentiate one type of bird from another or pick out the right kind of vegetable for the dinner menu, we are using our skills as naturalists. If our human forebears had not been expert at using those skills as hunters, gatherers, and growers of food and medicine, we would not be here.

While we all have some of the skills, some have special gifts as naturalists. John Muir and Margaret Murie, featured in this section, are two such people. From their earliest years, they exhibited a strong passion and affinity for the outdoors and fellow creatures that inhabit it. Along with others, such as Charles Darwin, Rachel Carson, George Washington Carver, and John James Audubon, Muir and Murie clearly embody the naturalist intelligence, as identified by neuropsychologist and brain researcher Howard Gardner, Professor of Education at Harvard University.

Howard Gardner, the father of the theory of multiple intelligences, identified the naturalist intelligence in 1997 as a complement to the seven other intelligences—linguistic, logical-mathematical, spatial, bodily–kinesthetic, musical, interpersonal, and intrapersonal—that he identified in his research on giftedness and impairment in brain function. A simple way to describe the multiple intelligence theory is to say that it seeks to identify how a person is smart, not how smart a person is. In a person's neurological system working without impairment, all of the intelligences operate collectively at various levels of proficiency. They do not operate individually. To Gardner, intelligence means a constructively creative human ability or problem-solving ability that is of value to some or many cultures. In his research, he identified the following criteria for determining a specific intelligence: a particular function in the brain represented by that ability, groups of people noticeably expert or noticeably impaired in an intelligence, and an evolutionary track record of the intelligence in species other than humans.

The naturalist intelligence fits those criteria perfectly. It is marked by the human ability to observe, understand, and organize flora, fauna, and geology. Gardner found specific brain functions dedicated to interpreting life-forms and landforms in humans and other animals. Some of the behaviors evident in naturalists include:

- Feeling comfortable in the outdoors.
- Feeling an affinity for other living things.
- Recognizing and classifying patterns in life-forms and landforms.
- Using the senses in exploration and discovery.
- Organizing information collected.
- Using natural objects constructively, in roles such as chef, florist, artist, and herbalist.
- Understanding biologic and geologic systems, in roles such as hunter, farmer, angler, and geologist.

Howard Gardner said that the naturalist intelligence, like the other seven, can be enhanced, especially in young people. Many educators have enthusiastically rallied around the theory of multiple intelligences. They see it as a more complete picture of the learning process (when compared with the IQ-based theory of intelligence, for example). Teachers are adapting the multiple intelligences theory extensively in their classrooms and curricula. An excellent resource for fostering the naturalist intelligence in young people is Norma J. Livo's *Celebrating the Earth: Stories, Experiences, and Activities* (Englewood, CO: Teacher Ideas Press, 2000).

Exploring the autobiographies of John Muir and Margaret Murie helps students define their own role as naturalists. The readings and **Learning Horizons** divisions of the chapters in **Young Naturalists** are designed to extend their experience from the writer's words to the realm of real life.

JOHN MUIR

CHAPTER 6

Born April 21, 1838 in Dunbar, Scotland. Died December 24, 1914 in Los Angeles, California. Childhood and young adult autobiography describes Scotland and Wisconsin.

AN APPRECIATION OF THE WRITER

This sudden plash into pure wilderness—baptism in Nature's warm heart—how utterly happy it made us! Nature streaming into us, wooingly teaching her wonderful glowing lessons, so unlike the dismal grammar ashes and cinders so long thrashed into us. Here without knowing it we were still at school; every wild lesson a love lesson, not whipped but charmed into us. Oh, that glorious Wisconsin wilderness! Everything new and pure in the very prime of the spring when Nature's pulses were beating highest and mysteriously keeping time with our own!

—John Muir on first arriving at their Wisconsin homestead, from *The Story of My Boyhood and Youth*.

Figure 6.1. John Muir, about 1870.

The stimulus of wild places developed many remarkable talents and skills in John Muir—and a powerful vision. From his earliest days in Scotland, his interest in the natural world and its creatures was unbounded. Muir's explorations in nature required feats of endurance in hiking, mountaineering, scaling glaciers, swimming, rock climbing, canoeing, and more. His inventions and mechanical aptitude are well known. A friend of both the rich and the poor, and especially of wild creatures, Muir was the prime mover in the designation of Yosemite and other national parks. Many consider him the father of the worldwide environmental movement. Earth Day is celebrated on his birthday. Today, Muir's vision for the well-being of the earth is shared by hundreds of millions of its residents.

Figure 6.2. John Muir's "scribble den" at his home in Martinez, California. Photo by John Stansfield.

For Muir, writing represented a many-faceted tool for recording his far-flung outdoor explorations and detailed natural observations. Although he grew to be very good at it, writing was not his primary vocation or occupation. It was sometimes his adversary. At times Muir wrote for no audience other than himself. Sometimes he wrote for very specific interest groups, and sometimes for a broader public. Whatever Muir's intentions in putting pen to paper, nature and wilderness lovers in the generations since his death in 1914 continue to celebrate his writings and his message.

And what is the powerful message in Muir's writing? Namely this: that human beings strive to understand and treasure the natural world that supports all life; that we work to sustain—not just consume—the natural environment, through techniques of education, conservation, and preservation; that all creation—rock, water, soil, air, plant, animal—is interrelated and valuable in nature's scheme.

Contemporary educators would say that John Muir was "expert at writing in the content areas." His subject matter, during almost 60 years as a writer of nonfiction, reflects his far-ranging interests and endeavors:

Naturalist and Scientist. Starting with his days as a student at the University of Wisconsin, Muir kept field notebooks with observations and drawings of flowering plants, trees, animals, glaciers, geology, and many other topics. This information, to varying degrees, appears in his speeches, in articles for magazines and scientific journals, and in all of his books.

Geographer and Traveler. John Muir traveled extensively, especially in North America. His observations about the people he encountered are as canny, if not as frequent, as those about the environments he visited.

Autobiographer. Most of Muir's books are autobiographical in some sense, based on his experiences in the outdoors. Of particular note here are those books involving his early years and young adulthood, *The Story of My Boyhood and Youth* and *A Thousand-Mile Walk to the Gulf*.

Despite (or perhaps because of) his love of outdoor experience, writing books about it was sheer drudgery for John Muir. Once, while at work on a book, he wrote to his sister Sarah that his life was an eternal grind, like the life of a glacier. Until the age of 70, he completed only three books, though he wrote many articles, speeches, and short papers. When he died at age 76 in 1914, according to biographer Edwin Way Teale, Muir left notes for 12 books that he never finished. (Six books under his name were published posthumously.) A second lifetime might not have even been enough for the dynamic John Muir.

IN HIS OWN WORDS

After settling Fountain Lake Farm in Wisconsin, John Muir's father Daniel Muir, encouraged his children to use the lake to learn to swim. "Go to the frogs," he told them, "and they will give you all the lessons you need." In their limited spare time that summer, the Muir children began to experiment with the frog style, swimming in a shallow basin at one end of Fountain Lake. Venturing beyond the basin, John Muir learned memorable lessons, which he recounts in the chapter titled, "Life on a Wisconsin Farm" from *The Story of My Boyhood and Youth*. (See page 131.)

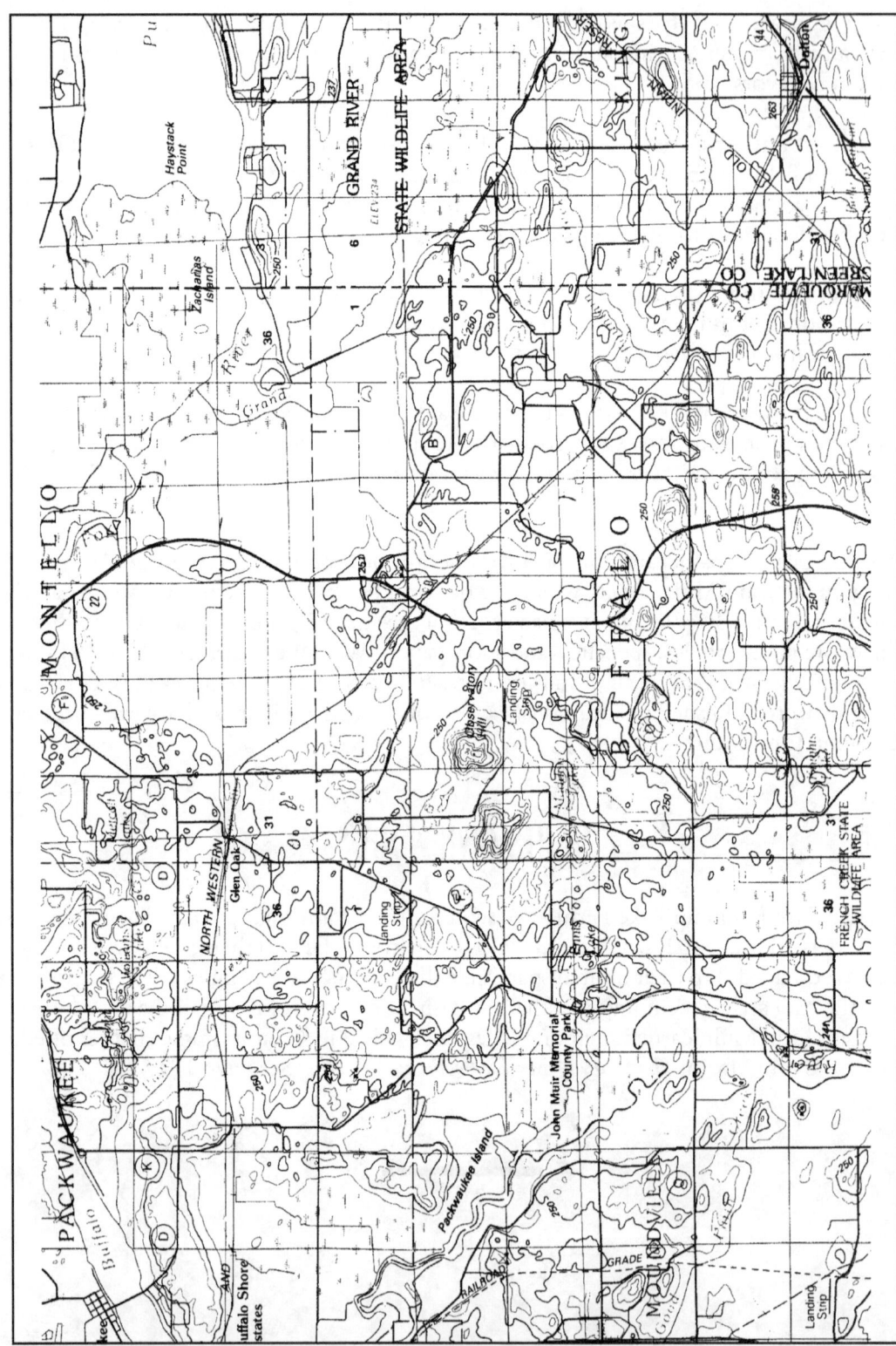

Figure 6.3. Contemporary map of John Muir's boyhood homelands in Wisconsin. John Muir Memorial County Park marks the site of Muir's first homestead. Public domain, courtesy of the U.S. Geologic Survey.

Note: The following is excerpted as punctuated and spelled in the original manuscript.

On the fourth of July of this swimming year one of the Lawson boys came to visit us, and we went down to the lake to spend the great warm day with the fishes and ducks and turtles. After gliding about on the smooth mirror water, telling stories and enjoying the company of the happy creatures about us, we rowed to our bathing-pool, and David and I went for a swim, while our companion fished from the boat a little way out beyond the rushes. After a few turns in the pool, it occurred to me that it was now about time to try deep water. Swimming through the thick growth of rushes and lilies was somewhat dangerous, especially for a beginner, because one's arms and legs might be entangled among the long, limber stems; nevertheless I ventured and struck out boldly enough for the boat, where the water was twenty or thirty feet deep. When I reached the end of the little skiff I raised my right hand to take hold of it to surprise Lawson, whose back was toward me and was not aware of my approach; but I failed to reach high enough, and, of course, the weight of my arm and the stroke against the overleaning stern of the boat shoved me down and I sank, struggling, frightened and confused. As soon as my feet touched the bottom, I slowly rose to the surface, but before I could get breath enough to call for help, sank back again and lost all control of myself. After sinking and rising I don't know how many times, some water got into my lungs and I began to drown. Then suddenly my mind seemed to clear. I remembered that I could swim under water, and, making a desperate struggle toward the shore, I reached a point where with my toes on the bottom, I slowly rose to the surface, gasped for help, and was pulled into the boat. This humiliating accident spoiled the day, and we all agreed to keep it a profound secret. My sister Sarah had heard my cry for help, and on our arrival at the house inquired what had happened. "Were you drowning, John? I heard you cry you couldna get oot." Lawson made haste to reply, "Oh, no! He was juist haverin [making fun]."

I was very much ashamed of myself, and at night, after calmly reviewing the affair, concluded that there had been no reasonable cause for the accident, and that I ought to punish myself for so nearly losing my life from unmanly fear. Accordingly at the very first opportunity, I stole away to the lake by myself, got into my boat, and instead of going back to the old swimming-bowl for further practice, or to try to do sanely and well what I had failed to do in my first adventure, that is to swim out through the rushes and lilies, I rowed directly out to the middle of the lake, stripped, stood up on the seat in the stern, and with grim deliberation took a header and dove straight down thirty or forty feet, turned easily, and, letting my feet drag, paddled straight to the surface with my hands as father had at first directed me to do. I then swam round the boat, glorying in my suddenly acquired confidence and victory over myself, climbed into it, and dived again, with the same triumphant success. I think I went down four or five times, and each time as I made the dive-spring shouted aloud, "Take that!" feeling that I was getting most gloriously even with myself.

Never again from that day to this have I lost control of myself in water. If suddenly thrown overboard at sea in the dark, or even while asleep, I think I would immediately right myself in a way some would call "instinct," rise among the waves, catch my breath, and try to plan what would better be done. Never was victory over self more complete. I have been a good swimmer ever since. At a slow gait I think I could swim all day in smooth water moderate in temperature. When I was a student at Madison, I used to go on long swimming-journeys, called exploring expeditions, along the south shore of Lake Mendota, on Saturdays, sometimes alone, sometimes with another amphibious explorer . . .

One calm summer evening a red-headed woodpecker was drowned in our lake. The accident happened at the south end, opposite our memorable swimming-hole, a few rods [33 to 50 feet] from the place where I came so near being drowned years before. I had returned to the old home during a summer vacation of the State University, and having made a beginning in botany, I was, of course, full of enthusiasm and ran eagerly to my beloved pogonia, calopogon, and cypripedium gardens, osmunda ferneries, and the lake lilies and pitcher-plants. A little before sundown the day-breeze died away, and the lake, reflecting the wooded hills like a mirror, was dimpled and dotted and streaked here and there where fishes and turtles were poking out their heads and muskrats were sculling themselves along with their flat tails making glittering tracks. After lingering a while, dreamily recalling the old, hard, half-happy days, and watching my favorite red-headed woodpeckers pursuing moths like regular fly-catchers, I swam out through the rushes and up the middle of the lake to the north end and back, gliding slowly, looking about me, enjoying the scenery as I would in a saunter along the shore, and studying the habits of the animals as they were explained and recorded on the smooth glassy water.

On the way back, when I was within a hundred rods or so of the end of my voyage, I noticed a peculiar plashing disturbance that could not, I thought, be made by a jumping fish or any other inhabitants of the lake; for instead of low regular out-circling ripples such as are made by the popping up of a head, or like those raised by the quick splash of a leaping fish, or diving loon or muskrat, a continuous struggle was kept up for several minutes ere the out-spreading, interfering ring waves began to die away. Swimming hastily to the spot to try to discover what had happened, I found one of my woodpeckers floating motionless with outspread wings. All was over. Had I been a minute of two earlier, I might have saved him. He had glanced on the water I suppose in pursuit of a moth, was unable to rise from it, and died struggling, as I nearly did at this same spot. Like me he seemed to have lost his mind in blind confusion and fear. The water was warm, and had he kept still with his head a little above the surface, he would sooner or later been wafted ashore. The best aimed flights of birds and man "gang aft agley," but this was the first case I had witnessed of a bird losing its life by drowning.

End of excerpted manuscript.

THE WRITER'S LIFE

It is not so unusual that John Muir begins *The Story of My Boyhood and Youth* by saying, "When I was a boy in Scotland I was fond of everything that was wild . . ." Many children love the outdoors—its freedom, its discoveries, its stimulus to the imagination. More unusual is the way he finishes that first sentence, " . . . and all my life I've been growing fonder and fonder of wild places and wild creatures." While many youngsters seem to be "born naturalists," curious about everything from ants to elephants, few adults continue to answer the call of the wild as keenly as John Muir did throughout his life.

Scotland

John was born April 21, 1838, in Dunbar, Scotland, to Ann Gilrye Muir, a mother and homemaker, and Daniel Muir, a storekeeper. He was the first-born son and third child of eight. Around Dunbar, "by the stormy North Sea, there was no lack of wildness" in the margins of farmer's fields and the tidal pools of the seashore. There, "with red-blooded playmates," John would ramble, "though solemnly warned that I must play at home in the garden and back yard, lest I should learn to think bad thoughts and say bad words." To no avail, for Muir continues, "In spite of sure sore punishments that followed like shadows, the natural inherited wildness in our blood ran true on its glorious course as invincible and unstoppable as stars."

With a little green book bag hung around his neck, young John began school while still three. With the alphabet taught him by his grandfather Gilrye, he spelled his way through his first reader and beyond. Poetry and stories about the sea and about animals ignited a fire in the boy's imagination. At home he learned hymns and Bible verses at his father's insistence, for a penny—the then-sizeable reward for success. Punishment for failure to learn lessons by heart was the same at home or school—a sound whipping with a switch or the taws, a leather strap.

Local boys played games of daring, called scootchers, amid the ruins of ancient Dunbar Castle. John often bested the others climbing up the thousand-year-old walls and down into the darkness of the deepest dungeon. Another death-defying scootcher lured John and younger brother David to climb out their bedroom window one night and up steep, slippery slates to the rooftop, three stories above the backyard. Getting down proved even more hazardous. These experiences in overcoming climbing challenges served Muir well later in life on hazardous peaks and glaciers.

For Dunbar boys, scootchers involved contests in cross-country running, wrestling, jumping, visiting supposedly haunted places, as well as climbing, which hardened them for an arduous life. Fighting was also a constant part of their play, whether in re-creating historical battles or in sparring for schoolyard supremacy.

After age seven, John moved to the grammar school to study Latin, French, and English, three lessons a day each, as well as spelling, history, arithmetic, and geography. He continued to learn Bible verses for his father every day until "by the time I was eleven years of age I had about three fourths of the Old Testament and all of the New by heart and by sore flesh."

On the night of February 18, 1849, as John and David sat, "at grandfather's fireside solemnly learning our lessons as usual, my father came in with news, the most wonderful, most glorious that wild boys ever heard. 'Bairns,' he said, 'you needna learn your lessons the nicht, for we're gan to America the morn!' " Daniel had sold his store. Following the guidance of religious leader Thomas Campbell, he sought more democracy in the practice of his religion. Daniel departed Glasgow the next night via sailing ship, accompanied by Sarah (13 years old), John (11), David (9), and a great pile of possessions. The rest of the family followed in the fall when a farm and house were established in North America.

Wisconsin

After a rough ocean crossing of more than six weeks, the Muirs traveled through New York City, up the Hudson River to Albany, and embarked for Buffalo on an Erie Canal packet boat. At Buffalo, Daniel decided to head west to the "oak openings" of southeastern Wisconsin. There, unlike Canada, a crop could be raised the first year, without need of clearing a dense forest. A lake steamer brought the Muirs to Milwaukee. An overloaded farmer's wagon brought them 100 miles northwest to Kingston. With the help of a pioneering fellow Scotsman, Alexander Gray, Daniel located an 80-acre tract on a small lake near the Fox River, which he named Fountain Lake Farm. A log shanty was soon built to house Daniel and the children.

Arriving at the farm in the height of spring, the boys felt "Nature streaming into us." As John states, "Here without knowing it we were still at school; every wild lesson a love lesson, not whipped but charmed into us." Almost the only schooling Muir would receive over the next decade would be from "that glorious Wisconsin wilderness" and what he taught himself.

But what "glowing lessons" Nature had for him. In *The Story of My Boyhood and Youth*, John Muir describes his discoveries in great detail. Birds, especially birds; from his first encounter with a crafty blue jay to the unforgettable sight of millions of migrating passenger pigeons (now extinct) "like a mighty river in the sky," Muir found Wisconsin a "paradise of birds." There were mammals, reptiles, amphibians, fish, insects, all in great diversity; many sustained by the waters of Fountain Lake. Farm animals had distinctly remarkable personalities; Jack, the herding pony; Nob, the affectionate plow horse; Watch, the good dog gone bad. Abundant flowers lured Muir on to explore ever more of their secrets through the science of botany.

Figure 6.4. Muir's sketch of Fountain Lake farm.

What was amazing about young John Muir is that he enjoyed and found time for learning despite having to work endlessly, exhaustingly hard. He was nearly worked to death several times. "I was put to the plough at the age of twelve," he says, "when my head reached but little above the handles, and for many years I had to do the greater part of the ploughing . . . And as I was the eldest boy, the greater part of all the work on the farm quite naturally fell to me." Planting, hoeing corn, harvesting, threshing wheat, woodcutting, mending things, tending animals, sharpening tools—John and his brothers and sisters did them all and more. All was overseen by the "excessively industrious" Daniel Muir, with his switch ever ready to whip his children, especially the spirited, independent John. The children regularly worked 16 hours a day in summer and 12 hours, often outdoors, in winter, six days a week.

After eight arduous years at Fountain Lake Farm, and despite John's arguments against it, Muir states, "father bought a half-section [320 acres, about six miles southeast] of wild land . . . and began all over again to clear and fence and break up other fields for a new farm, doubling all the stunting, heartbreaking chopping, grubbing, stump-digging, rail splitting, fence-building, barn-building, house-building, and so forth." This higher, drier tract, known as Hickory Hill Farm, needed a good well. After 10 feet of digging, the Muirs encountered sandstone. Daniel directed John to chip away at the rock with hammer and chisel, "from early morning until dark, day after day, for weeks and months." One morning, young Muir was overcome by carbonic acid gas, accumulated overnight in the deep pit. Near death, at his father's shouts, he revived enough to climb into the haul bucket and was hoisted out. After a day's recovery and learning how to dispel the gas, John finished the well, ultimately 90 feet deep, striking "a fine, hearty gush of water."

Daniel Muir allowed none but religious books in his house. But at age 15, through the influence of friends, John made the "great and sudden discovery that the poetry of the Bible, Shakespeare, and Milton, was a source of inspiring, exhilarating, uplifting pleasure." With the help of his sympathetic mother and sisters, he covertly hid his nonreligious books, both the borrowed and the ones he saved pennies to buy. Finding time for reading was another problem. Daniel commanded early bedtime for all the family most every night, but after some argument he permitted John to wake early, if so desired. John responded by waking at one in the morning, giving himself precious time of his own for reading—and for inventing.

On winter nights too cold for reading, Muir resorted to the cellar—right under his father's bedroom—to tinker with inventions. Like his father, John possessed a gift for designing practical devices and building them from materials at hand. A water-powered sawmill became his first creation. A variety of pendulum-powered wooden clocks sprang next from his fertile mind. One was designed to roll a sleeper from his bed and to start the morning fire. Another large timekeeper could be viewed from a great distance outdoors, as could a great iron thermometer. John dreamed of working as an inventor or machinist to earn money for future education.

Neighbor William Duncan encouraged John, then 22, to display his inventions at the State Fair in Madison. He left home with two wooden clocks and a thermometer made from an old washboard on his back. Muir's alarm clock-bedsteads turned into a huge Fair attraction, written up glowingly in newspapers. Near the fairgrounds, the University of Wisconsin, on its sunny hilltop, caught the eye of the young inventor.

After several months at various jobs (including making and selling a few alarm clock-bedsteads), the shy country boy summoned enough courage to seek enrollment to the University. The Dean welcomed Muir, despite his lack of formal schooling. Chemistry and geology, Greek and Latin, (still remembered from Dunbar) occupied his first semester.

John's invention-filled dormitory room became a showplace. There was the trick bed, his study desk, which at timed intervals automatically rotated textbooks in front of the student, and the Loafer's Chair. When anyone sat in the chair too long, a pistol fired a blank beneath it, instantly propelling the startled loafer up and out. Board, as for some other students, was a poor diet of bread, graham crackers, and milk, costing about one dollar a week. Hearing of this spartan fare, the often tight-fisted Daniel Muir sent money to his suffering son.

John Muir spent four years at Madison, studying what "was most useful," never receiving a degree. (In 1897 the University awarded him an honorary doctorate.) He worked summers for wages at Hickory Hill, continuing his studies, especially in botany, during spare moments. In 1864, Muir "wandered away on a glorious geological and botanical excursion," leaving "one University for another, the Wisconsin University for the University of the Wilderness."

The World

Figure 6.5. John Muir's home in Martinez, California, now part of the John Muir National Historic Site, administered by the U.S. Park Service. Photo by John Stansfeld.

In between naturalist treks, Muir successfully applied his mechanical aptitudes in factories in Meaford, Ontario, and Indianapolis, Indiana. But an industrial accident in the spring of 1867 nearly took his sight. When his vision returned, John turned away from machine trades and toward his other love, the natural world. Now that the Civil War had ended, the dream of a botanical excursion from Indianapolis to the Gulf of Mexico and to the Amazon became a reality. A bout with malaria in Florida redirected his ultimate destination from Brazil's rainforest to California's Sierra Nevada Mountains.

What might have resulted from a Muir Amazon exploration, we can only guess. What resulted from his explorations in California's Sierra has changed the face of the United States and the world. In the naturalist's paradise of Yosemite Valley, John Muir found, in the words of an old Shaker hymn, *Simple Gifts*, his "valley of love and delight." As years passed he became the prime force in the protection and designation of the world's second national park, Yosemite. His mountaineering exploits and accomplishments are legendary. His studies in California and Alaska helped establish a scientific understanding of glaciers and their power to shape the earth. Books Muir wrote have profoundly influenced millions worldwide to conserve natural resources, preserve wild places, and, in outdoor recreation, to seek the benefits and wisdom nature offers. To accomplish these ends, in 1892 Muir founded the Sierra Club, today one of the world's most effective environmental organizations.

As a loving husband and father of two daughters, successful agriculturalist, friend of presidents and common folk, internationally famous author, and more, John Muir's life was full of success and rich accomplishment. Yet, the things that made him richest of all, that cost him nothing but his time, were the things that John Muir, boy and man, gloried in from his earliest days—"wild places and wild creatures."

TEACHING ADVICE FOR JOHN MUIR

Autobiographical Writings

A classic autobiography of childhood, John Muir's *The Story of My Boyhood and Youth* is the primary focus of this chapter. All quotes in **The Writer's Life** section are taken from that book. Interested teachers and students can follow Muir's continuing adventures into manhood in *A Thousand-Mile Walk to the Gulf* and *My First Summer in the Sierra*, both written in the form of daily journals. *Stickeen*, an adventure-filled dog story published in book form, provides a wonderful read or read-aloud for fourth to eighth graders. All of these books are in print and available online, as of this writing.

Age Appropriateness

All of Muir's works read aloud well for listeners of any age. At times though, his language can be ornate and his descriptions lengthy. Good readers in fourth grade, fifth grade and up should have no problem mastering *The Story of My Boyhood and Youth*. If length is a problem for less-able readers, appropriate episodes can easily be excerpted from the book's mostly chronologically arranged text.

Muir's Spirituality

John Muir's personal relationship with the natural world was not just experiential and scientific; it was theological. Rooted in his rigorous Bible-based early education, he uses frequent religious references to describe the world's wonders in his writings.

Scotland and Wisconsin, Western?

Although Muir's childhood took place in Scotland and east of the Mississippi River in Wisconsin, he is included here for three good reasons. First, during Muir's boyhood, Wisconsin was widely considered to be part of the American northwest. Second, his boyhood homesteading experience makes for many interesting comparisons and a few contrasts with those who settled farther west. Third, few people have understood and influenced western North America as fundamentally as John Muir.

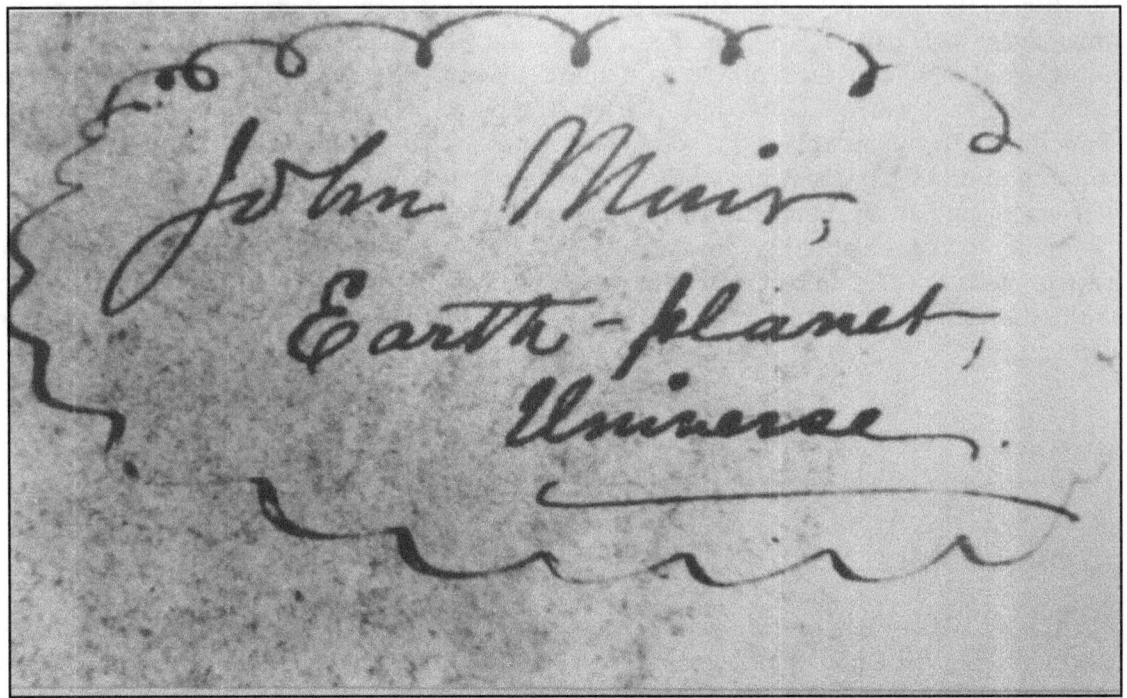

Figure 6.6. John Muir's famous signature on display at John Muir National Historic Site, Martinez, California. Photo by John Stansfield.

LEARNING HORIZONS

Literature Aloud Experiences

◆ *NARRATIVE POETRY AND BALLADS*

Level: Grades four and higher.

Student Learning Opportunities: Discussion; Cooperation; Selection of narrative material; Preparation of material; Presentation.

Background: The times when Daniel Muir played his handmade fiddle were cherished by his children. Their father's often harsh demeanor would soften as he played and they all sang together the old Scottish ballads and hymns. The Muirs grew up in a culture where rhythm, rhyme, and melody were tied to story in traditional ballads. As fondly described in *The Story of My Boyhood and Youth*, John Muir's glowing recollections of Robert Southey's dramatic narrative poem, "The Inchcape Rock," represent some of his earliest literary memories. Later, the poetic recitations of Wisconsin neighbors David Gray and David Taylor ignited an unquenchable fire for learning and literature in the 16-year-old Muir. He found memorization, though hard work, to be an asset, not a threat.

The poetic techniques and compelling storylines of narrative verse and ballads hold strong appeal for young people of any era. These poetic forms played a substantial role in

North American education in the nineteenth and early twentieth centuries. Unfortunately, they play a greatly diminished role today. Students can gain considerable exposure to the ancient and contemporary art forms of narrative poetry and ballad by preparing and performing them in a **Festival of Story Poetry and Story Song**.

Old Favorites: Compile a list of the story poems and story songs with which students and teachers are already familiar. Don't forget nursery rhymes, folk songs, or rap songs. Read aloud some of these favorites. Discuss the storyline of each piece and what elements—rhythm, rhyme, meter, melody, and others—make it appealing and memorable. Identify, define, and display for future reference vocabulary words pertinent to story poems and story songs.

New Favorites: Expose students to a wide variety of unfamiliar narrative poetry and ballads (especially the instructor's favorites) through read-alouds and their own reading, video and audio recordings, and live performances by "poemtellers" and folksingers. As with the previously identified favorites, discuss storyline and poetic and musical elements of each piece. A brief narrative poetry and ballad resource list includes:

Chase, Richard, ed. *American Folk Tales and Songs.* New York: Dover, 1971.

Cole, William, ed. *The Poets Tales.* New York: World Publishing, 1971.

———. *Story Poems, New and Old.* Cleveland, OH: World Publishing, 1957.

Fife, Austin, and Alta Fife, eds. *Ballads of the Great West.* Palo Alto, CA: American West, 1970.

Harrison, Michael, and Christopher Stuart-Clark, eds. *The Oxford Book of Story Poems.* Oxford, England: Oxford University Press, 1990.

Janeczko, Paul, ed. *The Music of What Happens: Poems That Tell Stories.* New York: Orchard, 1988.

Livo, Norma J. *Troubadour's Storybag: Musical Folktales of the World.* Golden, CO: Fulcrum, 1996.

Sandburg, Carl. *The American Songbag.* San Diego: Harcourt Brace Jovanovich, 1990.

An excellent teacher resource for orienting students to many types of poetry is:

Denman, Gregory A. *When You've Made It Your Own. . . : Teaching Poetry to Young People.* Portsmouth, NH: Heinemann, 1988.

Selection: As students become acquainted with the new poems and songs, ask them to identify one or several pieces they like and want to perform. Have students consult with the teacher on final selections based on the appropriateness of the selections for student level of performance skill and intended audience.

Organization: Determine whether each piece requires solo, duo, or ensemble performers and if live or prerecorded musical accompaniment is necessary. Recruit duo or ensemble performers and musicians from among students, as needed. Students can perform in more than one selection.

Preparation: With instructor's consultation, ask students to decide whether to memorize or read aloud their selected narrative poem(s). Ballads should be memorized, whether performed a cappella or with musical accompaniment. Whether memorized or read, selections require considerable rehearsal. Understanding the selections may require research into their history and the lives and experiences of the authors. Costumes, sets, and props are possible additions, but should be kept secondary in emphasis to the quality performance of the oral literatures.

Performance: As with other **Literature Aloud Experiences**, "the play's the thing." Student performance, with its complex of educational and life-skill benefits, is the desired outcome. Integrating adult performers into the event provides excellent role models, as well. Presentation options range from simple in-classroom performances, through multiclass or school assembly programs, to evening family performances and touring in the community.

Extensions: Incorporate narrative poetry and ballads in a Classroom Chautauqua (see **Literature Aloud Experiences,** chapter 3).

Teacher Evaluation Opportunities: Discussion; Cooperation; Selection of narrative material; Preparation of material; Presentation.

Language Arts Experiences

◈ *MEMORABLE FIRSTS*

Level: Grades four to eight.

Student Learning Opportunities: Personal memory; Reading aloud; Narrative writing; Six-Trait Writing—Ideas, Word Choice, Organization, Voice.

Background: There is an old adage, "First impressions are the most memorable." Writing in *The Story of My Boyhood and Youth*, John Muir describes his first sight of the Fountain Lake Farm in Wisconsin. Though 60 years had passed when he wrote it, you can still hear the excitement of new discovery in his voice. First sight, first impressions, first discoveries, first meetings or experiences—all are often especially memorable. For that reason, they make excellent writing topics.

Basics:
1. Introduce the concept of memorable firsts to students. Share a personally memorable first sight, impression, discovery, meeting or experience with them. Ask a few of them to briefly share a first of their own. If needed, use the **Learning Horizon**: Recollections, chapter 2, to help students develop oral stories of their memorable firsts. Read aloud John Muir's discoveries of blue jays and fireflies at Fountain Lake, from chapter 2 of *The Story of My Boyhood and Youth*. If desired, read examples of other memorable firsts. For example, Zitkala-Ša's first experiences at boarding school from "The School Days of an Indian Girl" in *American Indian Stories*; Hal Borland's first sight of his homestead in chapter 2 of *High, Wide and Lonesome*; Mardy Murie's first impressions of Fairbanks, Alaska, in chapter 2 of *Two in the Far North*; and Charles Eastman's first meeting with his father from the final chapter of *Indian Boyhood*.

2. Brainstorm with students a topic list of memorable firsts. Allow them some time for self-reflection to identify a personally memorable first about which they would like to

write. As needed, consult with individuals in finding the right topic. Be aware that some first memories may be disturbing to them and undesirable for this assignment.

3. When all students have chosen a memorable first sight, impression, discovery, meeting, or experience, present this writing assignment: Compose no more and no less than three powerful paragraphs describing your memorable first. Write in the first person. Choose words that vividly describe sights, sounds, smells, tastes, people, and places. Use strong verbs. Organize your text to tell an interesting short story. Let the audience know and feel why the event is a memorable first for you.

4. After composition and revision, ask some or all of the students to share their final versions with the class.

Extensions:
1. Ask students to write about the same (or a new) memorable first, using the same criteria as above except this time, have them write from the point of view of someone else, not their own. For example, instead of describing her own first successful bicycle ride, have Maria describe the event as her mother might have seen it.

2. After composition and revision, ask some or all to share their final versions of both stories of memorable firsts. If desired, promote group discussion of comparisons and contrasts between the versions, as well as other qualities of the writing.

Teacher Evaluation Opportunities: Memorable first story—written version; Memorable first story from a different point of view—written version; Oral presentation of written stories; Use of Six-Trait Writing techniques.

❖ WELL SEASONED WITH ADJECTIVES

Level: Grades four to eight.

Student Learning Opportunities: Parts of speech; Textual analysis; Descriptive writing; Six-Trait Writing—Ideas, Word Choice, Sentence Fluency, Conventions.

Background: Adjectives in writing are like seasonings in food. Used enough, they enhance the flavor; used too much, the fare is spoiled. John Muir was an expert in using the right number and kind of adjectives to flavor his writing. By analyzing and emulating this skill, students will improve the descriptive power of their own writing.

Basics:
1. Review with students the meaning of the part of speech, the adjective: a word used to limit or qualify a noun or noun equivalent; one kind of describing word. Solicit and suggest examples of sentences that contain adjectives. Be sure to include examples of coordinate adjectives and compound adjectives. An example of a coordinate adjective is, "Launched by his *long, thin* legs, Jerome soared for the rebound." An example of a compound adjective is, "The *Albuquerque–Denver* flight for the volleyball team was canceled."

2. Distribute copies of figure 6.7 to students, the first paragraph of John Muir's lessons learned from swimming from **In His Own Words**, this chapter. Ask them to underline adjectives and coordinate adjectives as they read. (There are no compound adjectives in the selection.) The paragraph contains more than 20 adjectives.

3. Solicit and record examples of the adjectives found by the students until all are identified. Discuss and analyze the quantity and quality of words Muir chooses as adjectives. He uses an average of two or fewer adjectives in his long sentences. Is that too many? Too few? Just right? What types of descriptive jobs do Muir's adjectives do in his paragraph? These jobs include numbering and measuring (such as, "few," "twenty or thirty"), expressing emotion (such as, "happy," "humiliating"), describing condition (such as, "smooth mirror," "thick"), position (such as, "high," "overleaning"), and others. Finally, discuss Muir's adjective word choice. Does it help to bring his experience more clearly to life? How?

Extensions:
1. John Muir kept track of his observations of the natural world in journals. He used his journal entries to help himself write books later in life. With the students, take a walk outside to observe nature in the schoolyard, park, neighborhood, or countryside. Like John Muir, make observations in preparation for creating a short nature journal entry. Use the Observation and Memory Walk strategy, as in **Learning Horizons**, chapter 1, or basic note-taking in the field to record observations.

2. Ask students to prepare a five- to eight-sentence nature journal entry describing their field observations. Remind them to include details of the date, time of day, weather, and location of the walk.

3. Ask students to underline all adjectives used in their journal entries. Then, have them review their entries and select three places where effective adjectives will add descriptive or clarifying power to the sentences. Have students add the adjectives to the entry and double underline them.

Teacher Evaluation Opportunities: Participation in discussion and nature walk; Identifying adjectives in Muir text; Nature journal entry—observation and note-taking, text, identification and addition of adjectives; Use of Six-Trait Writing techniques.

The Near Drowning of John Muir

Your Task: Underline every adjective you can find in this paragraph. Don't forget that the coordinate adjectives have more than one word.

On the fourth of July of this swimming year one of the Lawson boys came to visit us, and we went down to the lake to spend the great warm day with the fishes and ducks and turtles. After gliding about on the smooth mirror water, telling stories and enjoying the company of the happy creatures about us, we rowed to our bathing-pool, and David and I went for a swim, while our companion fished from the boat a little way out beyond the rushes. After a few turns in the pool, it occurred to me that it was now about time to try deep water. Swimming through the thick growth of rushes and lilies was somewhat dangerous, especially for a beginner, because one's arms and legs might be entangled among the long, limber stems; nevertheless I ventured and struck out boldly enough for the boat, where the water was twenty or thirty feet deep. When I reached the end of the little skiff I raised my right hand to take hold of it to surprise Lawson, whose back was toward me and was not aware of my approach; but I failed to reach high enough, and, of course, the weight of my arm and the stroke against the overleaning stern of the boat shoved me down and I sank, struggling, frightened and confused. As soon as my feet touched the bottom, I slowly rose to the surface, but before I could get breath enough to call for help, sank back again and lost all control of myself. After sinking and rising I don't know how many times, some water got into my lungs and I began to drown. Then suddenly my mind seemed to clear. I remembered that I could swim under water, and, making a desperate struggle toward the shore, I reached a point where with my toes on the bottom, I slowly rose to the surface, gasped for help, and was pulled into the boat. This humiliating accident spoiled the day, and we all agreed to keep it a profound secret. My sister Sarah had heard my cry for help, and on our arrival at the house inquired what had happened. "Were you drowning, John? I heard you cry you couldna get oot." Lawson made haste to reply, "Oh, no! He was juist haverin [making fun]."

Figure 6.7. **Finding Adjectives.**

Social Studies Experiences

◈ *GOING ON A WILDERNESS EXPEDITION? PLAN AHEAD!*

Level: Grades four to eight.

Student Learning Opportunities: Research skills; Cooperative decision-making; Written and oral reporting; Expository writing; Imaginative and narrative writing; Six-Trait Writing—Ideas, Voice.

Background: When Lewis and Clark set off in 1804 with more than 30 members of the Corps of Discovery to explore the West via the Missouri and Columbia rivers, they carried tons of equipment in a 55-foot-long keelboat and two smaller vessels. Meriwether Lewis planned the expedition for more than six months. It lasted 27 months. When young John Muir set out alone in 1867 on a naturalist trek of 1,000 miles from Indiana to the Gulf of Mexico, his physical preparations were few. He carried only a few carefully selected articles in a small backpack. But he had mentally planned the two-month journey for more than a year. Students can develop a keen understanding of what it takes to plan a journey of discovery by planning their own imaginary, weeklong wilderness expedition, following in the footsteps of explorers like Lewis, Clark, and Muir.

Basics:
1. Have students form expedition teams of four members to work cooperatively and successfully together. The teacher may want to organize teams based on the wild region in which the students are most interested—seacoast, forest, desert, rainforest, mountain, Arctic, Antarctic, river, lake, canyon, plains (or steppes), or island. Atlases or multiple copies of maps of the world are needed for reference.

2. Have each team discuss, decide, and collectively fill out the **Expedition Planning** form, figure 6.8. Their expedition site should be a real locale somewhere on the earth that offers (or did offer in the historic past) an opportunity for "muscle-powered" (non-motorized) wilderness exploration.

3. Ask each member to research the climate and geography of the wild locale and two of the eight categories from the **Essential Expedition Equipment** form, figure 6.9, page 146. Next, have them present tentative gear lists for their categories to the team for discussion, revision, and final decision-making. Have each team create a final list of essential equipment for each category. Back issues of *Backpacker* and *Outside* magazines, along with outdoor "how-to" and field guides, found at call numbers 796–798 in the library, provide excellent reference material for this task.

4. Have each team prepare a large-scale graphic representation, based on their completed **Expedition Planning** and **Essential Expedition Equipment** forms. They can use an overhead or computer projector, chart paper, markers or a blackboard, artistic renditions, maps, props, or other creative means in their presentations. Using its graphics, each team shares the results of its expedition planning with the other teams.

TEAM MEMBERS_____

Expedition Planning

Your team is preparing a seven-day expedition to explore a wild and remote portion of the earth. On the expedition, all travel will be "muscle-powered"—on foot, on bicycle, onboard a non-motorized boat, on animal back, or with pack animals to help carry your equipment. For the expedition to be successful and safe, teamwork and advanced planning are critical.

Your Task: To begin planning for your expedition, as a team, review the following questions, make group decisions about each one, and record your team's answers on this sheet.

1. What kind of wild region will you explore—seacoast, forest, desert, rainforest, mountain, Arctic, Antarctic, river, lake, canyon, plains (or steppes), or island?

2. On what continent is this region located? In what country? In what year will your imaginary expedition take place?

3. What kind(s) of "muscle-powered" transportation will you use on the expedition?

4. Will you need motorized transportation to get you to and from your wild region? What kind(s)?

5. How far will you travel during the seven-day trek? Will you take any days off during the expedition?

6. Why do you want to visit this wild place?

Figure 6.8. Expedition Planning Form.

TEAM MEMBERS_____

Essential Expedition Equipment

Selecting the right lightweight, portable equipment for the expedition is very important. Muscles alone will be moving you and your gear for seven days. You don't want to carry anything unnecessary, but you also don't want to leave behind something essential.

Knowing about the climate and geography of your wild region helps you choose the right gear. Is it cold, mild, or hot there? Dry, rainy, flooded? Is it flat, mountainous, buggy, steep, or deep? Are there any hazards of which to beware? In what season are you planning to travel?

Your Tasks: Each expedition team member should research the climate and geography of your wild region and research two of the following categories of equipment. Next, make a draft list of essential gear for each category. Talk over your list with the other team members. Be specific as to sizes, amounts, and types of gear. Choose the lightest weight equipment and food that you can. Finally, as a team, choose and list the essential equipment for each category.

Essential Equipment Categories

CLOTHING AND FOOTWEAR—Don't forget coats or rainwear and hats.

SHELTER AND SLEEPING GEAR—Will your shelter keep out bugs? How about rain or snow?

COOKING AND WATER PURIFICATION GEAR—Don't forget fuel for cooking.

PERSONAL ITEMS—Got your toothbrush, water bottle, sunscreen, pocket knife? Extra batteries?

FIRST-AID, REPAIR, AND EMERGENCY GEAR— Know how to perform first aid and fix your gear should it break?

MAPS, FIELD GUIDEBOOKS, AND CAMERAS—Know how to read your maps?

FOOD—Don't forget extra food for emergencies.

EQUIPMENT-CARRYING GEAR—Canoes or kayaks? Backpacks, bike packs, or horse packs?

Figure 6.9. Essential Expedition Equipment Checklist.

Extensions:

1. Before and during the expedition planning activity, read aloud or have students read appropriate segments from the following books: *Undaunted Courage: Meriwether Lewis, Thomas Jefferson, and the Opening of the American West* by Stephen E. Ambrose, chapters 7 to 11, and the introduction and early journal entries from *A Thousand-Mile Walk to the Gulf* by John Muir, edited by William Frederic Bade.

2. After each team's planning information is complete, have individuals use the data by creating an imaginary daily expedition journal, describing their experiences on the journey. An original map could accompany the journal.

Teacher Evaluation Opportunities: Cooperation in team activities; Expedition Objectives form; Essential Expedition Equipment form; Climate and geography reports; Graphic presentations; Oral presentations; Reading selections; Daily trip journal.

JOHN MUIR RESOURCES

Selected Books by Muir

Muir, John. *My First Summer in the Sierra*, The John Muir Library Series. San Francisco: Sierra Club Books, 1990 (1916).
Based on Muir's journals for the summer of 1869, it presents his memorable first experiences in what he called "the Range of Light," the Sierra Nevada Mountains of California, especially Yosemite Valley.

———. *A Thousand-Mile Walk to the Gulf*, The John Muir Library Series. San Francisco: Sierra Club Books, 1991 (1916).
Muir's journal paints a deft picture of the natural scene and the people encountered on his trek through the wilder parts of the American South just after the Civil War.

———. *Stickeen: Story of a Dog*. Bedford, MA: Applewood Books, 1989 (1885).
When Stickeen, the dog, follows Muir on his exploration of an Alaskan glacier in 1880, a danger-filled adventure ensues.

———. *The Story of My Boyhood and Youth*, The John Muir Library Series. San Francisco: Sierra Club Books, 1988 (1913).
Written late in Muir's life at the request of friends, it depicts the early days of one of America's true geniuses; his emergence from a childhood of sometimes dire hardship is a testament to creativity and the power of the human spirit.

Selected Muir Resources

Anderson, Peter. *John Muir: Wilderness Prophet*. Danbury, CT: Franklin Watts, 1995.
A brief, 60-page biography, well illustrated with photos and drawings, especially appropriate for fourth- to sixth-grade researchers.

Cornell, Joseph Bharat. *John Muir: My Life with Nature*. Nevada City, CA: Dawn Publications, 2000.
Muir expert and naturalist Joseph Cornell has edited many of Muir's own writings about his adventures and nature into an autobiographical collection for readers 10 to 16. Enhanced with illustrations and photos, this book is a companion, of sorts, for Muir's own *The Story of My Boyhood and Youth*.

Douglas, William O. *Muir of the Mountains*. Illustrated by Daniel San Souci. San Francisco: Sierra Club Books for Children, 1994 (1961).

    Written by a renowned conservationist, author, and former U.S. Supreme Court Justice, this 105-page biography for young adults details Muir's mountaineering exploits, as well as other aspects of his life, and makes an excellent read-aloud.

Naden, Corinne J., and Rose Blue. *John Muir: Saving the Wilderness. A Gateway Biography*. Millbrook, CT: The Millbrook Press, 1992.

    A basic biography in 48 pages, suitable for reading and research by students in grades four to eight; illustrated with a variety of scenic and historic photographs and sketches.

Talmadge, Katherine S. *John Muir: At Home in the Wild*, The Earth Keepers Series. Illustrated by Antonio Castro. New York: Twenty-first Century Books, 1993.

    An 80-page biography of Muir's life written for young readers and young adults; one of the excellent "Earth Keepers" series of naturalists' biographies.

Weitzman, David. *The Mountain Man and the President*. Illustrated by Charles Shaw. New York: Steck-Vaughn, 1993.

    Though a mere 40 pages, this young reader–young adult history of the conservation movement introduces two of North America's foremost conservationists, John Muir and Theodore Roosevelt, focusing on their milestone camping trip to Yosemite in 1903.

Wolfe, Linnie Marsh. *Son of the Wilderness: The Life of John Muir*. New York: Alfred A. Knopf, 1945.

    This Pulitzer Prize-winning biography for adults presents a remarkably clear portrait of the life and times of John Muir. A fascinating reading experience in itself, it provides a superlative background reference for anyone teaching about him.

Electronic Resources

The Canadian Friends of John Muir. Available: http://www.johnmuir.org (Accessed September 22, 2000).

    Historical information, links, contemporary travel tips and events, especially related to John Muir's time in Ontario, 1864–1866.

Dunbar's John Muir Association. Available: http://www.muir-birthplace.org/djma/index.html (Accessed September 22, 2000).

    An organization dedicated to educating the world about John Muir and conserving landscape and wildlife in Scotland. The Web site features details about the annual John Muir Festival in April, his family home (now a museum), the town of Dunbar, travel tips, and links.

Ecology Hall of Fame—John Muir. Available: http://www.ecotopia.org/ehof/muir/ (Accessed September 22, 2000).

    The Web site contains biography, quotes, appreciations of John Muir, bibliography, links, and more, all excellent resources for student research.

Haines, Alaska's John Muir Association. Available: http://www.johnmuir.wytbear.com (Accessed September 22, 2000).

    Muir quotes, biographical information, links, and travel tips, especially related to Muir's visits and discoveries in southeast Alaska.

The Sierra Club's John Muir Exhibit. Available: http://www.sierraclub.org/john_muir_exhibit (Accessed September 22, 2000).

    A superlative Web site with a great variety of historical and contemporary information about John Muir and his legacy. Of particular interest to educators and students are:

- The Student Page, an online resource for those learning about John Muir.
- The John Muir Day Study Guide, downloadable lesson plans for teachers, grades K–12.
- The John Muir Award, actually a unique series of awards, available to all ages, in recognition for valuable, achievable contributions to the natural world and education.
- An online Muir forum and an educators' discussion group and listserv.
- Online texts of excerpts, articles, and a number of John Muir's books, including *The Story of My Boyhood and Youth*, *A Thousand-Mile Walk to the Gulf*, *My First Summer in the Sierra*, and a short and long version of *Stickeen*.

Video Resources

John Muir: Environmentalist (1838–1914). Part of "Portraits: The Americans" Series, A GPN Production, color, 15 minutes, 1997. For grades 4–8. Available from Great Plains National Instructional Television, Lincoln, NE 68501-0669, Phone: (402) 472-2007 or Toll Free: 800-228-4630. Fax: 800-306-2330. E-mail: gpn@unl.edu. Available: http://www.gpn.unl.edu. Price: $39.95. Videocassette. Focuses on Muir's key role in the conservation movement, as well as roles that students can play in conservation today.

The Boyhood of John Muir. A Hott Production of Florentine Films, Produced by Diane Garey, Directed by Lawrence R. Holt, color, 78 minutes, 1997. Distributed by: Bullfrog Films, P.O. Box 149, Oley, PA 19547. Telephone: 800-543-3764. Fax: 610-370-1978. E-mail: Bullfrog@igc.apc.org. Price: Rental = $59.50, Sale = $137.50 for a single school or institution. Videocassette, 1/2 inch VHS format. A dramatic family film.

An Evening with John Muir: Conversation with a Tramp. A KQED-TV S.F. production, color, 90 minutes, 1992. Available from Lee Stetson's Wild Productions, Box 93, Midpines, CA 95345. Phone: 209-742-7838. E-mail: leestetson@sierratel.com. Available: www.johnmuirlive.com. Price: $19.95 (plus $3.00 per tape for postage and handling). Videocassette.
A video recording of Stetson's one-man stage play of John Muir, with occasional mild profanity in the dialogue.

John Muir: The Man, The Poet, The Legacy. A KRON-TV S.F. Production in Association with Chronicle Productions, produced by Ziggy Stone, color. Available from Panorama West Productions, P.O. Box 1255, Beverly Hills, CA 90213. Price: $24.95. VHS format videocassette.
A comprehensive historical recounting of Muir's entire life, appropriate for classroom use.

Audio Resources

The Glacier That Saved America: John Muir's Adventures in Alaska's Glacier Bay. Tim Hostiuck, 1993. Available from: Alaska On Tape, P.O. Box 21651, Juneau, AK 99802. Price: $12 postpaid. Audiocassette.
Storyteller Tim Hostiuck explores Muir's fascination with glaciers in general, and the Muir Glacier in Glacier Bay National Park in particular.

John Muir Tribute CD. John Muir Memorial Association, 1999. Produced by Jill Harcke and Dan McIlhenny. Compact Disc.
   A collection of music about or evocative of John Muir, together with quotations from John Muir read by a variety of Muir scholars and experts.

John Muir's The Yosemite. Read by Michael Zebulon. San Francisco, Sierra Club Audio Library, 90 minutes, 1990. Available from Audio Literature, Inc., 325 Corey Way, Suite 112, South San Francisco, CA 94080. Audiocassette.
   Three audiocassettes are available from Lee Stetson's Wild Productions, Box 93, Midpines, CA 95345. Phone: 209-742-7838, e-mail: leestetson@sierratel.com. Available: Lee Stetson's John Muir Live Available: www.johnmuirlive.com. Price for each audiocassette: $9.95 (plus $1.50 per tape for postage and handling).

Conversations with a Tramp. Lee Stetson, Wild Productions, 90 minutes, 1988. Audiocassette.
   Lee Stetson portrays Muir in 1913 recounting his eventful life and exploring his conservation philosophy.

John Muir's Stickeen. Lee Stetson, Wild Productions, 38 minutes, 1988. Audiocassette.
   Lee Stetson portrays Muir as he recounts his perilous adventure on an Alaskan glacier with Stickeen, a dog.

The Spirit of John Muir. Lee Stetson, Wild Productions, 50 minutes, 1990. Audiocassette.
   Lee Stetson celebrates Yosemite National Park's Centennial, featuring Muir's Yosemite adventures.

MARGARET MURIE

CHAPTER 7

Born August 18, 1902 in Seattle, Washington. Childhood and young adult autobiography describes Alaska.

Figure 7.1. Margaret Murie in Denali National Park, Alaska with North America's highest peak, Mt. McKinley, in the background. All photos in this chapter are courtesy of Murie Archive, National Conservation Training Center.

AN APPRECIATION OF THE WRITER

I would love to think that the world will survive its obsession with machines to see a day when people respect one another all over the world. It seems clear as a shaft of Aurora that this is our only hope. My prayer is that Alaska('s) . . . great wild places will remain great, and wild, and free, where wolf and caribou, wolverine and grizzly bear, and all the Arctic blossoms may live on in the delicate balance which supported them long before impetuous man appeared in the North.

—Margaret Murie from the Preface of *Two in the Far North*

On January 15, 1998, 95-year-old Margaret "Mardy" Murie received the Presidential Medal of Freedom, the United States' highest civilian honor, from President Bill Clinton. This tribute recognized her seven decades of devotion to preserving millions of acres of wildlands in western North America. Murie's fieldwork alongside her biologist–husband, Olaus Murie, her quiet determination, her activism for the environment, and her writing—all have positively influenced generations of wilderness-loving people worldwide.

Figure 7.2. A page from Mardy Murie's journal, the basis of her book, *Two in the Far North*, written at a camp in the Alaskan wilderness like the one shown here.

From her childhood, Mardy Murie kept a journal. She drew on it extensively for her two autobiographical works. *Two in the Far North* relates the story of her childhood and early married life in Alaska. *Wapiti Wilderness*, co-authored with her husband Olaus, tells of their family and community lives in Jackson Hole, Wyoming, and in the spectacular wild country surrounding it. Native life on St. Lawrence Island in the Bering Sea is the subject of her novel, *Island Between*.

Murie did not limit her writing to three books. From the first days of their marriage, Mardy was Olaus's secretary for everything from biologic field notes to the voluminous scientific reports he published. (She also edited Olaus's book, *Journeys to the Far North*, published after his death in 1963.) Add to this her numerous articles and correspondences written on behalf of wild creatures and places and those for the Wilderness Society (which she and Olaus helped found), and her accomplishments as a writer seem nothing short of remarkable. But, beyond her prolific output, Murie's gift for sharply defined description makes her experiences come to life on first reading and linger long, thereafter, in the reader's memory.

IN HER OWN WORDS

In the spring of 1918, young Margaret Thomas prepared for the first of many wilderness adventures in her life. Headed to Cordova on the southern coast of Alaska to visit her natural father, she was to travel alone more than 350 miles during nine days on the Northern Commercial Company's stageline over the Valdez Trail. There were no stagecoaches, though. Passengers, freight, and the mail traveled over snow and ice on horse-drawn sleighs and sleds, and by dogsled in winter. The stage stopped occasionally for food and rest at stations called roadhouses in Alaska. This was the last run before the ice melted in the rivers that spring—and the last run ever for the stageline. The Alaska Railroad was being built toward Fairbanks, to provide a fuller link to the outside world than the stageline or the Army Signal Corp's telegraph could ever give.

In chapter 8, "The Trail," and chapter 9, "And over the Mountains," of *Two in the Far North*, Margaret Murie describes her memorable journey (see page 154):

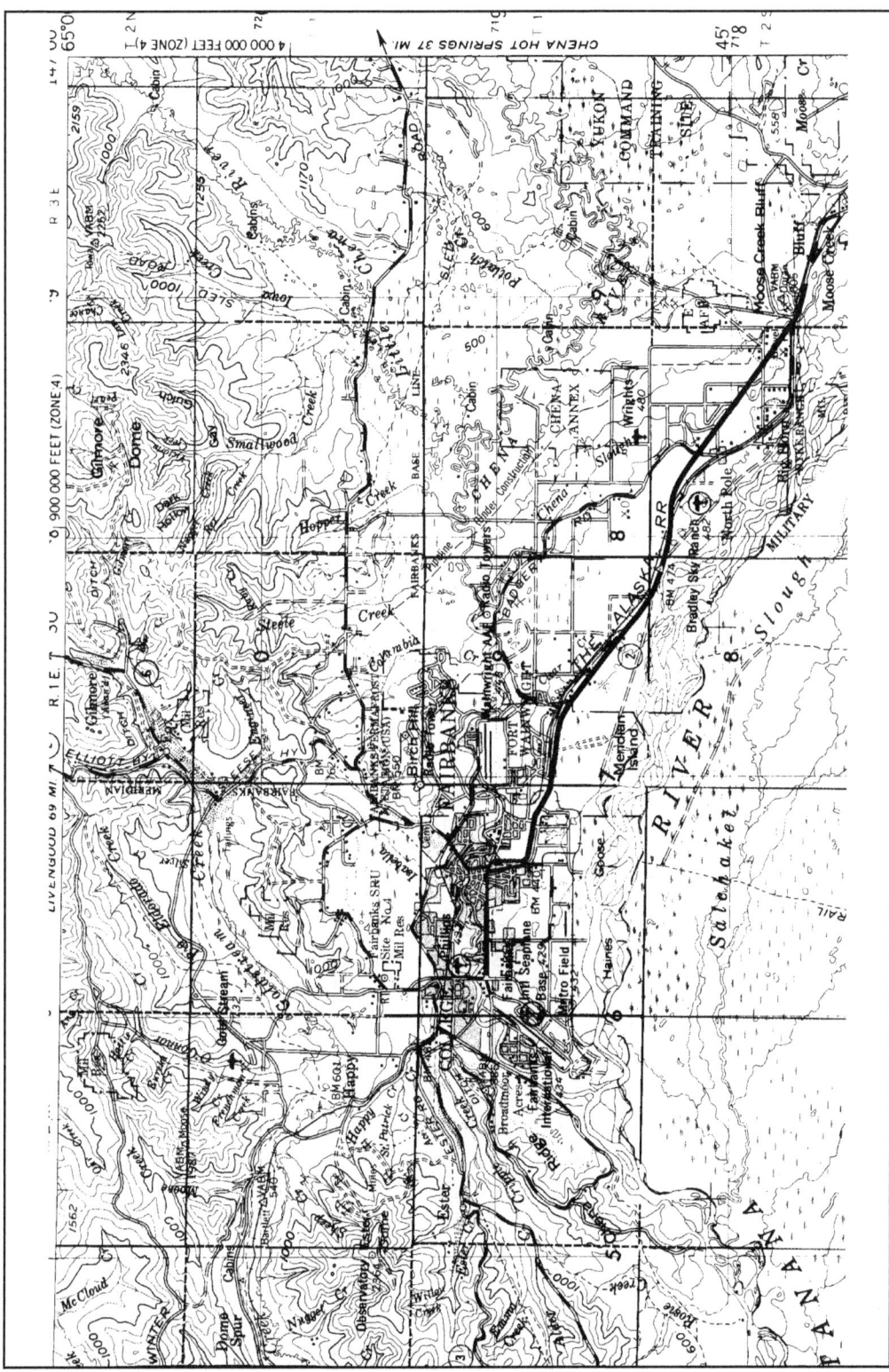

Figure 7.3. Contemporary map of Fairbanks, Alaska, childhood home of Margaret Murie. Public domain, courtesy of U.S. Geological Survey.

Note: The following is excerpted as punctuated and spelled in the original manuscript.

Fifteen, and shy, yet eager for adventure—scared, yet determined to go ahead. For it turned out that of all the eager crowd that had stood spellbound as the stage [to Fairbanks] went by, week after week, winter after winter, I was to be the one to go over that mysterious trail on the last trip of the stage line, the last trip before breakup, the last trip of all. The mere thought of it went whirling around and around all day long in my head. . . .

The last stage was leaving at midnight on May 4. . . . Travel must now be at night, while the trail was frozen. The trail was going; the snow would not hold up the horses in daytime. . . .

When Daddy and I arrived just before midnight, the driver and a warehouseman . . . were drawing up the big tarpaulin over the whole load and lashing it all tight to various parts of the sled. It was exactly like one tremendous package, neatly tied in waterproof canvas. It wasn't long before I found out why. "But we've got the young lady's bags well stowed in there too."

[Driver] Roy Rynearson, stalwart and good-looking, had twinkling blue eyes in a face burned to leather by the spring sun reflected off the snow. "She may get pretty tired before we make our first long stop—got to get across five rivers before they go out—but we'll take good care of her. Guess we're ready, Joe.". . .

The horses started at a trot; the warehouse porch and Daddy and the warehouseman standing there watching us were quickly lost to sight. We were moving through the dusky half-dark quiet streets, pulling over bare ground. The snow was all gone in town. The panicky emptiness inside me fought against the enormous thrill of unimaginable adventure ahead. I could fairly feel the presence of the big square schoolhouse when we passed Eighth Avenue. The kids would all be there in a few hours, and I—I would be out on the trail somewhere. . . .

We were bumping down a steep creek bank and the ridge of blue hills had moved to meet us. At the base of the hills, here across the creek, there were some neat log buildings, one of them two stories high. Salcha [Roadhouse]. And out in front of the buildings, stretching out at our right, the Tanana [River], broad and white.

"Well, she's still there. Got some mushy spots though." Roy was leaning toward the river, blue eyes flicking over it judiciously, while the horses sped along, crossed the bridge over the creek, and stopped exactly in front of the two-story house . . . Then we all went into [a] room beyond to a long white oilcloth-covered table, very clean, with benches on either side, and loaded with oval vegetable dishes and platters of thick hotel china, a great array of food. It was eleven in the morning and we had been going since midnight. . . .

"Now, young lady," said Roy, "I'm going to have you climb right up on top of the load here behind me. Hang on to the lash ropes and get a good grip, but don't be scared. Whatever happens, don't jump off. Stay right with the load."

He settled himself firmly and got his feet braced at the front of the load, and we started slowly down the long incline toward the river. Ahead of us was Old John [the roadhouse barnman], walking, holding a long pole, which he continuously drove into the ice, testing. The horses, a fresh team, were wise too. They went slowly, I thought, even reluctantly. . . .

Out over the ice we went. There were dark-looking spots here and there, with water on top. The river here was about a quarter mile wide. . . . I looked ahead again and realized that Old John had on hip boots, and that he now walked through water, very slowly, probing each step. Roy looked back at me and grinned and said softly: "Scared?"

"No, I think it's fun!"

But my fingers were wound pretty tightly around those lash ropes. We were in the water now, but Roy was reassuring me. "This is just surface water, on top of the anchor ice. So long as John finds the anchor ice, we're all right."

Out of the water now, John was wading through slush, but he didn't sink out of sight. In a sudden burst he fairly ran up the bank, turned, and yelled: "Lay it on 'em, Roy!"

Roy did, and in a great splashing, tipping, rocking flurry we were all on the bank and up among the black spruces again. Old John started right back. "Better get myself back now," he called. "Hope you make it across the Delta O.K. I bet you're the last outfit across the Tanana this year!" . . .

Delicious food—moose steak—and sweet sleep at Sullivan's [roadhouse]. We left in the dusky dark again, at midnight . . . Only a couple of hours; then the world began to wake up and we were reminded that spring was here, relentlessly, stageline or no. . . . It seemed we had been traveling along like this for weeks. But this morning I was faced with the knowledge that in a few hours, at Big Delta, I would be turned over to another driver. Roy would have to turn back. I had a cold, apprehensive sadness inside me. But Roy was preparing me for the next chapter. "Now when you get to Rapids, the dog mushers will be there to take you and the mail across the summit of the [Alaska] Range. You be sure you go in French John's sled. You'll have the time of your life. . . ."

. . . Late in the afternoon we arrived at Rapids, and there was deep snow all around, and outside the two-story log roadhouse were a great number of dogs, chained and howling at our approach. . . . After a few hours' sleep, I was tucked into a big wolfskin robe in French John's basket sled sometime around midnight. For now the snow even high in the mountains was thawing and we must still travel at night.

But not silently, for John poured forth one story after another of the North, of his dogs, even while he struggled to keep the sled on the thawing, sliding trail which led up and around and ever up, with the high peaks glistening above us. Sometimes John talked to his seven beautiful Huskies in French, and I almost drowsed, snug in the furs, in spite of the bouncing and sliding of the sled on the soft trail. Once I roused suddenly with John's face close to mine; he was crouching under the side of the sled, his shoulder under the rim of the basket, his voice exhorting the dogs. He was fairly holding the sled by main strength from turning over and rolling down the mountainside, for here the way led across a steep mountain face and the trail had

> thawed away. "Jus' sit still; don' be scare. We soon get to Yost's now; dis place here de worse one. Ah, dere's de bell!"
>
> Bell? I sat up. We had come onto a level pass, and out in the middle hung a large bell in a framework of heavy timbers. A few yards away there was a black hole in a snowdrift, and above the hole, smoke.
>
> "Funny places in dis worl', eh?" said John. "You know, snow still very deep up here, roadhouse still mostly covered. Dis is top of Alaska Range—summit. And dat bell, she is save much people since early days. Wind, she blow like son of gun here in winter—roadhouse always cover in snow. Bell, she only ting to tell us where Yost's is, you see? Wind so strong she ring bell. Whoa, Blackie, don' you know roadhouse when you right dere?"
>
> *End of excerpted manuscript.*

Mardy arrived at Yost's roadhouse after four days and nights of traveling, with five more to go on the Valdez Trail. Today, you can drive a car over almost the same route in less than a day on Alaska Highway 4, the Richardson Highway, and Highway 2, the Alaska Highway.

Figure 7.4. Young Margaret Murie rests along the trail during a day of dogsledding.

THE WRITER'S LIFE

Up to Alaska

The wilds of Alaska change your view of the world. Instead of development surrounding the occasional wilderness, as in much of western North America, the opposite is true in Alaska. Human settlement there is dwarfed by massive mountain ranges, mighty rivers, and vast expanses of forest and Arctic tundra.

Such a place can make a great and lasting first impression on an observant young girl, like Margaret Elizabeth "Mardy" Thomas. As Mardy writes at the beginning of *Two in the Far North*, "the Alaska most vivid in my memory is the one I saw first as a nine-year-old, traveling from Seattle to Fairbanks with Mother, in September [1911], on the last trip before 'freeze-up'." (Also vivid was her memory of a "gorgeous" Royal Canadian Mounted Policeman on a Yukon riverboat.) Their three-week journey to the Alaskan frontier aboard steamship, trains, and riverboats, reunited them in Fairbanks with Mardy's beloved stepfather, Louis Gillette, a newly appointed assistant U.S. Attorney.

Mardy's natural father, a Canadian-born fisherman and cannery owner in southeast Alaska, spent many years facing harsh northern seas. It is from him, Mardy claims, that she inherited her adventurous, curious spirit and love of the outdoors.

In 1911 Fairbanks was, in Mardy's words, "a flat platter of hodgepodge buildings and low log cabins . . . defying the cold and loneliness and all the powers of the unbeatable North." It was a pinpoint in a wilderness so vast it could not be visualized. The rhythm of life was dictated by the changing seasons. After the freeze-up of the rivers in fall, Fairbanks was nearly cut off from the rest of the world for eight months. The town's only connection to the "outside" (Alaskans' term for anywhere else in the U.S. or the world) was the 365-mile Valdez Trail, a sleigh and dogsled route to Alaska's southern coast.

Because there were so few children in Fairbanks, Mardy and her friends were cherished and watched over by the entire community. Mardy enjoyed her days at the little Fairbanks school, and apparently did well academically. But some of her clearest childhood memories have to do with being outdoors. Despite a temperature of 50 degrees below zero or more in winter, Mardy often visited friends by dogsled pulled by her pet "Husky." On the day the river ice finally broke up in the spring, school was canceled as the students—and the entire town—watched and celebrated. When the first crocuses appeared, the children and their teachers scampered to the hills surrounding town for a picnic. And when warm days arrived, the children, fighting hordes of mosquitoes, picked gallons of blueberries, raspberries, currants, and cranberries for summer baking and packing away for winter.

Despite the mosquitoes, hiking in the endless light of summer was Mardy's favorite pastime. Her stepfather called her part-gypsy because she loved to ramble so. She says she liked to be outdoors, by herself, wandering around, letting the quietness sink into her. It gave her strength.

The Gillette's log cabin at the edge of town bustled with activity year 'round. During the next seven years, the birth of half-sisters, Louise and Carol, and half-brother, Louis, kept Mardy busy helping Minnie, her mother, with household chores.

Especially from her stepfather, Mardy learned to love language. Reading aloud was a nightly family activity. She devoured Shakespeare's *King Lear* at age 10. Mardy also enjoyed writing, though she never took a course in it.

Because her family valued learning, Mardy was sent "outside" to Reed College in Oregon. During a summer visit to Fairbanks in 1921, a friend introduced her to a young scientist with the United States Biological Survey. Olaus Murie had recently been assigned to study the great Alaskan caribou herds. This young man, Mardy declared, "was *not* like any of the rest."

The next fall, Mardy attended Simmons College in Boston. But her heart was back in Alaska with her family, friends, and, more and more, with Olaus. In July 1922, Mardy made a trip with her parents to visit Olaus and his half-brother and fellow scientist, Adolph, who were studying caribou in Mount McKinley National Park. "At the end of five days of tramping about in a rosy haze in those enchanted mountains," she recalls, "we both knew there was no life for us except together."

In 1923, Mardy transferred to the two-year-old Alaska Agricultural College and School of Mines at Fairbanks (soon to be the University of Alaska). She struggled mightily with math courses throughout the year and missed Olaus in the winter and spring, when he traveled to Washington, D.C., and then to the mouth of the Yukon River for five months studying nesting birds. On June 13, 1924, Margaret Thomas became the first woman to graduate from the University of Alaska. In fact, she was the senior class. Amid great celebration, the Governor of Alaska Territory awarded the single graduate her diploma.

Travels Together

Two months later, Mardy, her mother, and friends headed down the Yukon River by sternwheel steamer to join Olaus, who was heading upriver from his bird project. At 2:30 A.M. on August 19, Mardy and Olaus were married by candlelight in the tiny mission church at Anvik, Alaska. Just as the ceremony ended, the sun rose. The newlyweds stood together and "watched a sunrise of promise. A beautiful world was waking to light here on the Yukon."

The young couple spent their honeymoon dogsledding through the winter wilderness of the Brooks Range. Olaus studied the movements and feeding habits of the caribou, while Mardy cooked, helped keep scientific records, and grew used to life "in the field" as Olaus's trail companion. This trip established the pattern of their marriage. Days on the trail taught them that there is always something to rejoice about, in spite of hardships. In the Alaskan wilds Mardy learned that once you experience such a place, you never can forget it. The wilderness would be forever a part of her.

By the time Olaus received his next assignment, a six-month study of Alaskan brown bears, Mardy was expecting their first child. So she stayed with her parents in their

Figure 7.5. Newlyweds Mardy and Olaus Murie in their dogsledding garb.

new home in Twisp, Washington. But both she and Olaus found the separation unbearable. They decided that their family would travel together on all future field trips. Year-old Martin went with them when they traveled the mosquito-infested Old Crow River to study nesting waterfowl. Friends protested, "The baby would be safer at home!" But the wilderness was the Murie's home. The family eventually grew to include two more children, Joanne and Donald. All three seemed to thrive on their wilderness upbringing.

Figure 7.6. Martin Murie and his mother, Mardy, onboard the motorboat on the Old Crow River, summer 1926.

Wyoming and the Nation

In 1927 the United States Biological Survey transferred Olaus to Jackson Hole, Wyoming, to study the largest elk herd in North America. The Muries moved their family to the Tetons, and before long became central figures in the tiny town of Jackson. Every summer saw the entire family moving to a high camp in the mountains, where Olaus spent his days studying elk, and Mardy spent hers cooking and caring for the children.

Both Olaus and Mardy became increasingly convinced that, if North America's wilderness were to be preserved, it would have to be through organized, political effort. So, in 1945, Olaus left government service to become director of the newly organized Wilderness Society. Mardy officially acted as his secretary, but was a real partner in the work. The living room in the Murie's log home in Moose, Wyoming, became the site of countless groundbreaking meetings. The couple saw their hard work pay off in a number of victories

Figure 7.7. Margaret Murie with President Lyndon Johnson on September 3, 1964, at his signing of the Wilderness Act.

for wilderness preservation in North America, especially the creation of the Arctic Wildlife Range (now the Arctic National Wildlife Refuge) in the eastern Brooks Range of Alaska in 1960, which they initially proposed.

Olaus Murie died in 1963, a victim of cancer. After a time of sorrow and doubt, Mardy decided that she must continue their work. In the fall of 1964 she stood beside President Lyndon Johnson as he signed the Wilderness Act into law. The landmark law provides protection for millions of acres of public wild lands.

Now in her nineties, Margaret Murie remains a mentor, guide, and inspiration to students and environmental leaders. She says of the future: "I would love to think that the world will survive its obsession with machines to see a day when people respect one another all over the world. It seems clear as a shaft of Aurora that this is our only hope. My prayer is that Alaska's . . . great wild places will remain great, and wild, and free, where wolf and caribou, wolverine and grizzly bear, and all the Arctic blossoms may live on in the delicate balance which supported them long before impetuous man appeared in the North."

Figure 7.8. Mardy and Olaus Murie, pioneering conservationists.

TEACHING ADVICE FOR MARGARET MURIE

Autobiographical Writings

Margaret Murie's childhood autobiography comprises approximately the first 10 chapters and 100 pages of *Two in the Far North* and is the focus of this chapter of *Writers of the American West*. Interested students are encouraged to read all of Murie's memoir, as well as the Muries' *Wapiti Wilderness*.

Age Appropriateness

Though definitely not inappropriate for younger children, *Two in the Far North* may be most effectively used with students in grades six and higher, due to its somewhat sophisticated writing style and content. The same is true of *Wapiti Wilderness*. Selected sections from either book make good reading and read-alouds for fourth and fifth graders.

Touchy Terminology

In chapter 3, there is mention of prostitutes and prostitution. In chapter 9 and a few other locations later in the book, there is mild profanity in the dialogue.

LEARNING HORIZONS

Literature Aloud Experiences

❖ *AUTOBIOGRAPHY ALIVE*

Level: Grades four and higher.

Student Learning Opportunities: Consultation; Cooperation; Selection and preparation of autobiographical material; Preparation of biographical introductory script; Illustration, costume, and set design; Presentation.

Background: Like the other writers featured in this book, Margaret Murie presents a series of personally significant episodes, edited down from her much longer life history. This is a common format for autobiography. But, just as the writer gets to "edit his or her life," so do we, as readers, choose our favorite concepts, anecdotes, and turns of phrase from an autobiography as we read and reflect. These reader choices form the basis for an involving, multidisciplinary student activity—Autobiography Alive.

Autobiography Alive (or Autobiography Fair or Writer's Recollections or whatyoumaycallit): Autobiography Alive bears some resemblance to History Fairs, in which students research, script, then orally and visually (often with costume and props) interpret a historical character or event for an audience. In Autobiography Alive, participants add the role of text editor to the list of skills required for a History Fair presentation.

Selection: Ask students to select a writer they like and read an autobiography they want to interpret in an oral presentation. In reading, have them make notes of page numbers of interesting sections of the text, as well as biographical facts about the writer. Teachers should consult on students' writer and text selections.

Preparation: Have students choose one section from the autobiography for retelling as a story—one that says something meaningful about the writer's life and can be read aloud in no more than five minutes.

Using the "Preparing a Story for Telling" process (**Literature Aloud Experiences**, chapter 1), have them develop the selected story for retelling in the first person, as the writer, or in the third person, as a narrator talking about the writer.

Ask students to develop a written script as a brief introduction to the life of the writer from biographical facts and other research. The introduction should be five minutes or less in length when read aloud. It should provide a clear connection somewhere in its text to the selected story.

Have them combine the introduction to the writer and the selected story. Have each student rehearse alone and also with a partner. The introduction may be read or told; the story should be told.

Have students create props, visual aids (books, illustrations, photos, maps, backdrops), and costumes (if appropriate) that help interpret the writer's life. Rehearse using these objects.

Performance: Present Autobiography Alive performances at "presentation stations" with small audiences rotating among them or with a fixed audience in a theater setting. Watch the autobiographies come to life.

Extensions: Incorporate narrative poetry and ballads in a Classroom Chautauqua (see **Literature Aloud Experiences**, chapter 3).

Teacher Evaluation Opportunities: Consultation; Cooperation; Selection of material; Preparation of material; Visuals, costumes, sets; Presentation.

Language Arts Experiences

❖ *HOW DID IT FEEL TO BE THERE?*

Level: Grades six to eight.

Student Learning Opportunities: Descriptive Writing; Six-Trait Writing—Ideas, Organization, Voice, Word Choice, Sentence Fluency, Conventions.

Background: Margaret Murie writes well, in part, because she uses rich, clear descriptions. She selects words that enable readers to visit her world through their sensory imaginations.

Basics:
1. Review with students the elements of descriptive writing—creating word pictures of people, places, things, events, and ideas; making the images believable to the reader; using images that relate to the five senses, as well as ideas, emotions, comparisons, and other concepts; and using innovative word choices, not trite or stereotypic language. Give examples of each element. Ask students to suggest their own examples.

2. Read aloud page 20, paragraphs two to four, of *Two in the Far North*, in which Mardy describes the scene of her departure from Seattle in 1911. Ask students to read the same passage silently. Have students identify a few examples of descriptive language in the selection, such as "great cavern of the dock warehouse."

3. Distribute copies of figure 7.9, page 164, **Making "Sense" of Descriptive Writing**. Students identify the Subject Being Described on this sheet as "Mardy's Steamship Departure, 1911." Then, they should write down at least two descriptive words and phrases from the selection in each of the six categories on the sheet. Review their responses as needed to assure mastery.

4. Ask students to identify a personal experience or imaginary scene as the topic for a short descriptive passage they will write. Use brainstorming or the Recollections activity (**Learning Horizons**, chapter 2) to stimulate topic ideas.

5. Using a blank **Making "Sense"** form, ask students to create a title and generate a number of descriptive words and phrases in each category for use in their descriptive passage.

6. Have the writers incorporate their word choices in a descriptive passage of up to three paragraphs long.

Extensions:
1. Ask students to apply the **Making "Sense" of Descriptive Writing** form to a previously written piece of their own narrative or creative writing, as they did with Murie's narrative. What do they discover about their descriptive writing in the selection? They may make revisions to improve descriptive elements of the narrative. Use the **Descriptive Writing** form as a pre-writing activity for future descriptive, narrative, and imaginative writing projects.

Teacher Evaluation Opportunities: Making "Sense" of Descriptive Writing forms—Murie's, students'; Descriptive writing passage; Revisions of narrative or imaginative writing; Use of Six-Trait Writing techniques.

Making "Sense" of Descriptive Writing

Subject Being Described:_____

Sight Descriptions	Sound Descriptions	Smell Descriptions
_____	_____	_____
_____	_____	_____
_____	_____	_____
_____	_____	_____
_____	_____	_____
_____	_____	_____
_____	_____	_____

Taste Descriptions	Touch Descriptions	Other Descriptions—emotions, ideas, comparison
_____	_____	_____
_____	_____	_____
_____	_____	_____
_____	_____	_____
_____	_____	_____
_____	_____	_____
_____	_____	_____
_____	_____	_____
_____	_____	_____

Figure 7.9. Making "Sense" of Descriptive Writing form.

◈ THE VOCABULARY OF TIME AND PLACE

Level: Grades four to eight.

Student Learning Opportunities: Reading; Vocabulary definition; Using content and context clues; Dictionary skills; Various forms of writing; Six-Trait Writing—Word Choice, Sentence Fluency, Conventions.

Background: In addition to her descriptive writing skills, Margaret Murie uses special vocabulary pertinent to her era and locale to color her writing. Students can use a variety of methods to define this special vocabulary and add new words, or new meanings of familiar words, to their command for speaking, reading, and writing.

Basics:
1. Read aloud or have students read the introduction and Murie's selection about traveling by sled in **In Her Own Words**, this chapter. In discussion, solicit student reactions to the selection. Discuss and define the word "stage" as it is used in Murie's first paragraph. For example: a vehicle for transporting the public and goods on an established route over ground, snow, water, or ice.

2. Distribute copies of figure 7.10, page 166, **Mardy Murie's Special Vocabulary** form. Ask individuals to create their own definitions of the listed words and phrases on the form, using any of the following tools:

   - the content clues within the word or phrase
   - the context in which the word or phrase appears
   - at least two different dictionary definitions
   - consultation with the teacher
   - their own common sense

Extensions:
1. Students can select five of the **Special Vocabulary** words from figure 7.6 to include in a fiction or nonfiction paragraph of their own creation, in any form of writing.

2. Students can select and define 10 words or phrases that are part of their own time and place and are important to them. For example, mountain bike, computer, snowboarding. Record the terms and definitions in figure 7.11, page 167, **Your Special Vocabulary**. Have them use five of these in another fiction or nonfiction paragraph of their own creation, in a written form of their choice.

Teacher Evaluation Opportunities: Participation in discussion; Special Vocabulary form; Original paragraph using Murie's vocabulary; Student vocabulary list and definitions; Original paragraph using their own vocabulary; Use of Six-Trait Writing techniques.

166 *YOUNG NATURALISTS*

Mardy Murie's Special Vocabulary

Your Task: Create your own definitions of the words and phrases Margaret Murie uses to describe her sled journey.

Stageline_____
_____

Breakup _____
_____

Warehouseman_____
_____
_____
_____

Roadhouse_____
_____

Lash ropes_____
_____
_____
_____

Mushers_____
_____

Basket Sled_____
_____

Husky_____
_____

Pass_____
_____

Summit_____
_____

Figure 7.10. Special Vocabulary.

Your Special Vocabulary

Your Task: Create your own definitions of favorite words and phrases common in your time and place. List the word or phrase first, then your definition.

1. _____

2. _____

3. _____

4. _____

5. _____

6. _____

7. _____

8. _____

9. _____

10. _____

Figure 7.11. Your Special Vocabulary.

Social Studies Experiences

◆ *EVERYDAY NECESSITIES—THEN AND NOW*

Level: Grades six to eight.

Student Learning Opportunities: Research; Note-taking; Participation in discussion; Self-assessment; Drawing conclusions; Graphic representation of concepts.

Background: Using Margaret Murie's informative snapshot of everyday life in remote Alaska, students can compare and contrast the ways basic necessities are provided in their lives with her early life. This experience increases understanding of the natural resources, commercial services, and governmental organization, often taken for granted, that are required to support and enhance our well-being. (Other autobiographies featured in *Writers of the American West* may also be used to motivate this experience.)

Basics:
1. Have students, individually or as a group, research and take notes on chapters 2 to 7 of *Two in the Far North* (page numbers are from Alaska Northwest Books edition). Find information about the provision of necessary products and services in early Fairbanks. Specifically, look to the following pages for details on necessities:

   - **Shelter**, pages 31, 36, 37, 45;
   - **Water**, pages 31–32, 41, 45;
   - **Food**, pages 34, 36, 37, 40, 42, 50, 54, 55, 57, 60–62;
   - **Energy**, pages 33, 34, 38, 47–48, 51–52;
   - **Communications**, pages 34, 46, 49–50, 55–56;
   - **Sanitation**, page 31;
   - **Transportation**, pages 35, 49–50, 52, 55–57;
   - **Household Chores**, pages 33, 34, 38, 41–42, 45, 55, 60–62;
   - **Occupations**, pages 31, 32, 34, 36–37, 38, 40, 42–43, 44, 45, 53, 54, 56, 57, 58.

2. Distribute the **Basic Necessities Survey**, figure 7.13. (This lists some, but not all, fundamental human needs.) Review Survey content and terminology at outset: "Source" means the thing(s) that provides the necessity; "Producer" means the person(s) or organization(s) that provides the necessity; and, "Means of Delivery or Disposal" indicates the way(s) a product or service is transported. Drawing from their research on Margaret Murie, discuss with the whole group what her responses might be to the Survey. Record the responses on a master **Basic Necessities Survey** form. To be complete, more than one answer may be necessary in some categories.

EXAMPLE:

NAME: Margaret Murie

HOME: Fairbanks, Alaska

YEAR: 1917

Necessity	Source	Producer	Means of Delivery or Disposal
Shelter	Log Cabin	Logger, Sawmill, Carpenter	Driver, Team of Horses, Wagon

Figure 7.12.

3. Next, have students fill out a **Basic Necessities Survey** about themselves, listing the products and services they require. This may involve additional research on their part. Information from parents and teachers (even educated guessing) may help with the responses.

4. Ask all students to compare and contrast the group's Margaret Murie Survey with their personal survey. To highlight contrasts, have them circle the responses on their personal surveys that are distinctly different from the groups' Murie Survey. For example, if their personal response is "Apartment," they circle it, for an apartment and a log cabin are very different forms of shelter, both in shape and materials.

5. To conclude, hold a discussion that compares and contrasts the basic necessities of Margaret Murie's era and the students'. Among the students' survey responses, which are generally like Margaret's? Which are mostly different? What do their answers say about the similarities and differences of their lives today compared with frontier life in early twentieth-century Alaska?

Extensions:
1. Ask students to create a graphic representation of a similarity or a difference between Murie's era and their own, labeled with an explanatory caption. An example of difference might be an illustration of two power plants. A natural gas pipeline, coal, or recycled waste is being delivered to one of the plants, while logs (or even bacon!) are delivered to the other plant. Captions on opposite sides would read "2015" and "1915," respectively. An example of similarity might be a photograph, cut from a magazine, of a rustic log cabin with phone and power lines and a satellite dish and a caption that reads, "Log Cabins—An Alaskan Tradition."

2. Students complete a **Basic Necessities Survey** based on the autobiography of a favorite writer whose works they have read. Compare and contrast that survey to the Murie Survey and to their own.

Teacher Evaluation Opportunities: Participation in Murie Survey development and closing discussion; Personal **Basic Necessities Survey**; **Basic Necessities Survey** of another autobiographer; Similarity or difference illustration project.

NAME _____
HOME _____
YEAR _____

BASIC NECESSITIES SURVEY

Your task: List an answer (or more than one answer, if needed) under "Source," "Producer," and "Means of Delivery or Disposal."

Necessity	Source	Producer	Means of Delivery or Disposal

Shelter _____

Water _____

Food _____

Energy _____

Sanitation _____

Communications _____

Figure 7.13. Basic Necessities Survey.

MARGARET MURIE RESOURCES

Selected Books by Murie

Murie, Margaret E. *Island Between*. Illustrated by Olaus Murie. Fairbanks, AK: University of Alaska Press, 1977.

Mardy's fictional account of what happened when the native people of St. Lawrence Island, Alaska, first encountered Europeans.

———. *Two in the Far North*. Thirty-fifth Anniversary Edition. Anchorage: Alaska Northwest Books, 1997.

The simple but moving account of Mardy's childhood and marriage in frontier Alaska, and her adventures in the Brooks Range with her beloved husband, Olaus.

Murie, Margaret, and Olaus Murie. *Wapiti Wilderness*. New York: Alfred A. Knopf, 1966.

After Olaus's death, Mardy edited their delightful remembrances of outdoor expeditions raising a family in Jackson Hole and the Teton Wilderness of Wyoming.

Selected Murie Biographies and Resources

Bryant, Jennifer. *Margaret Murie, A Wilderness Life*. Illustrated by Antonio Castro. New York: Twenty-first Century Books, 1993.

An 80-page biography of Mardy's life written for young readers and young adults; one of the excellent "Earth Keepers" series of naturalists' biographies.

LaBastille, Anne. "Margaret Murie, A Long Life in the Wilderness," in *Women and Wilderness*. San Francisco: Sierra Club Books, 1980.

"Woodswoman" Anne LaBastille discusses Mardy's life as a role model for other women who love wilderness.

Electronic Resources

The Murie Center Website. Available: http://www.muriecenter.org (Accessed January 23, 2000).

Founded in 1998 at the Muries' ranch within Grand Teton National Park in Wyoming, the nonprofit Murie Center is moving forward on several fronts—preserving Murie family history and the ranch, while sponsoring events and dialogues on wildland protection and environmental education. For more information: P.O. Box 399, Moose, WY 83012, 307-739-2246, e-mail—muriecenter@wyoming.com.

Portrait of a Conservationist: Mardie (sic) Murie. Available: http://www.lnt.org/Newsletter.MardyMurie.html (Accessed January 23, 2000).

A short Margaret Murie biography, circa 1996, posted by the Leave No Trace program of the National Outdoor Leadership School, Lander, WY.

Profiles in Conservation. Available: http://www.tws.org/profiles/pres_murie.htm (Accessed January 23, 2000).

In the Web site of the Wilderness Society, which the Muries' helped organize and run, are the brief, but notable remarks of President William J. Clinton on January 15, 1998, at the time he awarded the Presidential Medal of Freedom to Margaret Murie.

Video Resources

Arctic Dance: The Mardy Murie Story. Charlie Craighead and Bonnie Kreps. Moose, WY: Craighead Environmental Research Institute, color, 75 minutes, 2000. Videocassette.
    A thorough film biography of the life and times of Margaret Murie, narrated by Harrison Ford. Appropriate for age 8 and higher. For ordering information, call Craighead Environmental Research Institute at 800-345-9556.

WRITERS OF THE NEW WEST

Beverly Cleary

Gary Soto

Laurence Yep

What influences in their early upbringing and education help turn children into successful writers? For contemporary parents and teachers, there is cause for reflection in that question. At first, looking at the lives of the authors featured in **Writers of the New West** seems to offer little help in finding an answer. Laurence Yep and Beverly Cleary were read to and enjoyed literature at an early age. But Gary Soto had no positive early relationship with books, being little more than a self-described page-turner in elementary school. Cleary discovered her affinity for writing in the intermediate grades, Yep found his in high school, and Soto found his in college.

Look closer for the answer, however, and patterns begin to appear. Here is Beverly Cleary's straightforward assessment of her first eight years of formal education:

> *With forty and sometimes more pupils in a class, our teachers had taught us the fundamentals of survival in society. Every one of us could read. We had learned to speak distinctly and correctly and to cope with the arithmetic necessary for everyday life.... School was a businesslike place. Teachers and parents expected us to learn but not to think for ourselves; we expected to be taught.*
>
> —*A Girl from Yamhill*, Pages 170-171.

Neither Gary Soto nor Laurence Yep comment about any exceptional attributes in their parochial and public primary and intermediate schools, either. They leave us to assume that, like Cleary, they received a "good, basic education." Read on in their autobiographies, beyond their grounding in fundamental skills, however, and other common attributes in the writers' educational backgrounds emerge:

- Parents with expectations for attendance and satisfactory performance in school.

- A time somewhere in their young lives when they became "hooked on books."

- A teacher or teachers with a clear understanding of the writing process, appropriate assignments to offer, and high expectations of student performance.

- A desire to explore their own personalities and family backgrounds through writing.

- A determination to "write what they know," using familiar characters, settings, and situations.

- A willingness to explore the boundaries of creativity beyond the familiar.

- A dedication to hard work in writing tasks.

The autobiographies of Cleary, Soto, and Yep provide even more clues to the connections between their literary imaginings and their real-life roots. Taken together, these books give guidance as to what it takes for children to be successful writers. The readings and **Learning Horizons** divisions of the chapters in **Writers of the New West** help students explore the nature of these three writers' creative gifts—and their own.

BEVERLY CLEARY

Born April 12, 1916 in McMinnville, Oregon. Childhood and young adult autobiography describes Oregon and California.

CHAPTER 8

Figure 8.1. Beverly Cleary. Photo by Alan McEwen, 1999. Used by permission of HarperCollins Publishers.

AN APPRECIATION OF THE WRITER

Miss Smith pulled out a paper that I recognized as mine and began to read aloud. My mouth was dry and my stomach felt twisted. When she finished, she paused. My heart pounded. Then Miss Smith said, "When Beverly grows up, she should write children's books."

I was dumbfounded. Miss Smith was praising my story–essay with words that pointed to my future, a misty time I rarely even thought about. I was not used to praise.

—Beverly Cleary on the reaction of her seventh-grade librarian to her first piece of imaginative writing, in *A Girl from Yamhill*, pages 178 and 179.

As a child, Beverly Atlee Bunn was often told to remember her pioneer ancestors. So often was this repeated that young Beverly grew to resent those family symbols of strength, will, and skilled inventiveness—the covered wagon women, the millwright, the miller, the frontier farmer. Her father's family included some of Oregon's earliest settlers.

As an adult, Beverly Cleary is one of North America's most popular writers for children and young adults. Despite overcoming her disdain for "ancestor worship," she has never extensively mined her ancestral roots in factual or fictional writing. Her characters spring, instead, from her powerful imagination and potent observation of human—especially young peoples'—behavior. Yet, those characters often embody the same admirable pioneer traits so deeply ingrained in her as a child. In Cleary's fictional creations we meet the undying will of Ramona, the inventiveness of Henry Huggins and Ralph S. Mouse, the persistence of Leigh Botts, humor in the face of difficulty, and quiet triumph over adversity.

The budding writer is often reminded, "Show, don't tell." Don't just talk about characters. Let the story unfold through the characters' observations and actions. Beverly Cleary masterfully shows us her early life through her two autobiographies. In *A Girl from Yamhill: A Memoir*, she takes us from her days on the family farm in Yamhill, Oregon, through her earliest attempts at writing, to her high-school graduation. (An interesting companion to this book is the fictional, semi-autobiographical *Emily's Runaway Imagination*, depicting life in a small town much like Yamhill.) *My Own Two Feet: A Memoir* recounts Cleary's experiences in higher education, in early married life, and in writing her first book. Lovers of Cleary's fiction will enjoy all three books. What emerges from the autobiographies is the picture of a strong, motivated, self-directed young woman with whom her pioneer ancestors would be greatly pleased.

Figure 8.2. The historic Bunn house in Yamhill, Oregon, where Beverly lived to the age of six.

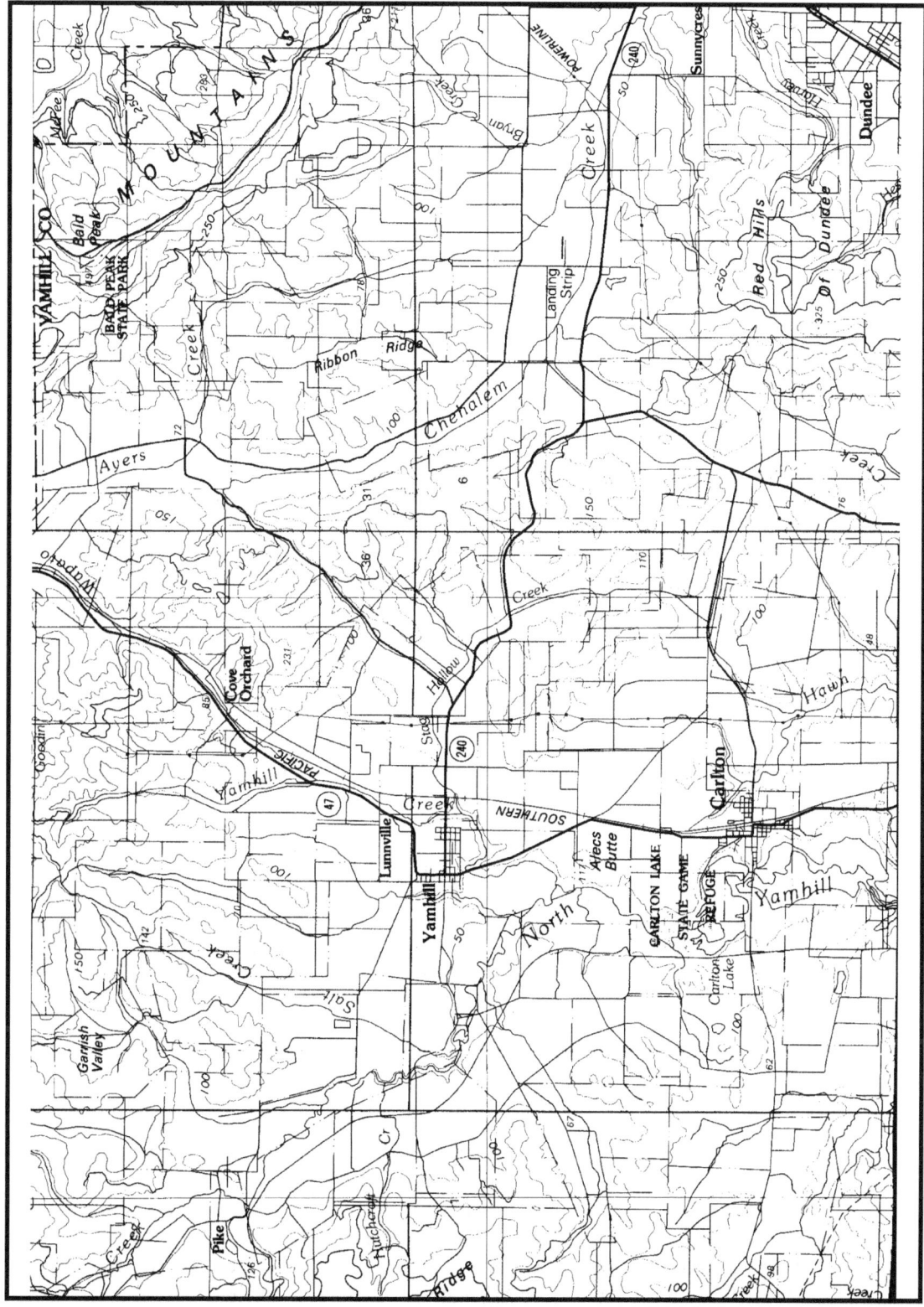

Figure 8.3. Contemporary map of the Yamhill, Oregon area, childhood home of Beverly Cleary. Public domain, courtesy of U.S. Geological Survey.

IN HER OWN WORDS

One of the first things Beverly Cleary discovered on returning to Fernwood Grammar School for her seventh year was that, "boys, awful in sixth grade, had become terrible in the seventh grade." Not all so terrible, though, that she didn't take an interest in a few of them. But, teachers, subjects, and the school day, itself, were also different. As she describes in the chapter "The Platoon System" from A Girl from Yamhill, some of those alterations made a substantial difference in her future.

Note: The following is excerpted as punctuated and spelled in the original manuscript.

In the seventh grade, changes took place, not only in boys but in the school curriculum. The platoon system was introduced. This meant we were taught some subjects—"Effie" (grammar and composition), reading, arithmetic, and United States history—in our homeroom but marched off in platoons to other rooms for music, art, nature study, library, an oddly named class called "auditorium," and double periods of domestic science or manual training. And, of course, gymnasium, where seventh-graders exercised with wands or marched while Claudine played "Napolean's Last Charge" on the piano.

Girls sewed in 7A or cooked in 7B while boys hammered, sawed, and sanded in another basement classroom. Many parents objected to the platoon system; schools should stick to basics. Mother felt the new system too strenuous. "It's just rush, rush, rush all day long," she said. At PTA she complained to Miss Stone that my handwriting had deteriorated and was difficult to read. Miss Stone replied that before long people would use typewriters.

We now had a school library with a librarian, Miss Smith, a young, brisk, well-tailored teacher who also taught reading. She taught us how to use the library and once made us line up alphabetically by our last names, as if we were books on shelves. After that, I found a place on the shelf where my book would be if I ever wrote a book, which I doubted.

Miss Smith introduced an innovation to Fernwood. Until Miss Smith entered our lives, our teachers forbade reading in the classroom, except for old copies of the National Geographic. No one enjoyed this except the terrible boys who knew, by ragged covers, which issues contained pictures of naked women in African tribes.

Not being able to read in school had frustrated me. During the first week, I held my reader under my desk and read it all the way through, even though teachers said repeatedly, "Do not read ahead." After that I hid books I wanted to read inside my geography, an ideal book, because of its size, for hiding other books. I was deeply grateful to Miss Smith, not only for letting us read but for letting me into the library first on the days when St. Nicholas magazine arrived.

Miss Smith had standards. We could read, but we must read good books. Cheap series books, traded around the neighborhood, were not permitted in her classroom. Miss Smith was also strict. She once made me stay after school until I could write on the blackboard, from memory and in order, all the presidents of the United States. I do not recall what I did to deserve this judgment, but I do recall thinking it more sensible than writing "I will not talk in gymnasium" one hundred times—a penalty once meted out by Miss Helliwell, our gym teacher.

Miss Smith also gave unusual assignments. Once, without warning, she said, "I want you to pretend you live in George Washington's time and write a letter to someone describing the experience."

Write something we had not learned in a book? This was unheard of. "But that's not fair," some protested.

Miss Smith assured us that such an assignment was perfectly fair. We knew she was right. Miss Smith was always fair. Strict, but fair.

"You mean now?" someone asked.

"Now." Miss Smith was always firm.

"But how?" someone else asked.

"Use your imaginations," said Miss Smith, unconcerned by the consternation she had created.

I was excited. All my life, mother had told me to use my imagination, but I had never expected to be asked, or even allowed, to use it in school. After a moment of pencil chewing, I wrote to an imaginary cousin, telling how I had sacrificed my pet chicken to feed Washington's starving, freezing troops at Valley Forge.

The next day, Miss Smith read my letter to the class, praised me for using my imagination, and said everyone else in the class had to try again. At Fernwood any written work even practice sentences, that did not measure up to teachers' standards, was rewritten—sometimes more than once. Smugly I read a library book while my classmates struggled with letters about their sacrifices of pet lambs and calves for Washington's troops. Copycats, I thought with contempt. Mother had told me authors found their ideas in their minds, not in the words of others. Besides, who ever heard of lambs and calves in the middle of winter? In Yamhill, they were born in springtime.

Next Miss Smith gave us homework: writing an essay about our favorite book character. This brought forth groans and sighs of resignation from most of the class. Nobody wanted to do homework, especially original homework.

That weekend, Mother happened to be visiting her parents in Banks, where Grandpa Atlee had bought back his store. (When he was seventy, after two years of retirement, he decided he was too young to be idle.) After I put together a Sunday dinner for my father, who gamely ate it and was enjoying his pipe and the Sunday paper, I sat down to write the essay. Which favorite character when I had so many? Peter Pan? Judy from Daddy-Long-Legs? Tom Sawyer? I finally solved this problem by writing about a girl who went to Bookland and talked to several of my favorite characters. I wrote on and on, inventing conversations that the characters might have had with a strange girl. As rain beat against the windows, a feeling of peace came over me as I wrote far beyond the required length of the essay. I had discovered the pleasure of writing, and to this day, whenever it rains, I feel the urge to write. Most of my books are written in winter.

As much as I enjoyed writing it, I thought "Journey Through Bookland" was a poor story because the girl's journey turned out to be a dream; and if there was anything I disliked, it was a good story that ended up as a dream. Authors of such stories, including Lewis Carroll, were cheating, I felt, because they could not think of any other conclusion.

I was also worried because I had used characters from published books. Miss Smith had lectured us on plagiarism and said that stealing from books was every bit as wrong as stealing from a store. But how could I write about a favorite character without having him speak?

When we turned our essays in during library, I watched anxiously as Miss Smith riffled through the papers. Was I going to catch it? Miss Smith pulled out a paper that I recognized as mine and began to read aloud. My mouth was dry and my stomach felt twisted. When she finished, she paused. My heart pounded. Then Miss Smith said, "When Beverly grows up, she should write children's books."

I was dumbfounded. Miss Smith was praising my story–essay with words that pointed to my future, a misty time I rarely even thought about. I was not used to praise. Mother did not compliment me. Now I was not only being praised in front of the whole class but was receiving approval that was to give direction to my whole life. The class seemed impressed.

When I reported all this to Mother, she said, "If you are going to become a writer, you must have a steady way of earning your living." This sound advice was followed by a thoughtful pause before she continued, "I have always wanted to write myself."

My career decision was lightly made. The Rose City Branch Library—quiet, tastefully furnished, filled with books and flowers—immediately came to mind. I wanted to work in such a place, so I would become a librarian.

End of excerpted manuscript.

THE WRITER'S LIFE

Yamhill

The "first fine house" in Yamhill, Oregon, constructed in the 1870s and now an Oregon landmark, belonged to John and Mary Edith Bunn, paternal grandparents of Beverly Cleary. Born Beverly Atlee Bunn on April 12, 1916, she spent the first six years of her life in that 11-room house, surrounded by her parent's farmland.

The house and farm offered Beverly a world to discover—wildflowers and trees, birds' nests and eggs, milking, plowing, chicken tripping (Beverly's favorite game), fruit picking, puddle splashing, banister sliding, and broom riding on stairs (which she only tried once). When her father told her that the world was round like an orange, Beverly set out to see for herself. He caught her climbing the neighbor's fence and asked where she was going. "Around the world, like you said," Beverly replied earnestly.

The small town of Yamhill presented Beverly with another world of wonder. Yamhill had small town character—and characters. In Yamhill everyone knew everyone, so they all knew Beverly. As she writes in *A Girl from Yamhill*, "Yamhill had taught me that the world was a safe and beautiful place, where children were treated with kindness, patience and tolerance."

For Beverly's parents, Mabel and Lloyd, life in Yamhill was not so idyllic. The big, old house and ever-present farm tasks meant constant work and worry. The tall, powerful Lloyd, raised as a farmer, enjoyed the challenge. But the endless work wore down Mabel, a petite former schoolteacher. "We had everything," Mabel later said about that time, "everything except money." The depressed farm economy forced the Bunns to lease their farm and move to the city of Portland, Oregon, in 1922.

Figure 8.4. Beverly, age six.

Portland

Lloyd found work as a bank guard, at first on the night shift. Mabel's tasks as a homemaker were eased somewhat by modern conveniences like a central furnace and gas cook stove. Beverly reveled in a neighborhood with lots of near neighbors, especially kids who had remarkable toys. She enjoyed roller skates, homemade stilts, elevator and escalator rides, trips to the public library, and the anticipation of starting first grade and learning to read.

But first grade was difficult, even fearful. As an only child, Beverly was overwhelmed by the size and regimen of Fernwood Grammar School. She missed much school due to bouts with chicken pox and smallpox. Her teacher was stern, punishing students, including Beverly, with often-unexplained hand raps from a bamboo pointer. Academically, Beverly fell behind her classmates—and her own expectations. She begged to stay home from school. But, as Mabel pushed her out the door to school, she told Beverly to think of her pioneer ancestors and to be brave.

Kind Miss Marius, her second-grade teacher, got Beverly's reading back on track and grade level. Still, the girl refused to read outside school until third grade. On a rainy Sunday, Beverly picked up *The Dutch Twins* by Lucy Fitch Perkins to look at the pictures. Soon she was reading, having discovered the joys of reading for pleasure. That night she devoured Perkins's *The Swiss Twins*.

The now-voracious reader received a copy of *The Story of Dr. Doolittle* in exchange for writing a newspaper review of the book. In fourth grade, Beverly entered a much-talked-about animal essay contest. After winning two dollars, she discovered that no one else had entered. The young writer learned a valuable lesson—try, you may succeed while others only talk.

After much soul-searching, Lloyd sold the family farm. With some of the proceeds, the Bunns bought a car and a house in Portland. The car carried them on Sunday excursions into the history and scenery of western Oregon. That summer they vacationed on a remote ranch run by Lloyd's sister, Aunt Dora, and her husband, Uncle Joe, in dry eastern Oregon. Riding a horse around the small ranch was a dream come true for Beverly.

Through eight grades of grammar school, writing became more important to Beverly. It gave her the uncommon opportunity to use her fertile imagination. Teachers praised her work. She dreamed of writing, perhaps for children, while supporting herself as a librarian.

Beverly sorely needed praise and approval. The older she grew, the more fretful and critical her mother became. Mabel rarely, if ever, expressed the affection for her daughter that Lloyd did. Friction between mother and adolescent daughter sparked frequent arguments.

The Depression years, beginning in 1929, were difficult times for the Bunn family. Lloyd lost his job for months before finding another, at lower pay. Always worrying and economizing, Mabel's life seemed joyless. Beverly worried, too, and not just about her parents' finances. Winter illnesses caused her to miss school and left her rundown. One summer Beverly was shocked by the lecherous advances of her Uncle Joe, which she resisted and disclosed to her parents. She never saw Aunt Dora and Uncle Joe again.

High School

Beverly entered Grant High School in the fall of 1930 with a homemade, hand-me-down wardrobe and a growing love of literature and writing. She invested her energy in creating stories, winning continued praise from teachers. Student cliques were a waste of time.

During high school years, there was no money for family summer vacations. Nor would Mabel allow her a summer job. When family or friends invited her to the country, Beverly gladly went. She was fascinated by a visit to her grandparents, the Atlees, and their lively general store in the rural town of Banks, Oregon. Swimming, dancing, and relaxing were wonderful at the rustic Pudding River cabin, owned by the family of Beverly's best friend, Claudine.

Dances provided Beverly with her first dates. At sixteen, during a ballroom dance class, she met 21-year-old Gerhart. Mostly at his own insistence, Gerhart was a frequent visitor to the Bunn household and Beverly's companion for more than two years. Usually, Mabel encouraged the relationship. But she and Gerhart overlooked an important fact—he and "his girlfriend" had little in common. In time, Beverly rejected his attempts to control—and marry—her.

Beverly enjoyed mastering a variety of writing skills. In addition to English assignments, she took journalism, wrote for the school newspaper, prepared and presented a debate, participated in literary club activities, and co-wrote an original school play in which she also performed a lead role. Outside of school, she began a diary and corresponded with students around the world.

Senior year was not all "happy days" for Beverly. She struggled with her unhappy, domineering mother, and the ever-present Gerhart. Worst of all, she saw no academic future for herself, though she desperately wanted one. "I seemed to be the only person at Grant with no plans and no place to go, although I knew this was not true," Cleary writes in *A Girl from Yamhill*.

College and Career

Then a letter arrived from California. Written by Mabel's cousin, Verna, a librarian at Chaffey Junior College, it offered Beverly a place to stay while attending the school, tuition-free, for the following year. At first, mother and daughter did not take the letter seriously. But Lloyd did. When her soft-spoken father told her to take the offer, Beverly agreed immediately.

Despite hard times, with the spirit of adventure and determination of her "pioneer ancestors," Beverly Bunn made the most of her opportunities. Helping herself with part-time jobs, she graduated from Chaffey with honors. Admitted for junior and senior years to the University of California at Berkeley, her parents managed to pay the $150 per year nonresident tuition. Cleary writes in *My Own Two Feet* that those were two very interesting years.

Academically, Berkeley was challenging, even for hard-working Beverly. There, she met a tall, lanky fellow student, Clarence Cleary. Despite busy schedules, they became close. Clarence attended school full-time, while working to support himself. As graduation approached, the couple admitted their love and began to discuss marriage—but only after Beverly finished library school and worked for a year. Clarence found work with state government in Sacramento. Beverly enrolled in the University of Washington Library School in Seattle. Its excellent children's library program drew her there.

Mabel and Lloyd did not approve of the wedding plans. Clarence was Catholic. The Bunns were Protestant. Beverly struggled with their disapproval, but continued a long-distance relationship with Clarence.

After library school, Beverly found work at the Yakima, Washington, Public Library. She dove into children's program preparation, background reading, storytelling, cataloging, more reading, community outreach programs, still more reading, developing a summer reading program, and adult reference work. All this left her no time for the writing she had long envisioned.

After more than a year in Yakima, Clarence and Beverly married on October 6, 1940, without her parents' consent or attendance. Living in Oakland, California, Clarence worked in accounting for the Navy, while Beverly learned another side of the book business, working seasonally in the children's department of a bookshop in Berkeley.

Then came World War II. Beverly spent the war years running libraries at Army facilities in Oakland. Working six days a week left her with neither time nor energy for writing. Only after the war ended and the Clearys settled in their first home in the hills of Berkeley, did Beverly answer the call of her childhood ambition. The problem was, she recalls in *My Own Two Feet*, she soon found that she did not know how to write a story. None of her teachers had ever suggested any improvements or changes.

Remembering that writing for children was written storytelling, she thought back to storyhours in Yakima. She recalled non-reading boys at her library desk asking for books about "kids like us." She began by telling herself and her typewriter, "Henry Huggins was in the third grade."

Reworking experiences and memories from her own life, as well as from her imagination, she created short stories that became a book's chapters. *Henry Huggins* was published in 1950.

Beverly Cleary's vague adolescent dream, of writing books for and about children, was now a reality.

TEACHING ADVICE FOR BEVERLY CLEARY

Age Appropriateness

A Girl from Yamhill and *My Own Two Feet* are especially appropriate for ages 10 and up. Excerpting segments for less-able fourth- and fifth-grade readers will enable them to deal with the length of the books, both nearly 350 pages. The autobiographical fiction of *Emily's Runaway Imagination* is shorter and excellent for fourth grade and older readers, and as a read aloud for even younger children.

Touchy Terminology

The description of Uncle Joe's lecherous advances (*A Girl from Yamhill*, in the chapter titled "Uncle Joe") may be disturbing to some students, as it certainly was for Cleary. Her frankness in sharing the incident provides an excellent opportunity for discussion of the dangers of sexual predation and other forms of child abuse.

LEARNING HORIZONS

Literature Aloud Experiences

◆ **READERS GUILDS DISCUSS NEWBERY AWARD–WINNING BOOKS ABOUT THE WEST**

Level: Grades four and higher.

Student Learning Opportunities: Newbery Award–winning books; Cooperation; Reading; Discussion; Development of book presentation; Presentation.

Background: When Beverly Cleary was in sixth grade, her teacher, Miss Stewart, read aloud *Smoky, The Cow Horse* by Will James, the 1927 Newbery Medal winner. As she writes in *A Girl from Yamhill*, "The whole class, even Ralph, sat silent, engrossed. Here was a book about the West, written in language we had heard spoken in Oregon . . . "

Obviously, Miss Stewart knew good books and her audience. She understood then what more contemporary educational research confirms now—it is important that parents and other educators share oral language experiences of all kinds with young people. Reading aloud, storytelling, poetry, plays, choral reading, fiction, nonfiction, ballad, and song—all are important for their growth. And not just for preschool or primary age children. Sharing "living language" with middle-school, high-school and college students (as well as for adults' own pleasure) is a critical, if often ignored, medium of education.

Since 1922, the American Library Association has presented the Newbery Medal annually to the most distinguished contribution to American literature for children. Other excellent works, Newbery Honor books, are also recognized. Several western states and provinces have their own awards that direct educators to additional quality books for students.

The Newbery Medal books present diverse geographies, cultures, and literary styles. But, many are set in the West. These offer opportunities to integrate good literature (including Cleary's own *Dear Mr. Henshaw*) into teaching and learning about the West. *After Smoky, the Cow Horse*, the list of Newbery winners with western settings includes:

1932—*Waterless Mountain* by Laura Adams Armer. Tales of mystery and magic are woven into the story of Younger Brother, a Navajo boy in training to be a medicine priest.

1936—*Caddie Woodlawn* by Carol Ryrie Brink. A lively fictionalized biography of the author's grandmother, who grew up on the frontier of western Wisconsin.

1954—*And Now Miguel* by Joseph Krumgold. In this beautifully crafted coming-of-age story, Miguel Chavez finds adventure among the mountains of northern New Mexico.

1961—*Island of the Blue Dolphins* by Scott O'Dell. Alone on an island off of California, Karana, an American Indian girl, fights for survival. O'Dell is a master of historical fiction.

1973—*Julie of the Wolves* by Jean Craighead George. Miyax has run away and is lost on the North Slope of Alaska. Only the wolf pack she observes can provide food. But will they?

1984—*Dear Mr. Henshaw* by Beverly Cleary. In this epistolary novel, comprised of young Californian Leigh Botts's letters to his favorite author, the boy's point of view on dogs, life, school, and his parent's divorce becomes crystal clear.

1986—*Sarah, Plain and Tall* by Patricia MacLachlan. Papa, widowed with two young children, puts an ad in Eastern newspapers for a mail-order bride. Then, a letter arrives from Maine, from Sarah, who is plain and tall.

1995—*Walk Two Moons* by Sharon Creech. Thirteen-year-old Salamanca Tree Hiddle heads west by car with her grandparents, in search of her mother who said she was going to Idaho.

1998—*Out of the Dust* by Karen Hesse. Set in the Dust Bowl days on a farm in Oklahoma and written in free-verse poetry, it is the story of how Billie Jo comes to deal with the death of her mother in a fire.

Basics:
1. Obtain multiple copies of Newbery Award books from the list above. Give a brief booktalk about each one.

2. Create Readers Guilds, book discussion groups, by assigning groups of four to six students with similar reading ability who can work together cooperatively. Select (or guide the students' selection of) a different western Newbery book for each Guild.

3. Determine the overall time to be devoted to this experience. Assign each Guild an appropriate number of chapters per day or week to read for classwork and homework. If desired, provide opportunities for brief, informal Guild discussions at intervals during the course of their reading and for comprehension and vocabulary assignments to assess individual progress and mastery.

4. Develop a standard agenda for a culminating book discussion by each Guild. Include topics such as overall reactions, favorite parts, least-favorite parts, responses to the storyline, responses to the author's writing style, and other topics. Identify a Guild member to act as secretary, taking brief notes on each member's response to the agenda topics for later reference.

5. Ask Guild members to develop a five to fifteen minute presentation about their book to share with the other Guilds. At a minimum, each presentation should include a contribution from each Guild member, responses to the topics in the culminating book discussion, and a short read aloud or reader's theater performance from their book involving one or more of the Guild members. (See **Reading Aloud** and **Readers' Theater** in **Literature Aloud Experiences** of chapters 5 and 10, respectively.) Encourage creativity and diversity of presentation styles.

Extensions: Share book presentations in other classrooms, school and public libraries, and with book discussion groups in the community.

Teacher Evaluation Opportunities: Cooperation; Reading; Comprehension and vocabulary assignments; Discussion; Development of book presentation; Presentation.

Language Arts Experiences

◈ STORIES OF EARLY MEMORIES

Level: Grades four to eight.

Student Learning Opportunities: Memory; Retelling; Listening; Cooperation; Narrative writing; Six-Trait Writing—Ideas, Organization, Voice.

Background: Beverly Cleary begins *A Girl from Yamhill* by writing brief vignettes about her earliest memories of childhood. She describes, for example, the Thanksgiving table with its long white tablecloth, which she was inspired to decorate all over with handprints in blue ink. Students can access powerful stories from their own early memories for retelling and writing. (For more preparatory information, see **Learning Horizons:** Recollection, chapter 2.)

Basics:
1. Read aloud "Early Memories" from *A Girl from Yamhill* and share some of your own early recollections.

2. Ask students to recall an early memory they enjoy revisiting. Give them brief, quiet time to visualize details.

3. Have pairs of students briefly share their memories with each other.

4. Ask for volunteers to tell their early memory stories again for a larger group.

Extensions:

1. Ask students to prepare a written version of their early memory in brief form—one to three paragraphs, maximum.

2. Have them prepare other early memories in the same form.

3. Use these as a "first chapter" for a longer student autobiography.

4. Have students write as a biographer, sharing a third-person version of their storytelling partner's early memory. Be sure they secure permission to retell the early memory from the original storyteller before writing. As needed, encourage students to interview their partners about the memory to develop the written story.

Teacher Evaluation Opportunities: Cooperation; Oral retelling; Written retelling(s); Use of Six-Trait Writing techniques.

❖ *THE SEVEN SECRETS OF HIGHLY SUCCESSFUL WRITERS*

Level: Grades four to eight

Student Learning Opportunities: Imaginative writing; Six Trait Writing—Ideas, Organization, Voice, Word Choice, Sentence Fluency, Conventions.

Background: Many fiction and nonfiction writers use seven questions to help conceive and organize their stories—Who?, Whom?, Where?, When?, What?, Why?, and How? Answering these questions helps young writers prepare for a writing task.

Basics:

1. In preparation, review with students figure 8.5, page 188, **The Seven Questions** form.

2. As an example of its use, read aloud Beverly Cleary's thoughts on preparing to write the first chapter of her book, *Henry Huggins*, in *My Own Two Feet*, pages 247 to 250. Also read the first chapter of *Henry Huggins*.

3. Present and discuss figure 8.6, page 189, **Seven Questions—Beginning *Henry Huggins***. Do the students understand how answering these seven questions helped Cleary conceive and organize her story? They should answer these questions before writing a story of their own.

Extensions:

1. Ask students to fill out a **Seven Questions** form, figure 8.5, in preparation for writing a short fiction piece. Have them identify a true personal experience they can incorporate in the story line, similar to the way in which Cleary borrowed from her experiences in developing *Henry Huggins*.

2. Before they begin writing their story, review the students' **Seven Questions** forms.

3. Have students use the form to guide their writing of the story.

Teacher Evaluation Opportunities: The Seven Questions form; Student writing; Use of Six-Trait Writing techniques.

188 WRITERS OF THE NEW WEST

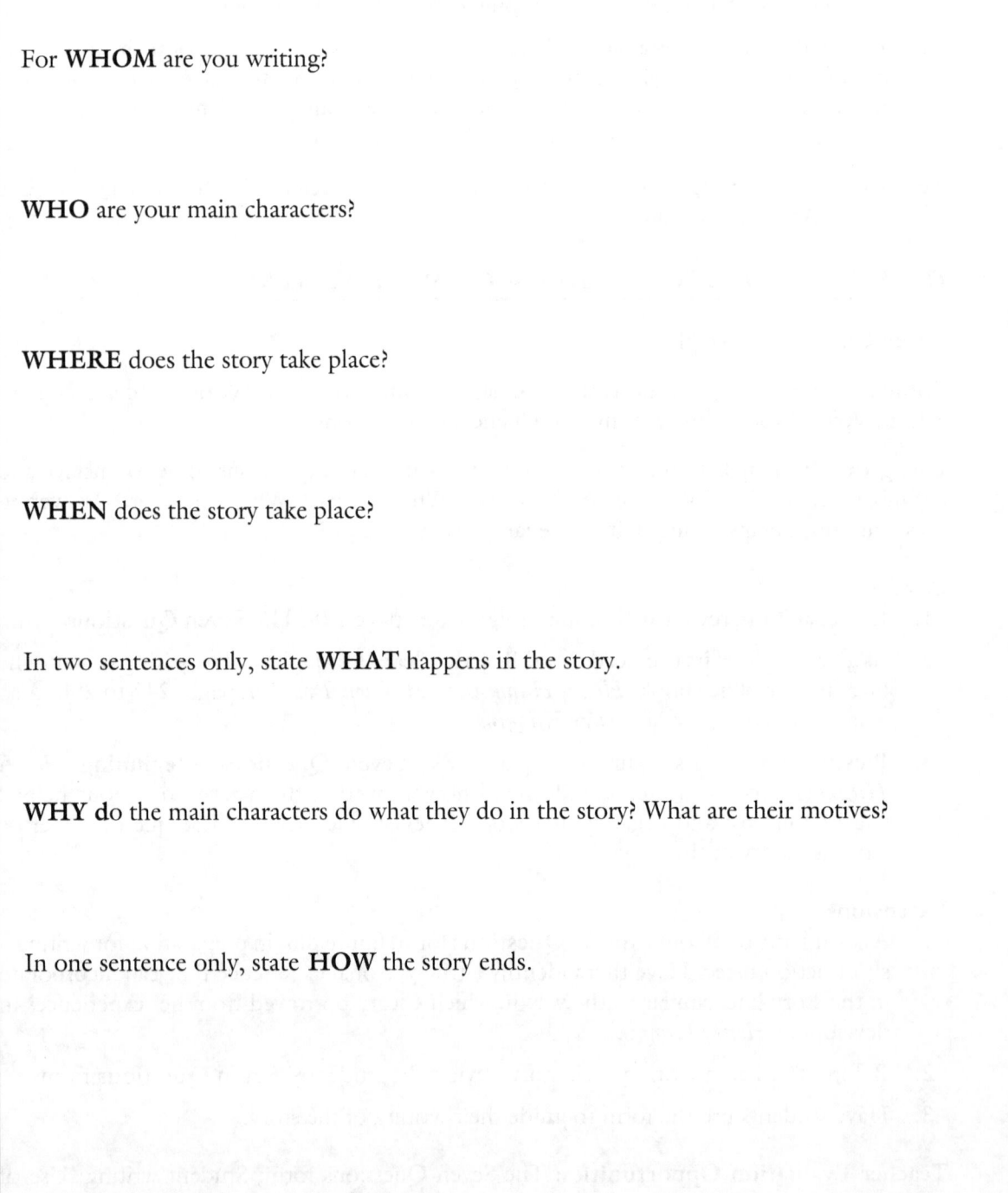

Figure 8.5. The Seven Questions.

If Beverly Cleary were filling out the Seven Questions form for the first chapter of *Henry Huggins*, it might look like this:

SEVEN QUESTIONS—Beginning *Henry Huggins*

NAME <u>Beverly Cleary</u>

DATE <u>January 2, 1949</u>

For **WHOM** are you writing?
I am writing *Henry Huggins* for children, especially boys, who want an easy-reading book about kids like them.

WHO are your main characters?
Main characters are Henry Huggins, a third grader, and Ribsy, the dog he adopts.

WHERE does the story take place?
The action happens in Portland, Oregon, at a drug store, on the bus, and on Klickitat Street at Henry's house.

WHEN does the story take place?
In the present time (circa 1950).

In two sentences only, state **WHAT** happens in the story.
Henry Huggins and a dog adopt each other, but Ribsy, the dog, can't ride the bus home without being in a box. Henry smuggles Ribsy on in a large bag, but the dog escapes, causing mayhem and laughter on the bus.

WHY do the main characters do what they do in the story? What are their motives?
Henry wants a dog, but has never had one. Hungry and homeless, Ribsy wants someone to take care of him.

In one sentence only, state **HOW** the story ends.
After getting a call from Henry's parents, the police find Henry and Ribsy on the bus and bring them safely home.

Figure 8.6. Seven Questions—Beginning *Henry Huggins*.

Social Studies Experiences

◈ GROWING A FAMILY TREE

Level: Grades four to eight.

Student Learning Opportunities: Inquiry; Research; Pictorial reporting; Oral reporting.

Background: We all stand at the tip-top of our own family tree. Our ancestors, and the past, are stretched out on the branches below us.

Basics:
1. Read aloud the chapters, "Those Pioneer Ancestors" and "The Little Schoolmarm," from *A Girl from Yamhill*. Discuss figure 8.7, page 191, **A Simple Family Tree for Beverly Cleary**.

2. Have students use family inquiry and research to identify the names of ancestors back to their great-grandparents or beyond. Adopted children can use their adoptive or birth families, as appropriate. In addition, locate birth dates, birthplaces, and photos, if possible. More ambitious researchers may also want to explore genealogical resources in libraries or on the Internet.

3. Ask the young genealogists to create a graphic depiction of their ancestry. Have them use figure 8.8, page 192, the **Family Tree**, or a larger format (see **Extensions** below) to organize and display information. Photos can be reduced and photocopied to a uniform size. If photos are unavailable, students can draw an imaginary picture of the ancestor.

Extensions:
1. Once students have collected genealogical information, they can display it in different ways:

    Brackets, like those used in tournaments. Start with the child in the center and expand to left (father) and right (mother) in bracketed pairs horizontally through the generations.

    Family Balloon Bouquet. Use oval-shaped copies of photo portraits as balloons connected with lines like strings. Start with the child at the bottom and expand upward through the generations.

    Up a Tree. This requires more extensive family information. Start with the earliest known or desired maternal or paternal ancestors at a tree's roots and build upward with all members of each generation of the family on the branches, ending with the child's generation of sisters, brothers, and various cousins on the highest tree limbs. Next, build a similar tree for the other side of the family.

2. Students can orally present their family tree displays to the class, including a pertinent family story or stories discovered in their research.

Teacher Evaluation Opportunities: Thoroughness of research; Family Tree display; Oral reporting.

Beverly Cleary creates her family tree in words from the chapters, "Those Pioneer Ancestors" and "The Little Schoolmarm," in *A Girl from Yamhill*. If we display her family in simple tree-form, it looks like this:

Beverly Atlee Bunn

Mabel Atlee   Chester Lloyd Bunn

Mary Francis Jarvis   William S. Atlee   Mary Edith Hawn   John Marion Bunn

_ Jarvis   Z. Jarvis   J. Slater   T. Atlee   H. Pierson   J. Hawn   E. Noel   F. Bunn

Figure 8.7. A Simple Family Tree for Beverly Cleary.

The Family Tree

YOUR TASK: Starting with yourself at the top, fill in the names of family members on both sides of your family as far back into the past as you can go. "F" stands for father's line, "M" stands for mother's.

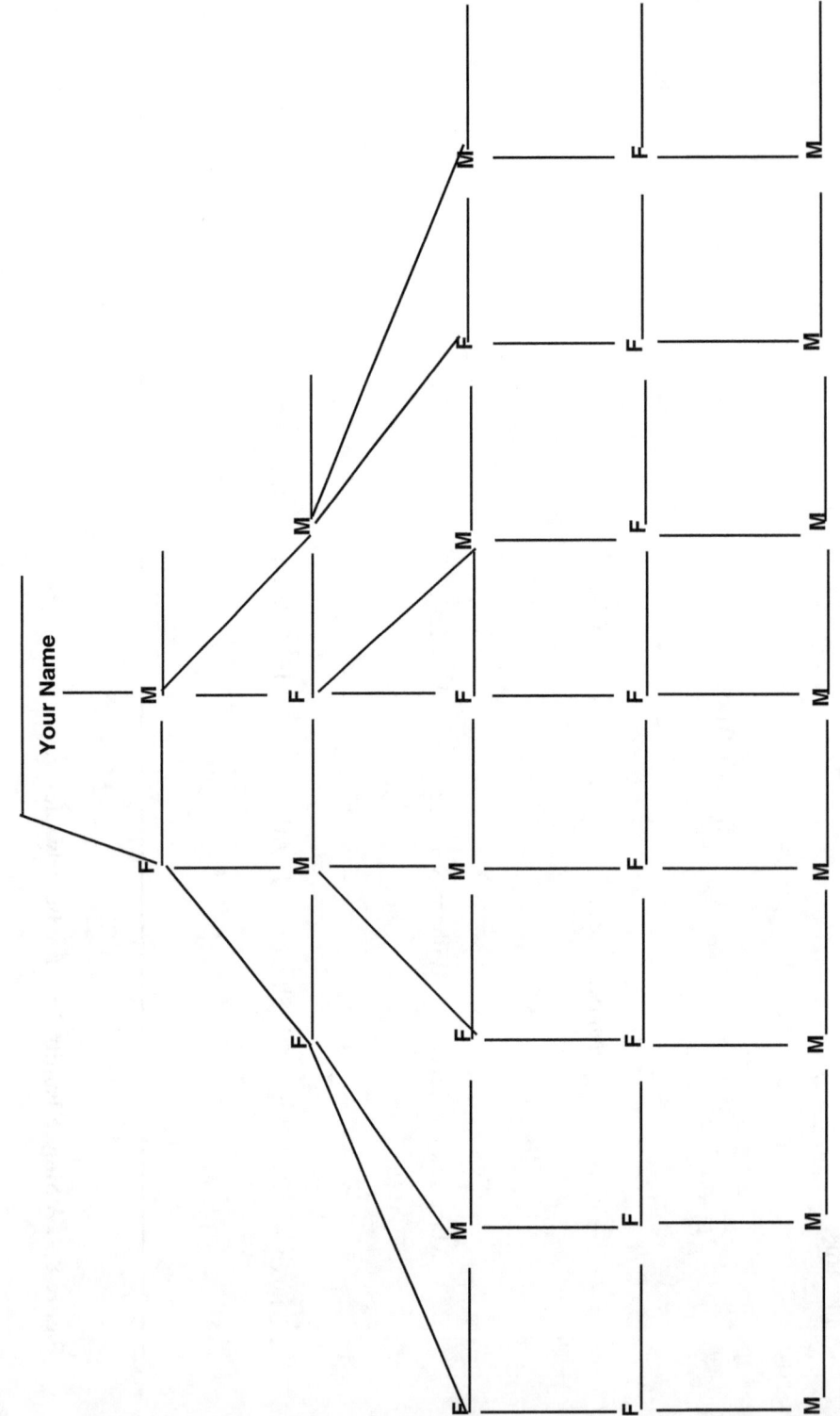

Figure 8.8. The Family Tree.

❖ FAMILIES IN MOTION

Level: Grades four to eight.

Student Learning Opportunities: Inquiry; Research; Map analysis; Mapmaking; Oral reporting.

Background: The families of western writers, like many other North Americans, have been very mobile through the generations. Beverly Cleary's ancestors are no exception. Neither, perhaps, are your students' families.

Basics:
1. Provide copies of the outline map of the United States, figure 8.9, and pages 10-22 of *A Girl from Yamhill* for students to read and analyze.
2. Have students map the movement of Cleary's family, using a distinctive symbol for the travel routes taken by each branch and a large **X** for their places of residence. For example, the Hawns's travels might be marked by dashed lines and the Atlees' by a line of circles. Each map should contain a key to the map symbols. Where Cleary provides the information, place-of-residence names should be labeled beside the **X**.

Extensions:
1. Ask students to research and map their own families' migrations. Students should use family inquiry and research to identify the places-of-residence of ancestors back to their great-grandparents or earlier.
2. Provide copies of outline maps of U.S. and Mexican states and/or Canadian provinces.
3. Have students follow the same mapping procedures, as with Cleary's family map.
4. Ask the young genealogists to present their family migration history and map to the class.
5. Merge individual maps onto one large map to get a picture of migration similarities, differences, and trends.

Note: An alternate activity will be required for students whose families have lived in the same locale for generations or whose migration information is not available. One possibility would have them use local or regional maps to trace the movements of their immediate family during vacations, weekends, or during a typical day or week or from house to house within the city.

Teacher Evaluation Opportunities: Amount and quality of research; Mapping—Cleary's family and student's families; Oral reporting.

194 WRITERS OF THE NEW WEST

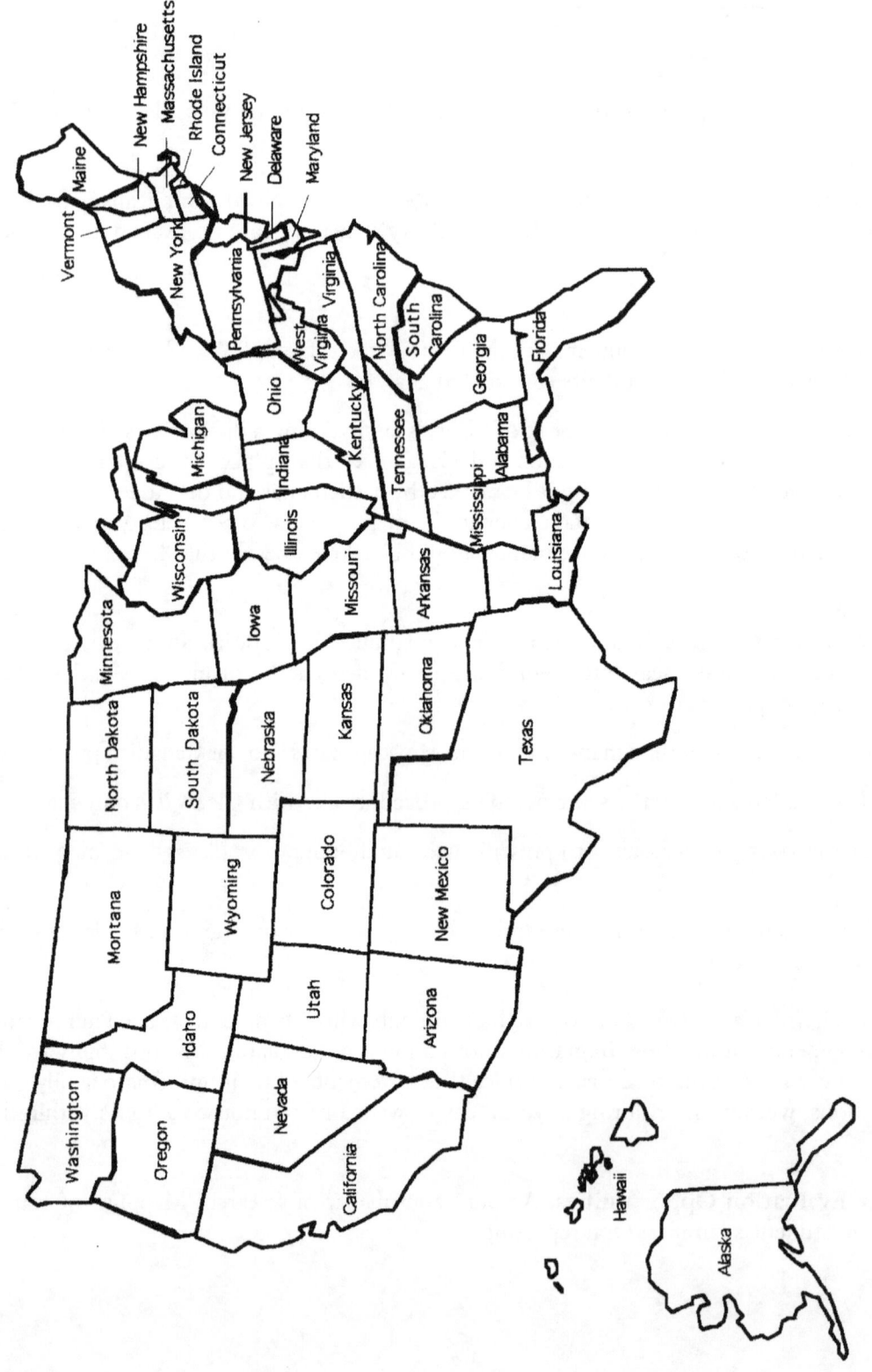

Figure 8.9. Outline map of the United States.

BEVERLY CLEARY RESOURCES

Selected Books by Cleary

Cleary, Beverly. *A Girl from Yamhill: A Memoir.* New York: William Morrow, 1988.
    This first volume of her autobiography takes Cleary from her days on the family farm in Yamhill, Oregon, through her earliest attempts at writing, to her high-school graduation.

——— . *Emily's Runaway Imagination.* New York: William Morrow, 1961.
    Young Emily's imagination runs away sometimes, often with humorous—and disastrous—consequences. This fictionalized or, more accurately, imaginary autobiography clearly recalls the town of Yamhill and Cleary's family as she knew them during her early childhood.

——— . *Henry Huggins.* New York: William Morrow, 1950.
    Cleary's first book is just as funny and on-target for its audience today as when it was published. Henry fits the description, "all boy," perfectly.

——— . *My Own Two Feet: A Memoir.* New York: William Morrow, 1995.
    Flowing seamlessly in style and content from *A Girl from Yamhill,* Cleary recounts her experiences in higher education, World War II, and early married life, with insights into her writing process.

Selected Cleary Biographies and Resources

Berg, Julie. *Beverly Cleary,* A Tribute to the Young At Heart Series. Edina, MN: Abdo and Daughters, 1993.
    A brief, 32-page biography for young readers, its focus is on Cleary's acquisition of writing skills.

Kelly, Joanne. *The Beverly Cleary Handbook.* Englewood, CO: Teacher Ideas Press, 1996.
    A complete reference and resource guide to Cleary and her works, it contains novel summaries, biographical links to her works, and extension activities for language arts and social studies, especially for grades 3–6.

Martin, Patricia Stone. *Beverly Cleary: She Makes Reading Fun.* Vero Beach, FL: Rourke Enterprises, 1987.
    This brief biography for young readers emphasizes goal setting.

Palumbo, Thomas J. *Integrating the Literature of Beverly Cleary.* Carthage, IL: Good Apple, 1991.
    Contains 162 pages of multidisciplinary activities based on 11 of Cleary's novels for children and young adults.

Electronic Resources

Beverly Cleary Teacher Resource File. Available: http://falcon.jmu.edu/~ramseyil.cleary.htm (Accessed November 15, 2000).
    As part of the Internet School Library Media Center, this site offers biographic and bibliographic information, as well as lesson plans and links to ERIC Clearinghouse resources and other sites.

Multnomah County Library Kids Page. Available: http://www.multcolib.org/kids/cleary.html (Accessed January 29, 2001).
    In addition to basic information and links on Cleary, this site features a segment on the Beverly Cleary Sculpture Garden in her hometown of Portland, that her young fans will enjoy visiting, electronically or in person.

The Unofficial Beverly Cleary Home Page. Available: http://www.teleport.com/~krp/cleary.html (Accessed November 15, 2000).

This is one-stop shopping for the Cleary fan: biography, bibliography, links, character sketches, frequently asked questions, a fan page, and a guest book.

GARY SOTO

CHAPTER 9

Born April 12, 1952 in Fresno, California. Childhood and young adult autobiography describes California.

Figure 9.1. Gary Soto. Photo courtesy of Gary Soto.

AN APPRECIATION OF THE WRITER

My advice to young poets is "Look to your own lives." What are your life stories? Can you remember incidents from your childhood? Some of you will say that your lives are boring, that nothing has happened, that everything interesting happens far away. Not so.

From the Foreword of Gary Soto's
A Fire In My Hands

As a boy, Gary Soto had no aspirations to be a writer. He wasn't surrounded by books. His family never read. They were too busy earning a living and making a life in urban Fresno, California. And Gary was too busy being a kid to read much outside of school.

Soto's intensity while doing "kid things" turned out to be a good thing. His experiences gave him many distinct childhood memories to write about later. According to Soto, his book-poor background made it unlikely that he would develop a desire to write poetry. But, as a young adult, he did. Then, after writing adult poetry for more than a decade and having several collections published, the writer, also a college professor, ventured into writing prose.

Gary Soto's first prose work, *Living up the Street: Narrative Recollections*, has the same subject matter as much of his poetry—growing up. He explores growing up in an extended family; growing up Mexican American; growing up on the edge of poverty and the edge of Fresno; growing up a little bit wild; and growing like kids everywhere through mysteries, discoveries, and disasters, and somehow surviving. Although Soto's prose and poetry most often involve Mexican American characters and neighborhoods, the themes he speaks to are universal. *Living up the Street*, published in 1985, won critical approval and an American Book Award from the Before Columbus Foundation. *A Summer Life*, published in 1990, continues his childhood recollections.

A prolific writer, Soto has extended his reach in poetry and prose to a broad audience beyond adults. He has written free-verse poetry for young children and young adults. Other works include young reader and adolescent novels, fictional and autobiographical short stories for all ages, text for juvenile picture books, plays, film scripts, a biography, and an opera libretto. What is remarkable is not just that Gary Soto has done all this varied writing, but that he has done it so expertly.

A prime reason Gary Soto can write in so many forms for so many audiences is that his writing "stays at home." He works the familiar, fertile ground of his own life, family, and neighborhood, the people, places, and things that he knows. He encourages young writers to do the same.

Read Gary Soto and you discover the poet's penchant for speaking to the reader with directness and honesty. Sometimes it is honesty so painful, it hurts; sometimes so honest, it makes you laugh out loud. His honesty acknowledges the remarkable in the commonplace object, in the everyday event. Soto is not afraid to wrestle with hard issues, like social and economic injustice, racism, ethnic discrimination, bullying, homelessness, and poverty. As a writer he is a tightrope walker, taking risks and meeting challenges with poise and balance. Soto deals with emotionally charged issues without preaching, while allowing the people about whom he writes (including himself) to retain at least a shred of their dignity, no matter how bad their behavior. Perhaps most important, he always leaves room for his readers to make up their own minds.

IN HIS OWN WORDS

From the time he was little, Gary Soto was, by his own admission, a scrappy kid. He got into lots of neighborhood and schoolyard fights—but not with Frankie T., the fifth-grade bully. In the chapter, "Fear," from *Living up the Street: Narrative Recollections* (see page 200), Soto deftly explores the motivation of bullies (and not just Frankie T.) without getting far from his own experience or too clinical. It is a powerful, moving piece of writing.

An advisory before reading: The name that Frankie T. calls Gary in the first paragraph, *cabron*, carries a profane meaning in colloquial Spanish.

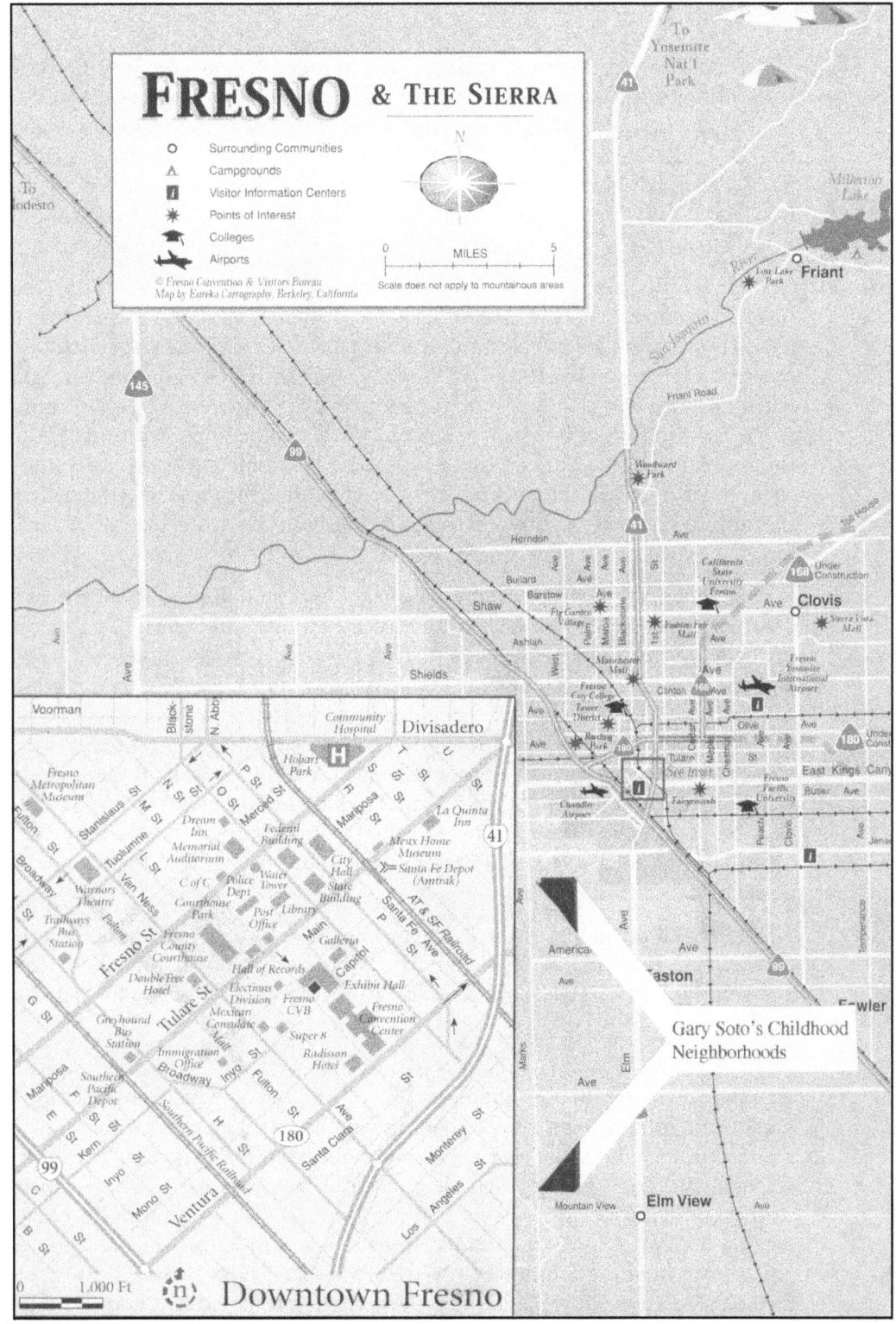

Figure 9.2. Contemporary map of the Fresno, California area, childhood home of Gary Soto. Used by permission of the Fresno, California Convention and Visitors Bureau.

Note: The following is excerpted as punctuated and spelled in the original manuscript.

A cold day after school. Frankie T., who would drown his brother by accident that coming spring and would use a length of pipe to beat a woman in a burglary years later, had me pinned on the ground behind a backstop, his breath sour as meat left out in the sun. "*Cabron*," he called me and I didn't say anything. I stared at his face, shaped like the sole of a shoe, and just went along with the insults, although now and then I tried to raise a shoulder in a halfhearted struggle because that was part of the game.

He let his drool yo-yo from his lips, missing my feet by only inches, after which he giggled and called me names. Finally he let me up. I slapped grass from my jacket and pants, and pulled my shirt tail from my pants to shake out the fistful of dirt he had stuffed in my collar. I stood by him, nervous and red-faced from struggling, and when he suggested that we climb the monkey bars together, I followed him quietly to the kid's section of Jefferson Elementary. He climbed first, with small grunts, and for a second I thought of running but knew he would probably catch me—if not then, the next day. There was no way out of being a fifth grader—the daily event of running to teachers to show them your bloody nose. It was just a fact, like having lunch.

So I climbed the bars and tried to make conversation, first about the girls in our classroom and then about kickball. He looked at me smiling as if I had a camera in my hand, his teeth green like the underside of a rock, before he relaxed his grin into a simple gray line across his face. He told me to shut up. He gave me a hard stare and I looked away to a woman teacher walking to her car and wanted very badly to yell for help. She unlocked her door, got in, played with her face in the visor mirror while the engine warmed, and then drove off with blue smoke trailing. Frankie was watching me all along and when I turned to him, he laughed, "*Chale!* She can't help you, *ese*." He moved closer to me on the bars and I thought he was going to hit me; instead he put his arm around my shoulder, squeezing firmly in friendship. "C'mon, chicken, let's be cool."

I opened my mouth and tried to feel happy as he told me what he was going to have for Thanksgiving. "My Mamma's got a turkey and ham, lots of potatoes, yams and stuff like that. I saw it in the refrigerator. And she says we gonna get some pies. Really, *ese*."

Poor liar, I thought, smiling as we clunked our heads like good friends. He had seen the same afternoon program on TV as I had, one in which a woman in an apron demonstrated how to prepare a Thanksgiving dinner. I knew he would have tortillas and beans, a round steak maybe, and oranges from his backyard. He went on describing his Thanksgiving, then changed over to Christmas—the new bicycle, the clothes, the G.I. Joes. I told him that it sounded swell, even though I knew he was making it all up. His mother would, in fact, stand in line at the Salvation Army to come away hugging armfuls of toys that had been tapped back into shape by reformed alcoholics with veined noses. I pretended to be excited and asked if I could come over to his place to play after Christmas. "Oh, yeah, anytime," he said, squeezing my shoulder and clunking his head against mine.

When he asked what I was having for Thanksgiving, I told him that we would probably have a ham with pineapple on top. My family was slightly better off than Frankie's, though I sometimes walked around with cardboard in my shoes and socks with holes big enough to be ski masks, so holidays were extravagant happenings. I told him about the scalloped potatoes, the candied yams, the frozen green beans, and the pumpkin pie.

His eyes moved across my face as if he were deciding where to hit me—nose, temple, chin, talking mouth—and then he lifted his arm from my shoulder and jumped from the monkey bars, grunting as he landed. He wiped sand from his knees while looking up and warned me not to mess around with him any more. He stared with such a great meanness that I had to look away. He warned me again and then walked away. Incredibly relieved, I jumped from the bars and ran looking over my shoulder until I turned onto my street.

Frankie scared most of the school out of its wits and even had girls scampering out of view when he showed himself on the playground. If he caught us without notice, we grew quiet and stared down at our shoes until he passed after a threat or two. If he pushed us down, we stayed on the ground with our eyes closed and pretended that we were badly hurt. If he riffled through our lunch bags, we didn't say anything. He took what he wanted, after which we sighed and watched him walk away peeling an orange or chewing big chunks of an apple.

Still, that afternoon when he called Mr. Koligian, our teacher, a foul name, we got scared for him. Mr. Koligian pulled and tugged at his body until it was in his arms and then out of his arms as he hurled Frankie against the building. Some of us looked away because it was unfair. We knew the house he lived in: The empty refrigerator, the father gone, the mother in a sad bathrobe, the beatings, the yearning for something to love. When the teacher mishandled him, we all wanted to run away, but instead we stared and felt shamed. Robert, Adele, Yolanda shamed; Nash, Margie, Rocha shamed. We all watched him flop about as Mr. Koligian shook and grew red from anger. We knew his house and, for some, it was the same one to walk home to: The broken mother, the indifferent walls, the refrigerator's glare which fed the people no one wanted.

End of excerpted manuscript.

THE WRITER'S LIFE

Growing Things

In the verdant Central Valley of California, things grow well, whether tended, or untended. Fields of grapes, beets, and cotton seem to spread out almost endlessly around Fresno, worked by machines and field hands, often migrant laborers. Weeds spring up in field margins, alleys, and vacant lots. (A weed is a plant that dares to grow where people don't want it or don't care.) Gary Soto's grandfather carefully tended fruit trees that grew in his backyard, near the Sun Maid Raisin factory on Braly Street where he worked for 30 years. Up the street, bean plants grew in the garden under young Gary's care, unless his older brother Rick wreaked some vengeance on them.

Gary, Rick, and their younger sister, Debra, didn't grow like weeds. They were wanted and cared-for. But, they were sometimes untended. Their grandmother and Mrs. Molina, a neighbor with many children, were not always able to watch every move of the energetic Sotos. Manuel and Angie, their parents, worked hard, manual jobs. The kids occasionally got into trouble and more often looked for it. As Gary Soto writes in *Living up the Street: Narrative Recollections*, the Soto kids were mean, especially the boys. They squashed and immolated thousands of ants, picked fights with neighbor kids and each other, threw rocks and bottles, and got as much punishment as they gave. In 1957, the summer when Gary was five, they tried to burn down their house. After lighting balled-up newspapers in the living room, the children joyfully put out the fire with a garden hose. Then they fought a war with cherry tomato "bombs" inside the house. When Angie returned home, their indiscretions were quickly punished.

That year, shortly after the Sotos moved to a home on the outskirts of Fresno, Manuel was hurt in an industrial accident. He died two days later. Family members rallied to help. Still, times were tough for Angie and the children. Somehow, she managed to send the children to St. John's Catholic school for a few years. Gary attended there from second through fourth grade, but, by his own admission, was not a star student. On Sundays, Angie Soto sent the children to church, especially Gary, whom she called her short-tailed devil. More than two years after Manuel's death, Angie remarried and gave birth to Gary's two half-brothers. As he grew, Gary often disagreed with his stepfather, a book warehouse worker.

For about five years, Gary's summer life centered upon games and activities at the nearby Romain playground. If the neighborhood kids weren't old enough to take long bike rides or hunt frogs and swim in irrigation canals, they were at the playground. Using terms from his childhood, Soto identifies the kids in his neighborhood as either "Okies," white kids, or "Mexicans," Mexican Americans. In *Living up the Street*, he writes extensively about the friends and adversaries he met there, the board games and ball games, the crafts and competitions, the "coaches" (recreation staff people), even a childrens' beauty contest. But everything at Romain playground wasn't all fun and games. Soto describes a racially charged incident in which a white father, mistakenly thinking that Gary's friend Rosie hurt his daughter while at play, verbally and physically attacks Rosie and her brothers who come, throwing wood chips, to defend her.

Growing Up

Beginning in fifth grade, Gary attended public school, Jefferson Elementary in Fresno. Outside of school, through the years, he worked at a variety of odd jobs, including weeding flower beds, raking leaves, mowing lawns, and cashing in returnable bottles. Money was always short in Soto's household. In junior high, Gary had to work to buy new school clothes or he would have had none. Summer jobs of any kind were hard to find in the 1960s, especially for kids under 16.

At dawn one day, Gary went with his mother to pick grapes outside town. That day and in days after, he discovered what his parents and grandparents had known for decades—that field work is laborious, boring, and low-paying. It requires large amounts of mental determination and physical stamina. Always bent over, working in the sun at the tough, springy vines with his grape knife, Gary cut tray after tray of grapes. That first day he worked eight hours and made $4.38. For 13 days of grape-cutting, he earned $53. In that time his mother earned $148. The next summer Rick and Debra joined Gary in cutting grapes. During high school, the brothers chopped cotton on spring weekends. The most they ever made was $14 a day, about $1.25 an hour, only equal to the minimum wage at that time.

Field work made Gary realize that, no matter how he and Rick laughed about it, that what their mother warned them of was true. She said that if they didn't work hard in school, they would be stuck for life doing field work or another manual job. She urged them to look to the future. Up to the age of sixteen, Gary didn't do well in school. He often wrangled with his stepfather who, along with others, told him he'd never amount to anything but a laborer.

From 1967 to 1970, Soto attended Fresno's Roosevelt High School. Instead of the schoolyard and neighborhood fighting of which he did plenty in the lower grades, Gary channeled most of his aggressive urges into wrestling. Competing for three years at a well-conditioned 103 pounds, the wrestler learned physical discipline and self-control.

In July 1969 Gary Soto ran away from home. After an emotional fight with his parents, he headed for southern California, ending up in Glendale, sleeping on the ground, living on his own. The work that he found on the tire recapping line at the Valley Tire Company was grimy, skin-blackening, hot, and arduous. Gary discovered that it was even worse than field work. At least, the job paid enough for food and room rental. The rest, $140 in all, was saved. In September he returned to Fresno for his senior year in high school. That year, or perhaps the next, he decided to take his mother's advice about working hard with his mind, not just his body.

Growing in New Directions

High-school graduation was followed by enrollment at Fresno City Junior College in the fall of 1970. Soto planned to study geography. A chance meeting with a book of contemporary poetry at the library changed the plan permanently. Gary liked the wild, unconventional energy of the unrhymed verse. He read more and was hooked. Particularly appealing were Spanish and South American poets, especially the Chilean Pablo Neruda and his odes to everyday things. American poets—James Wright, Gary Snyder, Edward Field, Philip Levine—also became favorites. Soto began writing poetry of his own, studies of people and places in the San Joaquin Valley, his home. In 1972 and 1973, Philip Levine became his teacher, sternly helping the young poet shape his "work of words."

Discovering his love and talent for writing ignited Gary Soto's academic career like the newspaper he had burned in his childhood living room. (It did not make him a genius overnight, however, as evidenced by the frank and painfully funny chapter "Being Stupid" from *Living up the Street*.) After completing junior college (*Junior College* is also the title of his 1997 poetry collection), he graduated magna cum laude from California State University at Fresno in 1974, with a degree in English. In 1976, Soto completed his Master of Fine Arts Degree in Creative Writing from California State University at Irvine. The next year his first book of poems, *The Elements of San Joaquin*, was published. This collection deals with aspects of the often grim lives of Mexican American farm workers in California.

In the middle of graduate school, Soto married Carolyn Sadako Oda, the daughter of Japanese American farmers from Fresno. The years following graduate school included a writing residency at San Diego State, a sojourn in Mexico City, a lecturer position in Chicano studies and then professorships in English and Chicano Studies at the University of California at Berkeley, and the publication of three more poetry collections. The birth of Carolyn and Gary's daughter, Mariko, highlighted that busy time.

In the 1980s, Gary Soto challenged himself with the task of writing prose, as well as poetry. The result was his autobiographical reflection on childhood and young adulthood, *Living up the Street: Narrative Recollections*, published in 1985. The personal challenge he accepted has resulted in a flood of prose since that time. Soto's explorations in narrative style have led him to wider audiences.

He now writes fictional, biographical, and autobiographical prose works, as well as free-verse poetry, for children, young readers, teens, and adults. Few North American writers explore so many forms for so many audiences at once.

Leaving teaching to become a full-time writer in 1993, Soto has produced several films based on his short stories. One of them, *The Pool Party* (a book of the same title followed the film), was awarded the Andrew Carnegie Medal for Excellence in Children's Video in 1993 by the Association for Library Service to Children of the American Library Association.

Gary Soto is a brave writer. Whether in poetry or prose, he does not hesitate to give of himself, sharing inner truths and outward joys, as well as failings. Readers of all ages benefit from his forthrightness and his literary artistry.

Figure 9.3. "The Bike," a short story from Gary Soto's collection A Summer Life, has been adapted as a short film. Illus. by John Stansfield.

TEACHING ADVICE FOR GARY SOTO

Autobiographical Writings

A large portion of Soto's work in prose and poetry is autobiography or autobiographical fiction. The main focus for this chapter is on Soto's *Living up the Street: Narrative Recollections*, a chronologically arranged volume of personal history sketches, not intended as a full childhood autobiography. The very short stories of *A Summer Life* fill in more of the history of the summers of his early years. Some of what Soto writes about in these two books shows up in his poetry in a different form. (It is interesting to compare and contrast the prose and poetry versions of the experiences.) Other Soto works of autobiography and memoir include *Small Faces, Lesser Evils/Ten Quartets*, and *The Effects of Knut Hamsun on a Fresno Boy*. He is also the editor of *California Childhood: Recollections and Stories of the Golden State*, which includes other writers who grew up in California.

Age Appropriateness

Both in reading level and content, *Living up The Street: Narrative Recollections* is most appropriate for students in grade six and higher. Most of the early chapters (about 75 pages) are excellent for elementary students, possibly if read aloud first by an adult. The same recommendations are true for *A Summer Life* up to about page 100. As for Soto's autobiographical poetry, *Canto Familiar* and *Neighborhood Odes* are appropriate for all ages, while poems from *A Fire in My Hands* are excellent for fifth grade and higher.

Touchy Terminology

Occasionally, mostly in the dialogue, there is profanity, in both Spanish (printed in italics) and English, in *Living up the Street: Narrative Recollections* and *A Summer Life*. There is also a brief sexual reference in the chapter titled, "Black Hair," from *Living up the Street*.

Mexican, Chicano, Latino?

Gary Soto's books use a variety of terms to describe his ethnic identity and that of his characters and subjects, including Mexican, Mexican American, and Chicano or Chicana. There are distinct differences among these terms and others, such as Latino or Latina and Hispanic, which refer to Spanish-speaking or Spanish-surnamed people. The most important thing to remember is that groups of people and individuals should be free to refer to themselves in any way they find appropriate and that others should respect those preferences. Some of the distinctions among these terms of ethnic reference are as follows:

> A **Mexican** is a native of Mexico, though the term, as Gary Soto describes its use in the period of the 1950s and 1960s, also identified people of Mexican ancestry living in the United States.
>
> **Mexican American** is a U.S. resident born in Mexico or of Mexican ancestry.
>
> **Hispanic** is a generic, often governmental, term used to refer to Spanish-speaking or Spanish-surnamed people.
>
> **Latino** (male) or **Latina** (female) are generic terms for Spanish-speaking or Spanish-surnamed people, often those from Central or South America and the Caribbean Islands.
>
> **Chicano** (male) or **Chicana** (female) is a term that Spanish-speaking or Spanish-surnamed people living in the United States, Canada, or other countries use to refer to themselves. Among other characteristics, it identifies their mixed Spanish and North, Central, or South American Indian ancestry. As a recognition of cultural identity, the term came into widespread use during the Civil Rights Movement of the 1960s. In various places in his writing, Gary Soto refers to himself as a Chicano.

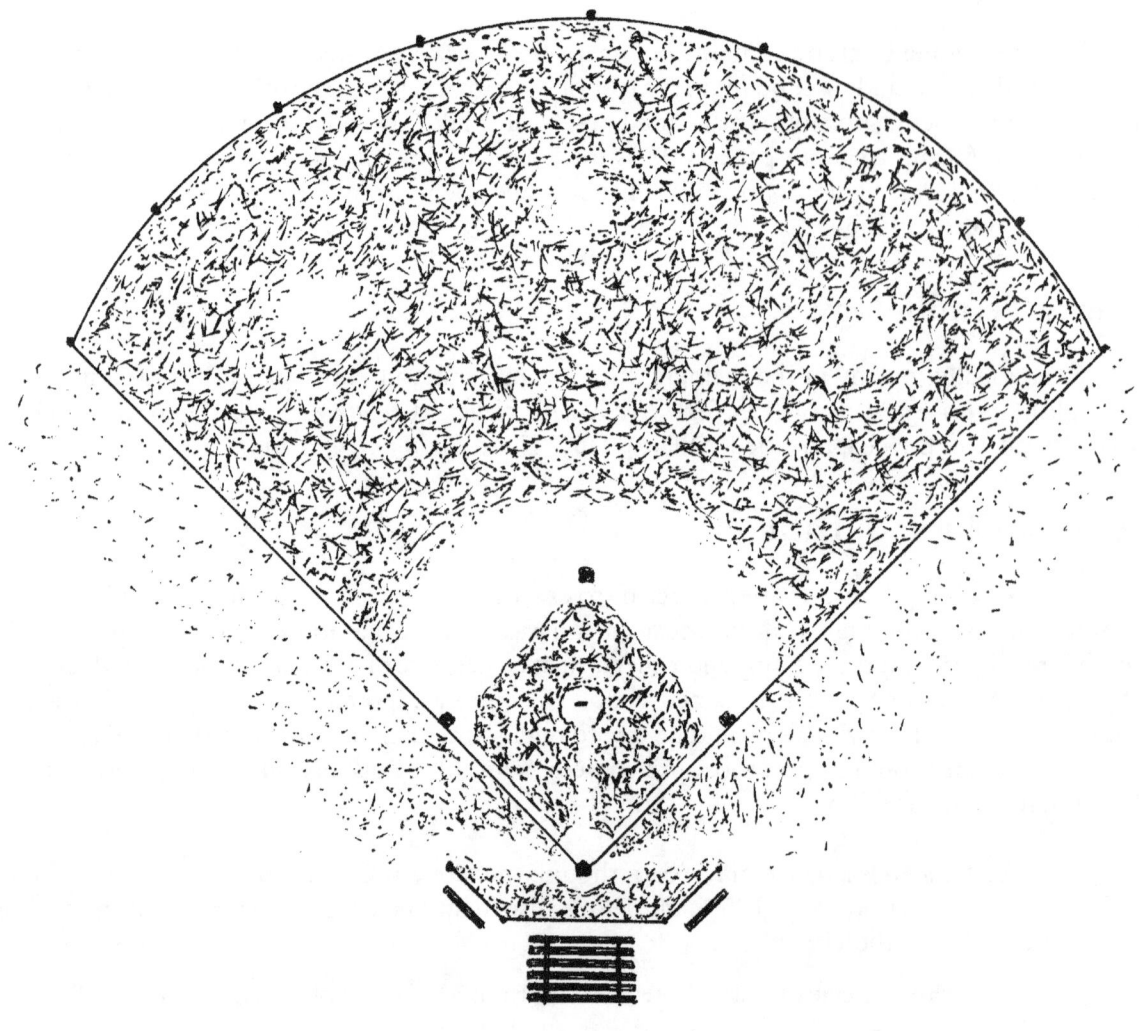

Figure 9.4. "Baseball in April" is the title of two works by Gary Soto, one a personal recollection from *Living up the Street*, the other a piece of autobiographical fiction and the title story of **Baseball in April and Other Stories**. Illus. by John Stansfield.

LEARNING HORIZONS

Literature Aloud Experiences

◆ *BARE-KNUCKLES POETRY READING*

Level: Grades four to eight and above.

Student Learning Opportunities: Cooperation; Selection of poetry; Preparation of material; Presentation.

Whether Gary Soto's poems are intended for young or older readers, their properties are the same—personal, hard-edged, clean as bone, sharply observant of living things. Even when Soto's words caress, warm, tickle, or enfold, the hands that shape them seem scarred and tattooed, like the knuckles of one of his short-story characters. Gary Soto poetry is bare-knuckles poetry. Sometimes bared-soul poetry, too, though not always. Like a beam of light spotlighting the uniqueness of an otherwise familiar object, Soto's poetry and prose highlight the fact that life, though often a struggle, can hold surprising happiness. Gary Soto makes strong connections with young people and adults through his writing.

Read the poems of Gary Soto aloud: Like most poetry, it only comes fully alive when read that way. Poetry readings of forthright poets, like Soto, are not for the weak-willed. They are for brave hearts.

Selection: Many excellent anthologies of poetry exist from which students and teachers may choose a poem or poems for reading aloud. Thematic anthologies offer age-appropriate selections to match individual interests, such as sports, adventure, and nature. Books by individual poets, literature textbooks, and original poetry (see **Under the Influence of Poetry**, this chapter) provide other sources. Whatever the source, there are three keys to selecting the right poem:

1. The performer must really *identify* with and like the poem.
2. The poem must make sense and *sound good* when read aloud. Some may not (acrostic poetry, for example).
3. The performer must master the *language and content* of the poem to share it well with the audience. Solo or ensemble performers may present the readings, depending on the requirements of the poem and the performers' creativity.

Consult with individual students to determine if the poetry they are considering matches all three keys to selection and is appropriate in length and content for classroom performance.

Rehearsal: Preparation is simple, but essential. Have students read the poem aloud at least 10 times. At first, it may sound different each time. When the delivery of the poem sounds nearly the same with each reading and the performer feels comfortable with it, it's ready for performance. Other than perhaps a prop to complement the poem, no costumes, stage movement, stage scenery, or other theatrical trappings are necessary. In fact, they may detract from the simple, bare-knuckles feel of the performance.

Performance: As with other **Literature Aloud Experiences**, student performance, with its complex of educational and life-skill benefits, is a desired outcome. Begin with simple in-classroom performances. Integrating adult performers into the event provides for excellent role-modeling.

Extensions: Presentation options range from multiclass or school assembly programs to evening family performances and touring in the community. There are often regularly scheduled, open poetry readings at libraries, universities, and coffee houses in which students may want to participate.

Teacher Evaluation Opportunities: Cooperation; Adherence to Selection keys; Rehearsal; Presentation.

Language Arts Experiences

❖ UNDER THE INFLUENCE OF POETRY

Level: Grades four to eight.

Student Learning Opportunities: Poetry reading; Self-expression; Oral interpretation of poetry; Writing poetry; Six-Trait Writing—Ideas, Voice, Organization, Word Choice, Conventions.

Background: If we let it, poetry can have a powerful influence in our lives. For Gary Soto, poetry represents a major tool for self-expression, for interpreting a sometimes-crazy world. It provided him with means and motive for much of his education. Through poetry, Soto shows us the cultural, if not economic, wealth of his childhood. Writing and teaching poetry and prose have also provided him with a well-deserved measure of professional and monetary success. Gary Soto is a poet worthy of emulation by students.

Basics:
1. Read aloud and have students read several of Gary Soto's poems from *Neighborhood Odes*, *Canto Familiar*, *A Fire in My Hands*, and other volumes. Also share with them the "Foreword" and "Questions and Answers About Poetry" from *A Fire in My Hands*.

2. In discussion, highlight elements of Soto's free verse:
   - Short in length of both line and poem, lean in style.
   - Without rhyme and meter, using mostly simple sentence structure.
   - Often conversational, and occasionally confessional.
   - Detailed in description, involving many sensory images.
   - Titles that often hint at the poem's meaning.
   - Rooted in personal experience and memory, although not always autobiographical.

3. Ask students to select a favorite Soto poem(s) whose style they can emulate in free-verse poetry and have them create their own poems. The subject matter should be of the student's own choosing.

4. Upon completion of writing and revision, have students share their poems aloud.

Extensions:
1. Explore and discuss the writing of other poets. There are many fine poems for young people among the works of John Ciardi, e. e. cummings, Kenneth Koch, Naomi Shihab Nye, and many others. Have students write poems in emulation of their styles.

2. Have them write more free verse or other types of poems in their own style and content.

3. Ask students to share poems, original and otherwise, at a Bare-Knuckles Poetry Reading (see **Literature Aloud Experiences**, this chapter).

Teacher Evaluation Opportunities: Free-verse poetry emulating Soto; Free-verse poetry emulating other poets; Original free-verse poems; Participation in discussions and oral sharing of poetry; Use of Six-Trait Writing techniques.

❖ TRANSFORMING AUTOBIOGRAPHY INTO AUTOBIOGRAPHICAL FICTION

Level: Grades four to eight.

Student Learning Opportunities: Reading; Text analysis; Oral interpretation of prose; Narrative writing; Six-Trait Writing—Ideas, Organization, Voice, Word Choice, Sentence Fluency, Conventions.

Background: An excellent example of adapting writing to fit differing literary needs is found in Gary Soto's two versions of his story, "Baseball in April." The version found in *Living up the Street: Narrative Recollections*, published in 1985, is autobiographical. With a few distinct changes, Soto transforms the story to autobiographical fiction as the title story for *Baseball in April and Other Stories*, published in 1990. Identifying and analyzing these changes assists students in making adaptations in their own writing for various needs and audiences.

Basics:
1. Briefly discuss with students the differences between autobiography, the recounting of personal experience in the first person, and autobiographical fiction, incorporating personal experiences and details in a fictional work.

2. At one sitting, have students first read Gary Soto's short story "Baseball in April" from *Living up the Street*, and then the version from *Baseball in April and Other Stories*. Discuss a few of the differences between the opening pages of each version.

3. Using the **Transforming Autobiography into Autobiographical Fiction** form, figure 9.5, page 210, ask students to record and analyze the changes in the text Soto makes to adapt "Baseball in April" from autobiography to autobiographical fiction. Discuss the examples given on the form with the students before they begin.

Extensions:
1. Have students write a short autobiographical story of one to two pages in length. (See **Learning Horizons: Recollection**, chapter 2, for pre-writing procedure.)

2. Have them transform the autobiographical story to autobiographical fiction, making either substantial or minimal changes, as appropriate.

3. Ask students to share both versions of their stories aloud with others.

Teacher Evaluation Opportunities: Transforming Autobiography to Autobiographical Fiction form; Student autobiography; Student autobiographical fiction; Oral presentation of stories; Use of Six-Trait Writing techniques.

TRANSFORMING AUTOBIOGRAPHY INTO AUTOBIOGRAPHICAL FICTION

Your Task:

1. Compare the autobiographical version with the autobiographical fiction version of the story "Baseball in April" by Gary Soto.

2. On this form, find and record some of the changes Soto makes to create the autobiographical fiction version of the story. Include the page number or numbers from *Baseball in April and Other Stories* and your own brief description of what changed.

PAGE NUMBER(S)   WHAT CHANGED IN AUTOBIOGRAPHICAL FICTION?

Examples:

All Pages   Soto changed from first-person to third-person narrator.

Page 46   Rick and Gary become Michael and Jesse.

Figure 9.5. Transforming Autobiography into Autobiographical Fiction.

❖ POINT OF VIEW: WRITING LIKE A BULLY

Level: Grades six to eight.

Student Learning Opportunities: Reading; Discussion; Behavioral analysis; Imaginative writing: Six-Trait Writing—Ideas, Voice, Word Choice.

Background: Nobody likes to be bullied. Yet bullying behavior is a fact of childrens' lives and sometimes of adults' lives, too. For those who are victims of it, it is often hard to understand. In the chapter, "Fear," from *Living up the Street: Narrative Recollections*, Gary Soto clearly recognizes both sides of a bullying situation he encountered as a fifth grader, even while writing from his own perspective as a victim. But how would a bully write about such an experience? Writing from the bully's point-of-view and coming to better understand bullying are the objects of this lesson.

Basics:
1. Read aloud or have students read the chapter, "Fear," from *Living up the Street*. Note the **Touchy Terminology**, *cabron* in Spanish, in paragraph one of the story.

2. Discuss the stated or potential reasons for the bullying behavior of Frankie T. and Mr. Koligian in the story. Discuss how Gary Soto responded to the bullying advances of Frankie T. Ask for volunteers to briefly describe bullying situations they have experienced, without naming any of the parties involved other than themselves. What reasons, if any, can they give for the bully's behavior? Can other students suggest additional reasons?

3. Have students write a fictional two- to five-paragraph, imaginative story about a bullying situation from the bully's point of view. Rather than dwelling only on the potential mayhem involved, ask them to explain, somewhere in the narrative, the reason or reasons for the bully's behavior that motivates the conflict.

4. After revision and upon completion of the stories, ask for volunteers to share them aloud with the class for consideration and further discussion.

Extensions:
1. Find other age-appropriate literature dealing with bullying behavior to share with the students or for them to read independently. Discuss them, as desired. See **Resources**, below.

2. Hold a culminating discussion, soliciting the students' explanations for bullying's consequences and motivations. Discuss appropriate actions to take should students find themselves being bullied.

Teacher Evaluation Opportunities: Discussions; Story from a bully's point-of-view; Oral sharing of stories.

Selected Resources on Bullying: There is a sizable list of recent nonfiction, fiction, and video resources dealing with bullies and bullying, including:

Nonfiction

Paulsen, Gary. *My Life in Dog Years.* New York: Delacorte Press, 1988.
    Parts of the well-known writer's life are retold through his relationships with his dogs, including one that protected him from bullying. 137 pages.

Romain, Trevor. *Bullies Are a Pain in the Brain.* Minneapolis: Free Spirit, 1997.
    A humorous look at a serious subject, dealing with bullying behavior. 105 pages.

Yee, John William. *The Bully Buster Book*, Streetproofing for Kids Series. Toronto: Outgoing Press, 1997.
    This 124-page guide discusses how to prevent bullying and school violence.

Fiction

Capote, Truman. *The Thanksgiving Visitor.* Illustrated by Beth Peck. New York: Alfred A. Knopf, 1996.
    Advice from a Thanksgiving guest helps an Alabama boy in the 1930s deal with a school bully.

Nickle, John. *The Ant Bully.* New York: Scholastic, 1999.
    Though this is a juvenile picture book, older readers will appreciate the story. The message is too good to miss (and Gary Soto would love it!). Lucas is pulled into an ant colony he has been tormenting.

Yep, Laurence. *Cockroach Cooties.* New York: Hyperion Books for Children, 2000.
    And speaking of insects, Teddy and little brother Bobby plan to use bugs to defeat the school bully.

Video Resources

Dealing with Bullies, Troublemakers, and Dangerous Situations, Peace Talks Series. Produced and directed by Jim Watson, 26 minutes, color. San Francisco and Plainview, NY: HeartLand Media, 1997. Distributed by the Bureau for At-Risk Youth. Videocassette.
    Michael Pritchard talks with a teen panel about the reasons for violence and preventing it.

Social Studies Experiences

❖ AN ANTI-ACTIVITY

Level: Grades four to eight.

Student Learning Opportunities: Personal expression; Discussion; Behavioral analysis; Six-Trait Writing—Ideas, Organization, Word Choice; Narrative writing.

Background: Kids don't just say the darnedest things, they sometimes do them. The consequences of their actions range from kind and funny to cruel and catastrophic. As children, Gary Soto and his siblings were no exception to the rule of childhood unpredictability. In *Living up the Street: Narrative Recollections,* Soto honestly, nonjudgmentally portrays their frequent mean-spiritedness. They were hard on pets, on playmates, on possessions, on houses, on each other, and especially hard on ants. This Anti-Activity (or "Ant"i-Activity, in the Soto childrens' case) doesn't ask much, just a simple and (if we can be as forthright as

Soto) potentially far-reaching discussion on two topics in which young people are often deeply involved and invest a great deal of time, energy, and worry—being mean and being kind.

Basics:
1. Read aloud or have students read the first chapter, "Being Mean," from Gary Soto's *Living up the Street*. Discuss a few of the things Soto calls mean. What do students perceive as the reasons for these actions? Why do they think Soto wrote about them?

2. Share your own and ask student volunteers to share their own personal stories about doing mean things in childhood. Talk about reasons for the behavior. What consequences resulted from the action?

3. Share your own and ask student volunteers to share their own personal stories about doing kind things in childhood. Talk about reasons for the behavior. What consequences resulted from the action?

4. Discuss what conclusions can be drawn from the personal stories about mean and kind behaviors. Categorize student and teacher responses to bring meaning and resolution to the discussion. For example, try categories such as, "I'd Never Do That Again," "I'd Do That Again in a Second," "Hard Lessons Learned," "One of the Smartest Things I've Ever Done," or "If I Knew Then What I Know Now."

Extensions:
1. Have students develop autobiographical short stories on the topic "Being Kind" or "Being Mean" out of their responses from the discussion.

Teacher Evaluation Opportunities: Participation in discussion; Autobiographical short stories, use of Six-Trait Writing techniques.

◆ THE TIME OF OUR LIVES

Level: Grades four to eight.

Student Learning Opportunities: Personal and family research; Graphic, oral, and/or written project; Project presentation; Narrative writing; Expository writing; Six-trait Writing—Ideas, Organization, Voice, Word Choice, Sentence Fluency, Conventions.

Background: In the chapter titled, "The Savings Book," from *Living up the Street: Narrative Recollections*, Gary Soto uses the deposits and debits from his old bankbook to measure and describe a portion of his young life. Using an external benchmark, like a bankbook, can be an excellent measure of personal and family history that young people can explore.

Basics:
1. Read aloud or have students read "The Savings Book" from *Living up the Street*. Discuss the chapter's content, time span, and how Soto uses the information from the bankbook to develop his themes: personal history, saving, spending, and the impact of poverty on his outlook.

2. Students identify an external benchmark they would like to use to display the passage of time during a segment of their personal and/or family history. Some possible benchmarks include:

> Childrens' growth marks on a doorframe
>
> A timeline
>
> A calendar recording events on various dates
>
> A diary or journal
>
> Hand-me-down clothes
>
> A bankbook or statement
>
> A photo album or scrapbook
>
> A season or seasons of the year
>
> Family holiday or birthday celebrations

As with Gary Soto's savings book, the chosen benchmark becomes a storytelling device tying their life story together. In addition, students identify the span of time and the significant themes their personal history presentation will cover. Have students document a benchmark, the time span, and themes in writing.

3. Give students the option to represent their personal history in one of four ways: visually, verbally, in writing, or in combinations of these three. Some examples of visual presentation are photo, video, and original illustration. Examples of verbal presentation include oral storytelling, lecture–demonstration, and dramatic reenactment. Written presentation could take the form of narrative recollections, diary entries, autobiographical fiction, or explanatory text written to accompany visual displays. After determining a preferred presentation style, students must decide how to incorporate their benchmark into the presentation as a narrative tool.

4. After students develop their personal history presentations, have them present them to teachers and classmates in the way best suited to their chosen presentation style.

Extensions:
1. Make sure students find an opportunity to deliver their presentations for parents and other family members, at home or at school. (An option for public presentation at school is an **Autobiography Alive Fair**. See **Literature Aloud**, chapter 7.)

2. Create a personal history exhibit in the school featuring the presentations so that other students and adults can view them. Verbal presentations can be audio or videotaped, providing content for a multimedia listening/viewing and reading station that highlights verbal and written personal histories. The display of visual presentations accompanies it.

Teacher Evaluation Opportunities: Personal history project—development and execution; Presentation of personal history—in school and at home; Participation in the personal history exhibit; Use of Six-Trait Writing techniques.

GARY SOTO RESOURCES

Selected Books by Soto

Soto, Gary. *Baseball in April and Other Stories.* San Diego: Harcourt Brace Jovanovich, 1990.

Short stories of fiction and autobiographical fiction written about Latino children and teenagers from California's San Joaquin Valley, Soto's childhood home. Written for intermediate grade readers and young adults, no matter what their cultural background.

——— . *Canto Familiar.* Illustrated by Annika Nelson. San Diego: Harcourt Brace & Company, 1995.

Canto Familiar, "familiar song," is a 79-page book of short poems, appropriate for elementary and middle-school students, that celebrates ordinary things, surprising things, enjoyable things, and frustrating things that give life a piquant flavor.

——— . *A Fire in My Hands.* Illustrated by James M. Cardillo. New York: Scholastic, 1990.

Sharp pictures in poetry, mostly autobiographical, especially for intermediate grade readers, young adults, and adults. Soto gives each poem a scene-setting introduction. The "Foreword" and the "Questions and Answers About Poetry" that he adds to this 64-page volume help explain important aspects of his writing process.

——— . *Jessie De La Cruz: A Profile of a United Farm Worker.* New York: Persea Books, 2000.

Jessie De La Cruz was a quietly remarkable woman. A farm worker in the fields of California's central valley for decades, she became the first woman organizer for the United Farm Workers Union, fighting for adequate pay and proper working conditions. Soto's first biography, this 128-page book, illustrated with photographs, is appropriate for young adults, ages 12 to 18, and adults.

——— . *Living up the Street: Narrative Recollections.* New York: Laurel-Leaf Books, 1992 (1985).

Not a complete autobiography of childhood and adolescence, but a series of clearly drawn sketches about growing up a Mexican American in Fresno, California. Often painfully honest, sometimes straight-facedly funny, the 167-page volume is most appropriate for middle-school readers and up, with most of the early chapters excellent for elementary students, as well.

——— . *Neighborhood Odes.* Illustrated by David Diaz. San Diego: Harcourt Brace & Company, 1992.

A collection of 21 odes to life in a Mexican American neighborhood, as seen through the eyes of children. Especially appropriate for grades four through seven.

——— . *A Summer Life.* New York: Laurel-Leaf Books, 1991 (1990).

With a style and chronological arrangement similar to *Living up the Street*, this 150-page collection of very short stories continues with lucid descriptions of characters, places, and experiences from Soto's youth and adolescence.

Electronic Resources

The Internet School Library Media Center Gary Soto Page. Available: http://falcon.jmu.edu/~ramseyil/soto.htm
(Accessed October 30, 2000).

A "full-service" Web site with Soto biography and bibliography, units and lesson plans, Hispanic and Mexican American resource materials, and lots of links to related Internet sites.

McDougal Littell Author Spotlight—Gary Soto. Available: http://www.mcdougallittell.com/lit/guest/soto/
(Accessed October 30, 2000).

A textbook publisher's Web site. Site contains a question-and-answer session with Soto that includes student questions, a partial bibliography, worksheets for Soto stories in their textbooks, and links to information about other Young Adult authors.

The Official Gary Soto Website. Available: http://www.garysoto.com (Accessed October 30, 2000).

Administered by Gary Soto & Friends, the Web site includes photos, updates on Soto's latest projects, and a list of his awards and honors. Most interesting is the catalog and order form enabling Soto fans to order books direct from the author. Support Your Local Poet (and Writer)!

Teacher Cyberguide: Short Stories by Gary Soto. Available: http://www.sdcoe.k12.ca.us/SCORE/soto/sototg .html (Accessed October 30, 2000).

Five student activities, keyed to California education standards, involving online research (links listed) and a variety of writing tasks: short-story writing, speech writing, preparing a biographic sketch, storyboarding, and letter writing. The activities grow out of Soto's *Baseball in April and Other Stories* and *Living up the Street: Narrative Recollections*, as well as Hispanic art and customs and the life of United Farm Workers leader Cesar Chavez.

Video Resources

Gary Soto. Color, 60 minutes. Santa Fe, NM: Lannan Foundation, 1995. Videocassette.

Gary Soto is interviewed by Alejandro Morales and he reads from his poetry in this video. Most appropriate for older teenagers and adults.

The Bike. John Kelly and Gary Soto. Color. Berkeley, CA: Gary Soto Productions, 1991. Videocassette.

The video is adapted from an autobiographical sketch of the same title, found in Soto's *A Summer Life*. It is a story that drives all ages through a great range of emotions, in only three pages.

The Pool Party. John Kelly and Gary Soto. Color. Berkeley, CA: Gary Soto Productions, 1993. Videocassette.

Carnegie Award-winning film based on Soto's book of the same title. A perfect story for and about adolescents.

According to Gary Soto, neither *The Bike* nor *The Pool Party* videos are commercially available, as of this writing. However, they may be available for viewing through library systems. Don't forget to check out the possibility of interlibrary loan.

LAURENCE YEP

Born June 14, 1948 in San Francisco, California. Childhood and young adult autobiography describes California.

Figure 10.1. Laurence Yep.

AN APPRECIATION OF THE WRITER

When I wrote, I went from being a puzzle to a puzzle solver. I could reach into the box of rags that was my soul and begin stitching them together. Moreover, I could try out different combinations to see which one pleased me the most.

Laurence Yep from *The Lost Garden*, chapter 8

When you read *The Lost Garden*, an autobiography by Laurence Yep, you can understand why so many of his fictional characters are outsiders. He sees himself as one, too. A Chinese American born in America, Laurence is definitely not Chinese, but as a child he is often made to feel not quite American by others. Awkward son in an athletic family; growing up in a mostly African American neighborhood rather than San Francisco's Chinatown, often tied to his chores at the family store when other children were at play—all reminded him that he was different. Yep even titles one of the chapters, "The Outsider."

But *The Lost Garden* is not just about the experience of alienation, of being on the outside. It portrays Yep's growing understanding of himself, his family, and cultural history. Most important, the book recounts how Yep acted on his feelings of alienation, how he solved his own identity issues, as a young man and, simultaneously, as a writer. Laurence Yep's characters may be outsiders, but they, like their author, find some satisfaction in their life situations, while resisting the pressure to become an insider. It is no surprise that most of Yep's books have been written for—and are very popular with—adolescents who are often struggling with issues of identity, alienation, and insider–outsider social conflict.

Laurence Yep has been an exceedingly prolific writer, both in number of publications and in their literary variety. As of this writing, he has published nearly 50 books. His publications encompass historic, realistic, and science fiction; mystery, fantasy, and retellings from folklore; short stories, novels, and plays, penned over more than 30 years. He has received numerous awards, including two Newbery Honor Book citations for *Dragonwings* (1975) and *Dragon's Gate* (1993).

In any subculture there are many stories that go unheard and many remarkable people who go unnoticed by the dominant culture in a society. Laurence Yep's writings perform the valuable role of presenting to the world previously little-known elements of the Asian American experience in the West and elsewhere. At the same time, his work explores themes universal to all humanity. These are roles admirably suited for such a talented outsider.

IN HIS OWN WORDS

Throughout all of his childhood and adolescence, Laurence Yep toiled in his family store, called La Conquista. Though tiresome, the daily tasks helped him learn good work habits, which carried over into his discipline as a writer. La Conquista also gave him the opportunity to regularly observe an endless variety of people and their behavior. He describes Jimmy, the Italian beer delivery driver, who called stupid-acting people (or anyone with whom he disagreed) salamis. There was kind Mr. Woodrow who laughed loudly at Yep's niece Franny's daily joke, even though it was always the same one. There was Cal, the cutthroat rival store owner, and friendly Saul the Junkman. Yep also records the physical toll the store took on his parents. The power of all these observations enriches his writing.

In this excerpt from chapter 2 of *The Lost Garden*, Laurence Yep records some of the smells, the sights, and the tasks connected with the store (see page 220):

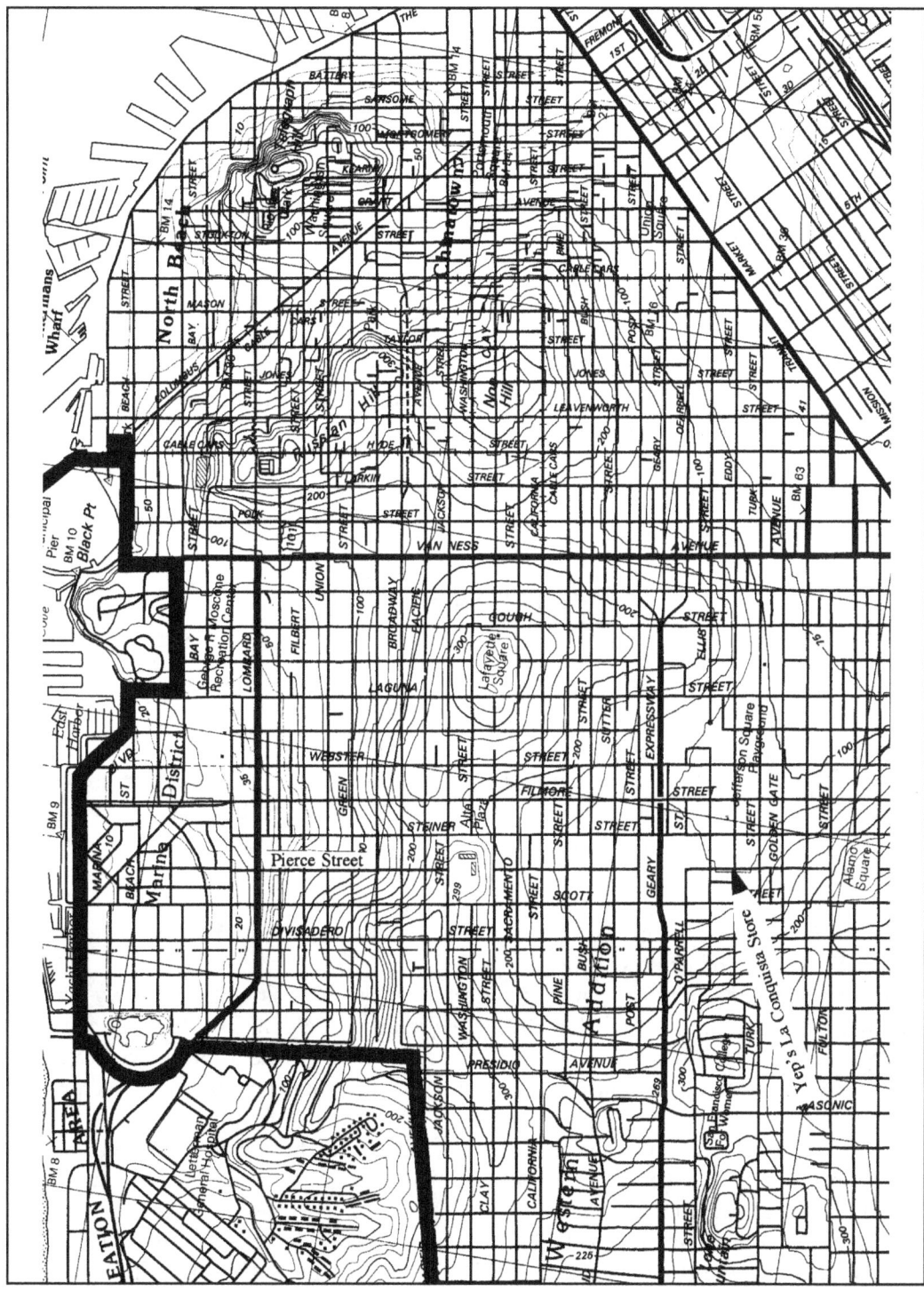

Figure 10.2. Contemporary map of a portion of San Francisco, California, showing the neighborhoods where Laurence Yep spent much of his youth. Public domain, courtesy of U.S. Geological Survey.

Note: The following is excerpted as punctuated and spelled in the original manuscript.

> The one thing that ruled my family's life was our grocery store. I can still smell it. Even today, if I smell old plaster, I feel almost as if I am back in our old storeroom where the plaster was crumbling off the wooden laths. Or if I smell the coppery odor of liver, I think of washing out the bloody porcelain pans in which we used to display that kind of meat. If I smell old dollar bills, I can imagine myself back in the dark, quiet store, helping my mother put away the day's receipts.
>
> A small grocery store is like a big beast that must be continually fed and cared for. Cans, packages, and bottles have to be put on shelves to take the place of things sold, produce like greens and celery have to be nursed along to keep them fresh as long as possible, and there are hundreds of other details that the customers never notice—unless they aren't done. In a small, family-owned store, certain chores must be done at a specific time each day. There is no choice. . . . My chief job was feeding the beast.

End of excerpted manuscript.

THE WRITER'S LIFE

Living over the Store

Using money saved and borrowed, Thomas and Franche (Lee) Yep bought the La Conquista store near the end of World War II. With their son Thomas, known as Spike, they moved into the Pearl Apartments above the small grocery, at the corner of Pierce and Eddy streets in the ethnically diverse Western Addition section of San Francisco. A second son, Laurence, was born June 14, 1948. As with his parents and brother, the store became the center of Laurence's life. Running a family grocery business is physically taxing and endlessly time-consuming work. In his autobiography, *The Lost Garden*, Laurence Yep compares a store to a beast constantly in need of care and feeding. The Yeps were the beast's keepers.

With her eldest son in school and early afternoon business slow at the store, Franche took little Laurence on excursions in Jezebel, a 1939 Chevrolet, to Golden Gate Park, Ocean Beach, the zoo, the aquarium, or to visit relatives in the Chinatown section of San Francisco. Even standing still, Jezebel served well as a play vehicle for the boy's imaginary journeys by rocket, stagecoach, and boat.

When old enough for kindergarten, Laurence, like Spike before him, was sent to St Mary's Grammar School, a Catholic school in Chinatown. Unlike most of his classmates from Chinatown, he spoke little Chinese, which made him feel different. (Both Thomas and Franche Yep spoke Chinese and English, but grew up and worked as adults in primarily English-speaking environments.) When after-school Chinese classes began at St. Mary's, fourth-grader Laurence disliked the attitude of his teacher so much that he vowed to pass the class, but not really learn Chinese. He succeeded. He felt uncomfortable with the opinion expressed by many native-born Chinese in Chinatown, including his teacher, that American-born Chinese were lazy and disrespectful of tradition. He knew he should respect the "old-timers," but they made him unsure of who he really was, Chinese or American.

As he grew older, experience taught Laurence that although he considered himself to be an American, others did not think him so, mostly because of his appearance. In neighborhood games of war, he was always the "all-purpose Asian," always the Japanese or North Korean enemy, not the American G.I. Unlike many of their relatives, Thomas and Franche Yep's family did not live in or near Chinatown with its network of family and community connections. In the mid-1950s, their neighborhood was mostly torn down and rebuilt with high-rise government housing. The former racial and ethnic mix of the area became predominantly African American. The Yeps lost many of their old friends and customers. Though they eventually gained new ones, it was a long time before the housing projects were finally completed and occupied. Racial tension and incidents of vandalism increased in the unsettled neighborhood.

In the meantime, Laurence lost his playmates. He worried that he was being punished for something he had done to drive his friends away. He resorted more to reading and imaginary games of his own. The boy was too awkward and slow to win friends through athletics, the way his parents had when they were young. Bouts with asthma kept him indoors for extended periods.

Puzzle Solver

As Laurence Yep approached his teenage years, he looked inside his family for answers to his identity puzzle. He kept a file of family stories he heard at get-togethers. Yep also looked outside for answers—to the Catholic Church, of which he became a member, and to literature. His church membership led him to numerous misadventures as an altar boy and, eventually, to St. Ignatius, a Jesuit high school on Stanyan Street. His interest in literature, especially fantasy at first, grew from the reading his mother did for him while he was laid up with asthma attacks. Trips to the Chinatown branch of the public library became a regular routine.

St. Ignatius exposed Laurence to something startling—and very different from St. Mary's—an almost completely white student body. Still, the Jesuit faculty, in consort with the growing Civil Rights movement of the 1960s, urged their students to be conscious of racism and avoid racist behavior.

Laurence was placed in the honors class in his freshman year of high school. Among these hard-working, creative students, good grades were important; a means of earning respect. Diligence in school tasks meant something else important for Yep. His parents excused him from the drudgery of chores in the store during the school year.

Many excellent instructors, Jesuits and lay people, taught the honors students at St Ignatius. Some student favorites were the teachers of physics and chemistry. Laurence and his classmates developed an affinity for explosive compounds, derived from the chemistry lab. Small-scale bombs erupted around the school, until Father principal experienced the sting of explosive paste on his doorknob. Then the explosions stopped.

Yep's interest in science ran parallel to his interest in science fiction, developed during elementary school. Robert Heinlein and Andre Norton were favorite authors. During his senior year, Father John Becker was Yep's English teacher. Becker taught English by asking his students to write in many styles and forms, often imitating well-known writers. He also challenged some of them, including Laurence, to submit their own articles for publication in national magazines. All tried, though none were accepted. But, after the experience, Yep discovered that he was bitten by the writing bug. He found that writing original stories was as much fun as bomb-making. (Yep dedicates *The Lost Garden* to Father Becker.)

Writing pushed Yep toward further self-discovery. From the confusing jumble of pieces he perceived himself to be—too American for Chinatown, too Chinese for his neighborhood, too awkward for his athletic family—patterns emerged. Yep states in *The Lost Garden* that writing helped him move from feeling like the scattered pieces of a puzzle to a solution of that puzzle.

His interest in writing drew him to the college of journalism at Marquette University in Milwaukee in 1966. For the California kid, Wisconsin was a real shocker. Winter with snow that turned quickly to treacherous ice, few Chinese in the community, and a student body even more predominantly white than St. Ignatius made Laurence feel homesick and alienated. And, journalism school taught him that his real interest lay in fictional, not factual, writing. That winter Yep wrote and submitted his first science fiction short story, "The Selchey Kids." To his surprise, a science fiction magazine printed it, paying him a penny a word. The young writer's career in fiction had begun.

A mutual interest in writing and literature fostered Yeps' friendship with New Yorker Joanne Ryder, the editor of the campus literary magazine. She shared her love of children's literature, introducing him to the *Chronicles of Narnia*, *Winnie the Pooh*, and *Alice in Wonderland*. Three years later, Joanne, working as an editor in a publisher's children's department, encouraged Laurence to write *Sweetwater*, a science fiction novel for children and his first book. Their friendship grew and they eventually married. Today, Joanne Ryder is a successful and remarkably prolific writer, working in fiction and nonfiction, especially nature subjects, for children. She and Laurence live in the San Francisco Bay area.

After two years at Marquette, Yep transferred closer to home to the University of California at Santa Cruz, graduating in 1970. He received his Ph.D. in English from the State University of New York at Buffalo in 1975, the same year his second novel, *Dragonwings*, was published.

Figure 10.3 Dragons play a substantial role in Chinese folklore and in the work of Laurence Yep. Illus. by John Stansfield.

Dragonwings earned its author much deserved praise. Its prose has the clarity of first light on a mountain. Its seamless blend of fiction and factual history suggests that a great amount of research went into its creation. *Dragonwings* delves into a little-known historical reality. For more than 75 years, a subculture of Chinese men existed in North America, separated from their families in China, most often working arduously to send money back home. Like Moon Shadow in *Dragonwings*, Laurence Yep's own father was part of this story, coming from China to join his businessman father in San Francisco in 1923. Various aspects of this remarkable mass migration are explored in other Yep books, as well. Another trait found in *Dragonwings*, the voice of the first-person narrator, is common in many of Yep's later books.

Laurence Yep has undertaken a challenging task. He has embraced a number of roles for himself as a writer. Creator of highly imaginative fantasy realms; commentator on social and historical issues; collector and reteller of folktales; explorer in personal, family, and cultural legacy; examiner of the human relations of insiders and outsiders—each role requires extensive research, thought, and diligence in writing to master successfully. Beyond these, perhaps Yep's finest achievement is as an interpreter of Chinese, Chinese American, and other Asian cultures for North American audiences, especially young people. The puzzle solver continues to lay out the pieces of the puzzle for us, and for himself, to assemble into new portraits of the past, the present, and the future.

TEACHING ADVICE FOR LAURENCE YEP

Autobiographical Writings

Although this chapter focuses primarily on *The Lost Garden*, it is fascinating to discover how real elements of Yep's life show up quite clearly in his fiction, especially his early work. For example, he integrates some of his childhood experiences and the family store into *Sea Glass*; he blends characteristics of his grandmother with her Chinatown neighborhood and apartment into *Child of the Owl*; and he models Windrider, the father in *Dragonwings*, after his own kite-making father. Yep's work exemplifies the adage often given to young writers, "Write what you know."

Touchy Terminology

In chapter 3, "The Neighborhood," there is a brief reference to topless clubs and dancing.

Yep on His Writing and the Writing Process

With an eye toward middle grade and older students, Yep spices the *The Lost Garden* with information about his books, his creative process, and excellent tips on the writing process for young writers. Because this advice, even without the rest of the book's content, might enhance a writing curriculum, the excerpts that contain Yep's guidance for the writing process are listed and briefly described here:

Chapter 2, pages 21 to 23. The writer's routine and story ideas.

Chapter 3, pages 28 and 29. Observing human behavior as a tool for writing.

Chapter 8, pages 90 to 92. Learning to write by imitation and writing what you know.

Chapter 10, pages 103 to 106. Memories as seeds for writing and how story ideas grow.

Chapter 10, page 106. Narrative voice.

LEARNING HORIZONS

Literature Aloud Experiences

◆ READERS THEATER

Level: Grades four and higher.

Student Learning Opportunities: Cooperation; Literature source and excerpt selection; Script development; Rehearsal; Presentation.

Background: As a child, Laurence Yep fought bouts with asthma that sometimes confined him to his bedroom. His mother, Franche, often read to the bedridden boy. Through her oral presentation of the Oz books, Laurence discovered a love of fantasy. He searched the public library for more of it to read on his own, expanding his interests to science fiction. As he proceeded to high school and college, what Yep loved to read became what he attempted to write. His first published story, "The Selchey Kids," and novel, *Sweetwater*, were science fiction, as are a number of his later works for young adults and adults.

Young people can creatively celebrate their favorite books and authors through their own oral presentation of literature—readers theater presentations. At the same time, they explore new relationships with familiar text—selection, script writing, and performance—which go beyond the primary act of reading. Readers theater, the "open book" form of dramatics, is simple to stage effectively. Ensemble performers, often including a narrator, read from a rehearsed script, usually without costumes, stage movement, and stage scenery or other theatrical trappings. What is central to a readers theater presentation is the literature, and the performers love of it, which they share with their audience.

Selection There are many excellent collections of readers theater scripts in print for performers of varied age and ability levels. Most of these scripts are based on folklore, history, or literary sources. Examples include *Readers Theatre for Young Adults: Scripts and Script Development* and *Readers Theatre for Children* by Kathy Howard Latrobe and Mildred Knight (Englewood, CO: Teacher Ideas Press, 1989 and 1990, respectively), *Readers Theatre for American History* by Anthony D. Fredericks (Englewood, CO: Teacher Ideas Press, 2001), and *Social Studies Readers Theatre: Scripts and Script Development* by Mildred Knight Laughlin, Peggy Tubbs Black, and Margery Kirby Loberg (Englewood, CO: Teacher Ideas Press, 1991). If time for this project is limited, selections from these anthologies enable students to move directly to the rehearsal and performance stages.

If more project time is available, student development of original scripts from a favorite piece of literature offers a great opportunity for skill-building—text analysis, script content decisions, script writing, creation of additional narration as needed, application of writing conventions, and more. Enhanced creativity and pride of authorship are major benefits, as well.

Selection: Have individuals select an excerpt from a favorite fiction or nonfiction book. The excerpt should tell a coherent story by itself, have opportunities for two or more readers to participate, and be readable in a maximum of approximately 15 minutes. Before finalizing selections, consult with each student on the text, discussing its content, its appropriateness for the intended audience, and how it would work best for ensemble performance. For example, does the selection have dialogue for several characters and what role, if any, would a narrator play? Revise selections as necessary.

Script Writing: Using a theater or readers theater script as an example, familiarize students with the format into which they will recast their literary selections. In addition to title, author, and student adaptor credits, the format should include setting, character list, and, optionally, stage directions. Have students rewrite the literary selections in script form, using as much of the author's original narration and dialogue as possible. As necessary for clarity, ask them to add dialogue for the narrator to introduce or end the script, or to explain details of plot not covered in the selection.

Rehearsal: Have scriptwriters recruit additional cast members, as needed. Rehearsals require reading practice, not memorization. Selections are ready for performance when script readings are fluid; the performance tells a clear, effective story; and any staging logistics—lights, music, props—are smoothly integrated into the overall presentation.

Performance: As with other **Literature Aloud Experience**, "the play's the thing." Student performance, with its complex of educational and life-skill benefits, is the desired outcome. Integrating adult performers into the readers theater presentations provides an excellent role model, as well.

Extensions: Presentation options range from multiclass or school assembly programs to evening family performances and touring in the community. Opportunities may exist at libraries, senior citizen centers and residences, and book discussion groups.

Teacher Evaluation Opportunities: Cooperation; Material selection; Script development; Rehearsal; Presentation.

Language Arts Experiences

◈ SENSE + MEMORY

Level: Grades four to eight.

Student Learning Opportunities: Personal memory; Reading aloud; Descriptive writing; Six-Trait Writing—Ideas, Word Choice, Sentence Fluency, Voice.

Background: The opening paragraph of chapter 2 in *The Lost Garden* presents a wonderful example of writing to the senses, in this case the sense of smell. The odors of old plaster, beef liver, and rumpled dollars stir Laurence Yep's recollections of his family's store. The senses prime a person's memory pump. They help us vividly revisit things, places, and people from our past. Senses provide potent prompts for writing, too.

Basics:
1. Read aloud the opening paragraph of chapter 2 in *The Lost Garden*. Point out how Yep uses his memory of smells to begin a description of place, La Conquista store. (Also note how the opening sentence, unrelated to smell, sets the theme for the chapter.) Share a personal example of a memory prompted by the sense of smell. For example, the tangy, sour smell of vinegar fills a kitchen during an Easter egg–dyeing session. Ask students to briefly share their own smell-related memories, pleasant or unpleasant.

2. Using the **Sense + Memory = Descriptive Writing** sheet, figure 10.4, page 227, have students compose a paragraph describing a person, place, or thing based on the smell or smells associated with it. Share the paragraphs aloud.

Extensions:
1. Using another **Sense + Memory = Descriptive Writing** sheet, ask students to write another descriptive paragraph using a different sense as a prompt. When revised, share them aloud.

2. Read aloud more of chapter 2 in *The Lost Garden*. As Laurence Yep does, have students incorporate a Sense + Memory paragraph into a longer, more varied description of a person, place, or thing from their memories.

Teacher Evaluation Opportunities: Sense + Memory = Descriptive Writing sheet; Descriptive paragraph based on another sense; Expanded description of person, place, or thing.

◆ METAPHOR—A CHINESE PUZZLE

Level: Grades four to eight.

Student Learning Opportunities: Discussion; Six-Trait Writing—Ideas, Word Choice.

Background: Metaphor is like a Chinese puzzle. Like a puzzle, metaphor holds something surprising and rewarding inside, even if it's sometimes hard to open. A metaphor involves direct comparison of one object or idea with another dissimilar one, without using comparative words (as or like, etc.) as in a simile. From the first page of *The Lost Garden* to the closing paragraph, Laurence Yep uses a number of powerful metaphors to explain to his readers his own adolescent self-discovery process and that of his book characters. Even the title of the book is a metaphoric statement. Unlocking the metaphor puzzle greatly benefits students' thinking, reading, speaking, and writing abilities.

Basics:
1. Read aloud the introduction to *The Lost Garden*. Discuss with students the metaphor stated in the title and its meaning for Yep. Read from chapter 1, page one through page two, paragraph three. Discuss the ways Yep compares the owl to Casey Young, a character in his *Child of the Owl,* and to himself. Note that without directly using a metaphor, he introduces us to the human-owl metaphoric comparison—and to the theme of the book.

SENSE + MEMORY = DESCRIPTIVE WRITING

The five senses prime a person's memory pump. They help us vividly remember things, places, and people from our past. Senses provide excellent prompts for descriptive writing, too.

Your Task:

1. Choose a sense related to a memory you have about a person, place, or thing. Write the name of the sense on the line after SENSE, below.

2. After JOTLIST, below, list several sense-related words to describe the memory. Words like wail, howl, siren, roar, crackle, hiss.

3. Write a three- to five-sentence descriptive paragraph using the sense you chose to describe the person, place, or thing in your memory.

SENSE:_____

JOTLIST:_____

MY
MEMORY:_____

_____

_____

_____

_____

_____

_____

_____

_____

_____

Figure 10.4. Descriptive Writing Process.

2. Read aloud from chapter 2, page 13 through the first sentence of paragraph four, page 15. Comment to students on the store-as-beast metaphor, then finish reading that paragraph through the top of page 16. Briefly discuss the reasons that Yep calls the store a beast.

3. Ask students to locate other metaphors used on pages 23 (buildings as hills), 31 (Saul as watch dog), 70 (not a metaphor, but an important metaphoric comparison, Yep as Chinese puzzle, compared in a simile), and 91 (Yep as cloth pieces). Briefly discuss each metaphor. Note that Yep often uses metaphors to mark important text passages for the reader and to help explain complex and difficult emotional struggles. In discussion, ask students to suggest a few metaphors of their own.

4. Using the **Making Metaphors** sheet, figure 10.5, page 229, have students create and use more original metaphors.

Teacher Evaluation Opportunities: *The Lost Garden* metaphors discussion; Making Metaphors page.

Social Studies Experiences

◆ A SENSE OF PLACE—LAURENCE YEP

Level: Grades four to eight.

Student Learning Opportunities: Map analysis; Map-making; Six-Trait Writing: Word Choice.

Basics:
1. In reading *The Lost Garden*, teacher and students build a list of specific geographic places and features in San Francisco identified by Yep

2. Obtain a detailed map of the City of San Francisco. Figure 10.2 may help.

3. Have students identify locations from the text and mark them on individual or group maps. For example, Chinatown, Golden Gate Park, Ocean Beach, Eddy Street, North Beach.

4. Using the map, verbally guide students on an imaginary journey around San Francisco. Can they follow your directions? Ask students to guide other imaginary journeys.

Extensions: Though it may be challenging, ask students to trace some of the movements of Laurence Yep and his family from clues on their marked maps and in the text. Historians and writers do this kind of detective work in their attempts to re-create the past and past lives.

1. Have students create their own maps tracing the Yeps' movements.

MAKING METAPHORS

Metaphors create powerful mental pictures by comparing things that are in many ways unlike each other.

Your Task, Number One: Complete the following metaphors by filling in all or part of the blanks with your ideas. Try to come up with original metaphors; not just ones used before by someone else.

Examples: Edison <u>was a giant among inventors</u>.

The sailboat <u>knifed</u> through the waves.

My brother's head is a <u>compass</u>. His hair points in every direction.

George Washington _____.
Questions for the speaker _____ down from the people in the balcony.
When it comes to free-throw shooting, my sister is _____.
Cancer _____.
The ancient car _____ in the intersection.
My neighbor makes me look tiny. He's a _____.
Hunger _____ in my stomach.
The wind _____ through the trees.
Prejudice _____.
My brother can never make up his mind. His brain _____.

Your Task, Number Two: Include your favorite sentence, above, in a three- to five-sentence paragraph. Before writing, decide if it opens, fits in the middle, or closes the paragraph.

Figure 10.5. Making Metaphors Process.

2. Have students create individual maps of what they define as their own community. Use copies of these maps to record the movements of the map-makers and their families during a defined period of time, such as a week, a month, or longer.

Teacher Evaluation Opportunities: Map of locations from *The Lost Garden*; Student-guided imaginary journeys; Map of the Yep family movements; Map of the student's community; Map of student's family movements.

❖ NATIONAL PARKS TRAVELOGUE

Level: Grades four to eight.

Student Learning Opportunities: Research; Written reporting; Oral reporting; Map-making; Graphic design; Expository writing; Six Trait Writing—Organization, Word Choice, Sentence Fluency, Conventions.

Background: As a child, Laurence Yep traveled vicariously to national parks and other natural habitats through the stories of his itchy-footed Uncle Francis, his Aunt Rachel, and their family. (See *The Lost Garden*, chapter 5, "Rambling Through America.") Francis was famous in the family for driving great distances to camp, fish, and enjoy scenic splendor. Later in life, Laurence got to visit many of those storied places in person. The national parks of the United States and Canada motivate many a visitor, young and old, to share stories of their own.

Basics:
1. Display maps of the United States and/or Canada that include national parks. Discuss with students the definition of a national park: a large area of remarkable ecological, geographic, or cultural value; set aside by a government; and managed by a park service to protect its special qualities forever for the enjoyment of people from the nation and around the world. **Note:** For the purposes of this experience, be sure to differentiate between national parks and other sites administered by the Park Services, such as national monuments, recreation areas, and historical parks and sites. These other preserves protect smaller areas and individual features. In this experience, the focus is on national parks.

2. Inquire if any of the students have visited national parks and which ones. Locate and temporarily mark those on the maps. Locate and mark the parks that teachers have visited, as well. Point out the additional unmarked national parks on the maps.

3. Have each student select a different national park on which to do research and prepare a short multimedia travelogue presentation, designed to inform others about that special place. Selection may be a park previously visited by the student or one new to them. As of this writing, there are 56 national parks in the United States and 35 in Canada.

4. Information sources for student research include libraries, atlases and encyclopedias, topical books, the Internet, and the Park Services. Each national park publishes brochures and other detailed information, available to the public upon request. Particularly helpful are the Web sites of the U.S. National Park Service (http://www.nps.gov. Accessed December 12, 2000) and Parks Canada (http://parkscanada.pch.gc.ca/. Accessed December 12, 2000), with educational material and contact information for each park.

5. Basic elements of student travelogue presentations include:

    - An overall script or outline to guide the oral travelogue.
    - A written description of the park—its location, size, natural resources and other special features; and its history, including the reason(s) for its protection as a national park.
    - Pictures or student-created illustrations of the park, drawn or projected large enough for display to a group.
    - A simple student-created map detailing the route the student takes to reach the park and important landmarks along the way, drawn or projected large enough for display to a group.

6. Ask students to present their travelogues orally to classmates, other classes, and community groups. Set a maximum time limit on presentations, if desired, that they work toward in rehearsal.

Extensions:
1. Have students supplement the travelogue fundamentals listed in **Basics**, step 5, with additional materials related to their chosen park. Maps, posters, postcards, photos, videos, CD-ROMs, memorabilia, facsimile artifacts, and other items—all add interest to the travelogues.

2. Hold a culminating discussion about national parks: future interest in visitation, careers in the Park Service, follow-up questions about specific parks, and more.

Teacher Evaluation Opportunities: Thorough research; Graphic design and illustration; Original map(s); Overall organization of travelogue; Oral presentation; Use of Six-Trait Writing techniques.

LAURENCE YEP RESOURCES

Selected Books by Yep

Yep, Laurence. *Child of the Owl*. New York: Harper & Row, 1977.
   A novel about Casey Young, the streetwise daughter of a ne'er-do-well father, who comes to live with her grandmother in San Francisco's Chinatown, discovering her Chinese heritage for the first time.

———. *Dragon's Gate*. New York: HarperCollins, 1993.
   When a deadly accident forces young Otter to leave China, he flees to the Sierra Nevada Mountains of California to join his stepfather and legendary Uncle Foxfire. This Newbery Honor Book details the arduous life of Chinese workers building a tunnel for the transcontinental railroad and is the sequel to *The Serpent's Children* and *Mountain Light*.

———. *Dragonwings*. New York: Harper & Row, 1975.
   Moon Shadow comes from China to join Windrider, his father, whom he has never met, in San Francisco in 1903. Together they struggle against poverty, prejudice, and an earthquake to make a dream of flying come true. This beautifully crafted novel, a Newbery Honor Book, is inspired by a true story of an early Chinese American aviator.

———. *The Lost Garden*. Englewood Cliffs, NJ: Julian Messner, 1991.

A finely detailed autobiography of coming of age in post–World War II San Francisco in a hard-working Chinese American family. For Yep, solving the puzzle of his own identity is the hardest work of all. Written for young adults and up, the narrative is infused with much information about his books and writing process.

———. *Sea Glass*. New York: Harper & Row, 1979.

In this semi-autobiographical novel, eighth-grader Craig Chinn moves from Chinatown to a small seaside California town. He feels like a total misfit with his schoolmates, his father, and almost everybody, until he discovers old Uncle Quail, who shows him the beauty of the ocean and its marine life.

Selected Yep Resources

Kutzer, M. Daphne, ed. *Writers of Multicultural Fiction for Young Adults: A Bio-Critical Sourcebook*. Westport, CT: Greenwood, 1996.

A teacher's reference, including Yep, among others.

McElmeel, Sharron L. *Bookpeople: A Multicultural Album*. Englewood, CO: Libraries Unlimited, 1992.

This teacher's resource book contains a unit on Laurence Yep (and 14 other authors who write or illustrate multicultural materials), including activities based in his works.

Electronic Resources

ERIC Database. Available: http://www.indiana edu/~eric_rec/ieo/bibs/yep.html (Accessed October 12, 2000).

A general reference for all ages with links, citations to articles, lesson plans, and books related to Yep's writing.

Internet School Library Media Center. Available: http://falcon.jmu.edu/~ramseyil/index.html (Accessed October 12, 2000).

Another general reference to Yep for all ages.

Learning About Laurence Yep. Available: http://www.scils.rutgers.edu/special/kay/yep.html (Accessed October 12, 2000).

An excellent teacher's resource including a brief biography, a bibliography of works by and about Yep, and critical reviews and commentaries on some of his books.

Scholastic Books. Available: http://www.scholastic.com (Accessed October 12, 2000).

A reference for all ages featuring a brief biography and booklist, with a lengthy transcript of an interview with Yep.

SCORE (Schools of California Online Resources for Education) Cyberguide. Available: http://www.sdcoe.k12.ca.us/score/cyberguide.html (Accessed October 12, 2000)

SCORE Cyberguides, composed of teachers' guides and student activities, present supplementary, Web-delivered instructional units on literary works, based on California education standards. The Cyberguide for Yep's *Dragonwings* contains compelling interactive student experiences on the San Francisco earthquake and an early-aircraft flight simulation, among others.

Video Resources

A Talk with Laurence Yep. Produced by Tim Podell. Directed by Sean Otis. Color. 20 minutes. Scarborough, NY: Tim Podell Productions, 1998. Videocassette.

Laurence Yep interviewed on books and writing.

ADDITIONAL READINGS AND LEARNING EXPERIENCES IN THE AUTOBIOGRAPHIES OF WESTERN WRITERS

In addition to the 10 writers featured in this book, there exist many others who have written about their experiences growing up in the West. Some of these write only a few chapters about their early years as part of longer life stories. Some write for adult audiences, including content inappropriate for use with elementary and middle-school students. And, some write in a style and content eminently suitable for young people. If this book were more than twice its length, this last group would be featured here, as well. However, creative educators can adapt many of the activities to the authors listed below. Beyond their style and content differences, all these writers share a role as contributors to a story of the North American West as remarkable and diverse as its landscape.

Here is a selected, annotated list of autobiography and autobiographical fiction by western writers for further reading and study. Following the author entries are brief student learning experiences for oral expression, language arts, and social studies that are related to each book.

RUDOLFO ANAYA

Anaya, Rudolfo. *Bless Me, Ultima*. Berkeley, CA: TQS Publications, 1972. 250 pages.

A classic of Chicano literature, this autobiographical novel explores the mystic wonders of a New Mexico childhood with touches of folklore and magic realism. Young Antonio learns much about the natural world and human behavior from his grandmother Ultima, an herbalist and *curandera* or healer. Appropriate for young adults to adults and, when excerpted, for young readers.

Oral Expression

◆ *CUENTOS—TRADITIONAL TALES*

Level: Grades four to eight.

Read a variety of *cuentos*, traditional Spanish American folktales from Mexico, Texas, New Mexico, Arizona, or California. An excellent source is *Cuentos: Tales From the Hispanic Southwest* (Santa Fe, NM: The Museum of New Mexico Press, 1980. By Anaya and José Griego y Maestes). Learn to retell a favorite one. Share it with family and classmates, incorporating both Spanish and English into the retelling, if possible.

Language Arts

◆ *AN ELDER'S GIFT*

Level: Grades four to eight.

In writing, have students describe both a special object, experience, or lesson received from an older person and the situation in which it was received.

Social Studies

◆ NEW MEXICAN HISTORY

Level: Grades four to eight.
Ask students to investigate and report on some aspect of the rich history of New Mexico. For example, New Mexico's American Indian cultures, ancient or modern; life in Spanish New Mexico; What happened there in 1846?; American Indian rock art; Carlsbad Caverns; Taos; Santa Fe; Albuquerque; the Rio Grande River.

DEE BROWN, A. B. GUTHRIE, JR., DAVID LAVENDER, WRIGHT MORRIS, CLYDE RICE, WALLACE STEGNER, AND FRANK WATERS

Backes, Clarus, ed. *Growing up Western.* Foreword by Larry McMurtry. New York: Alfred A. Knopf, 1990. 220 pages.

Seven of the West's best-known male writers share recollections of their western upbringings. Contributing short essays, and often photos, to this collection are Dee Brown, A. B. Guthrie, Jr., David Lavender, Wright Morris, Clyde Rice, Wallace Stegner (see separate listing, page 247), and Frank Waters. The editor adds a brief biography and personal comments on each writer to their essay. Appropriate for young adults to adults and, in most cases, as a read-aloud for younger children.

Oral Expression

◆ ORAL HISTORY

Level: Grades four to eight.
Have students develop a list of 10 questions to ask a family member (or other older person) concerning their personal history. Using a video or audio tape recorder, ask them to conduct an oral history interview using the question list. Students need to be ready to ask follow-up questions if the interview heads in new and interesting directions. Provide the interviewee with a recorded or written copy of the interview, when complete.

Language Arts

◆ AUTHOR BIOS

Level: Grades four to eight.
Have students research and write a short (one to two pages of text) biography of a favorite author. Ask them to include at least one drawing or photo of the writer with the bio.

Social Studies

◆ A PLACE TO GROW

Level: Grades four to eight.
Have students research, map, and report (in written and oral form) on a place important in the childhood or young adult life of one of the writers in Backes's book or any other writer from the West. Examples of such places include: Choteau, Montana, for A. B. Guthrie; Telluride and Paradox Valley, Colorado, for David Lavender; the Platte River Valley of Nebraska for Wright Morris; Eastend, Saskatchewan and Salt Lake City,

Utah, for Wallace Stegner; Colorado Springs, Colorado, for Frank Waters. Be sure to discuss the reason(s) why the place was important for the writer.

JENNIFER OWINGS DEWEY

Dewey, Jennifer Owings. *Cowgirl Dreams: A Western Childhood.* Honesdale, PA: Boyds Mills Press, 1995. 141 pages.

This bittersweet autobiography deals with growing up on a New Mexico ranch, surrounded by animals and, often, by family conflict. *Navajo Summer* (Boyds Mills Press, 1998) continues Dewey's story in autobiographical fiction. The artist–naturalist author also presents illustrations and a personal story about rattlesnakes and a snake bite in *Rattlesnake Dance: True Tales, Mysteries, and Rattlesnake Ceremonies* (Boyds Mills Press, 1997) and her observations of crawly critters in *Bedbugs in Our House: True Tales of Insect, Bug, and Spider Discovery* (New York: Marshall Cavendish, 1997). All books are written for young readers and young adults.

Oral Expression

❖ CRITTER TALES

Level: Grades four to eight.

Ask students to recollect and prepare a brief story for telling about a personal experience with an animal, wild or domestic. Have them tell the story to family and classmates.

Language Arts

❖ ARTIST–NATURALIST

Level: Grades four to eight.

Have students research, write, and illustrate with original drawings a detailed description of a species of wild mammal, reptile, amphibian, insect, or spider. Text should include physical description and measurements, life history, information about the creature's environment, and other pertinent data.

Social Studies

❖ RAISING CRITTERS

Level: Grades four to eight.

In a factual written and illustrated report up to four pages, ask students to describe the personal experience of raising a domestic animal from a baby until it's full-grown or research and report on the process of raising a specific species of domestic animals.

ANNE ELLIS

Ellis, Anne. *The Life of an Ordinary Woman.* Lincoln, NE: University of Nebraska Press, 1980 (1929). 150 pages.

Plain-spoken Anne Ellis was hardly an ordinary person; she lived an extraordinary, vagabond youth, spent almost always in poverty in the mining camps of the nineteenth-century West. Her memories are patched together here like the pieces of a crazy quilt. This book is suitable for young readers to adults. Two additional autobiographies, most appropriate for adults, continue the story of her adult life: *"Plain Anne Ellis": More About the Life of an Ordinary Woman* (Boston: Houghton Mifflin, 1931) and *Sunshine Preferred: The Philosophy of an Ordinary Woman* (Boston: Houghton Mifflin, 1934).

Oral Expression

◆ *EVERYBODY MAKES MISTAKES*

Level: Grades four to eight.

Some of our strongest childhood memories are of mistakes from which we learn and later laugh. Anne Ellis clearly remembers being a little girl feeding caged baby mountain lions whose claws destroy her first and only good dress. Ask students to recollect and prepare a brief story about a childhood mistake and the lesson(s) learned from it. Have them consult with family members on the details. And retell the story to family and classmates.

Language Arts

◆ *SAY, THEN WRITE*

Level: Grades four to eight.

Reading Anne Ellis aloud seems almost like listening to her speak. Ask students to try to capture the sound of the spoken word in writing. Have them audiotape a retelling of the "mistake story" (as above) or another brief personal experience story. (See **Stories of Early Memories**, Chapter 8 for guidelines on retelling.) Then have them transcribe to written words the audio retelling as exactly as possible, read the transcription aloud, and play the tape again for comparison. In discussion, have students compare the written and recorded retelling to the original writing.

Social Studies

◆ *MINING THE PAST*

Level: Grades four to eight.

The history of western North America in the past four centuries is intertwined with the history of miners and mining. Ask students to investigate and report on some aspect of mining in the West. For example, Aztec uses of gold; Spanish explorations for precious metals; great mineral discoveries and discoverers; everyday life in a Colorado mining town, as described by Anne Ellis and others; famous mine disasters; benefits derived from mining; the environmental impacts of mines.

JOHN D. FITZGERALD

Fitzgerald, John D. *The Great Brain*. Illustrated by Mercer Mayer. New York: Dial Press, 1967.

In the first in a series of entertaining autobiographical novels, the Great Brain is John D.'s older brother, Tom D. Fitzgerald, a boy genius growing up in a small Utah town in the early twentieth century. Unfortunately for John D., the narrator of the books, as a boy he was often the accomplice and sometimes the victim of Tom's brainstorms. As a writer, however, his brother's antics make highly entertaining subject matter, continuing with *More Adventures of the Great Brain* (1969), *Me and My Little Brain* (1971), *The Great Brain at the Academy* (1972), *The Great Brain Reforms* (1973), *The Return of the Great Brain* (1974), and *The Great Brain Does It Again* (1975). All are written for young readers and young adults.

Oral Expression

❖ OH, BROTHER/OH, SISTER

Level: Grades four to eight.
Brothers, sisters, and other family members present some of the best prompts for personal experience storytelling. Ask students to recollect and prepare a brief story involving a family member. Consult with them on the details, if necessary. Have them retell the story to family and classmates.

Language Arts

(This activity should follow Economics 101, below.)

❖ A BUSINESS PLAN

Level: Grades six to eight.
Tom D. Fitzgerald's Great Brain was always working overtime to turn his ideas into moneymaking propositions. Have students write and illustrate a plan, up to three pages in length, for a moneymaking venture. It should include: a detailed description of the product or service to be offered; the purpose of the business; the need and intended audience for the product or service; a list of materials needed for the business; and a budget listing estimated income sources and expenses required for doing business successfully. Next, find an opportunity to put the business plan into action.

Social Studies

❖ ECONOMICS 101

Level: Grades four to eight.
Select as an example and read aloud an excerpt about one of the Great Brain's money-making ventures. For example, charging admission to see the Fitzgerald's cesspool dug in *The Great Brain*, chapter 1. Discuss with students and list details of Tom's business plan for this venture, as identified in A Business Plan, above. Identify excerpts describing other of Tom's business ventures as found in the Great Brain series. Direct individual students to read an excerpt and create a business plan that describes Tom's venture.

LEWIS H. GARRARD

Garrard, Lewis H. *Wah-to-yah and the Taos Trail*. Norman, OK: University of Oklahoma Press, 1955 (1850).
Few teenagers experienced the adventures that the 17-year-old Lewis Garrard did on the Santa Fe and Taos trails in 1846 and 1847, in the midst of the war between the United States and Mexico. None wrote so eloquently about it as Garrard, describing overland trail travel, mountain men, and life and trade among American Indians and at Bent's Old Fort, among other topics. This book is an excellent companion to *Down the Santa Fe Trail and into Mexico: The Diary of Susan Shelby Magoffin, 1846–1847* (below), written by another teenaged Santa Fe Trail traveler. Appropriate for young adults to adults.

238 ADDITIONAL READINGS AND LEARNING EXPERIENCES

Oral Expression

◆ MOUNTAIN MAN LINGO

Level: Grades six to eight.

Lewis H. Garrard had a good ear for dialects and faithfully transcribed in text form some of the best examples of the fascinating speech of the mountain man era ever recorded. A brief example for reading aloud is found on pages 104 and 105 of *Wah-to-yah and the Taos Trail*. Many other examples are also found in the book, especially in chapter 19, "Wah-to-yah." **Touchy Terminology:** Scattered throughout the passages of mountain man dialect are profanity, descriptions of graphic violence, and racial slurs, about which teachers should be aware before assigning the text to students.

Language Arts

◆ DESCRIPTIVE TRANSITIONS

Level: Grades six to eight.

In "The Fort," chapter 5 of *Wah-to-yah and the Taos Trail*, from the last paragraph of page 72 to the next-to-last paragraph of page 73, Garrard artfully describes his transition from a cold, bleak horseback journey to a warm and happy condition inside Bent's Old Fort. He clearly tries to make us feel what he felt through his word choice and descriptions. Read the passage aloud. Discuss with students his word choice and imagery. Have students create a fictional or factual descriptive passage, up to one page in length, depicting a marked transition of some kind.

Social Studies

◆ BENT'S OLD FORT

Level: Grades six to eight.

The trading post established by Bent, St. Vrain & Company on the Arkansas River in 1833 played a central role in the human history of the entire southern plains region of North America, though it stood for only 16 years. Bent's Old Fort makes an interesting subject for research and reporting. A replica of the original post has been created by the U.S. National Park Service. Information is available from the Park Service at 35110 Highway 194 East, LaJunta, CO 81050-9532 and their Web site at http://www.nps.gov (Accessed December 12, 2000). Another excellent resource is *Bent's Fort* by David Lavender (Lincoln, NE: University of Nebraska Press, 1954).

SUSAN SHELBY MAGOFFIN

Drumm, Stella M., ed. *Down the Santa Fe Trail and into Mexico: The Diary of Susan Shelby Magoffin, 1846–1847*. Various editions, 1926 to the present. 250+ pages.

The diary of an 18-year-old newlywed, who journeys West with her merchant husband at the outset of the United States–Mexico War. Her portrait of travel on the Santa Fe Trail and El Camino Real is one of the most famous in the history of the West. Excellent footnotes by the editor help explain the people and places Magoffin wrote about. Appropriate for young adults to adults or, when excerpted, for young readers.

Oral Expression

❖ INTERPRETING SUSAN'S DIARY

Level: Grades four to eight.

Select an interesting portion of Magoffin's diary entries. Ask each female student to review one or two day's entries. Ask each male student to review one of Drumm's footnotes for the same diary entries. Have students read aloud the diary entries and footnotes as they appear in the text. (Footnote readers present their readings after the sentence in which the footnote appears.) Upon completion of readings, discuss the content of the diary and footnotes.

Language Arts

❖ TRAVEL DIARIES

Level: Grades four to eight.

As with the journey of Susan Shelby Magoffin, trips often make for interesting stories. One reason for this is that the shape of a trip parallels the shape of a good story with beginning, varied and detailed middle, and satisfactory conclusion. From a personal traveling experience, whether as short as a walk to the park or as long as a cross-country trek, ask students to develop a one- to two-page (or longer) written travel narrative in diary form.

Social Studies

❖ HISTORICAL PARALLELS

Level: Grades six to eight.

Analyzing primary source material, like diaries and letters, gives historians valuable information to help them understand the past. Ask students to read Susan Magoffin's 1846 diary entries from June 19 at Council Grove through July 27 at Bent's Old Fort and Julia Archibald Holmes's 1858 letters (see chapter 4) describing the same section of the Santa Fe Trail from Council Grove on June 2 to Bent's New Fort on June 28. Have them title two sheets of paper, one "Comparisons" and the other "Contrasts," both with two columns headed "Magoffin" and "Holmes." Ask them to record on the appropriate sheet and column the similarities and differences in the narratives of Magoffin and Holmes. For example, on the Contrasts sheet it might read, "Magoffin describes Council Grove's appearance" and, "Holmes does not describe Council Grove."

N. SCOTT MOMADAY

Momaday, N. Scott. *The Names: A Memoir*. Tucson, AZ: University of Arizona Press, 1976. 170 pages.

A Pulitzer Prize–winning writer explores his mixed American Indian and Caucasian family history and his own childhood and young adult memories. Momaday's writing style is often direct, sometimes poetic, and always purposeful. We hear his view of the Kiowas, his father's people, and the Navajo and Jemez Pueblo peoples with whom he and his parents lived and worked. A companion text, with more personal and family history, as well as a history of the Kiowa people and the author's illustrations, is Momaday's *The Way to Rainy Mountain* (Albuquerque: University of New Mexico Press, 1969). Both books are appropriate for young adults and adults.

Oral Expression

◆ CREATION STORIES

Level: Grades four to eight.

Woven into both *The Names* and *The Way to Rainy Mountain* by Scott Momaday are creation myths, the origin stories of the Kiowa people. Learning and retelling creation myths from any country or culture offers young storytellers the unique opportunity to "time travel" and explore from within the worldview and creative powers of ancient people. In addition to Momaday's retellings, an excellent resource for creation stories is *In the Beginning: Creation Stories from Around the World* (San Diego: Harcourt Brace, 1991) by Virginia Hamilton. For guidance on preparing a creation story for telling, see **Retellings of Traditional Tales**, chapter 2.

Language Arts

◆ ONE TOPIC, THREE PERSPECTIVES

Level: Grades six to eight.

Many chapters of *The Way to Rainy Mountain* are only about three paragraphs long—one retelling Kiowa myth, one relating historical events, and one recounting Momaday's personal history—all related to a single topic. Read aloud and have students read a number of these chapters, starting with chapter 1 of "The Setting Out." In discussion, identify the topic(s) of each chapter and analyze Momaday's literary devices of using three perspectives and different voices. Ask students to write a chapter exploring one topic from three brief perspectives. For example, describe an aspect of Yellowstone through Native American myth, geology, and personal experience.

Social Studies

◆ HORSE CULTURE

Level: Grades four to eight.

The introduction of the horse into the West by the Spanish had a revolutionary effect on its native peoples. Ask students to research and report on the many ways in which the horse influenced their lives.

MOURNING DOVE

Mourning Dove. *Mourning Dove: A Salishan Autobiography*. Lincoln, NE: University of Nebraska Press, 1990. 265 pages.

Mourning Dove was the pen name of Christine Quintasket, a determined writer who, in 1927, was perhaps the first Native American woman to publish a novel, *Cogewea, The Half Blood* (University of Nebraska Press, 1981). Mourning Dove also published the collection *Coyote Stories* (University of Nebraska Press, 1990). Her autobiography, unfinished at the time of her death in 1936, has been expertly assembled by editor Jay Miller from rough drafts. The first 50 pages deal with her youth as a Salish member of the Colville Confederated Tribes of eastern Washington State. Substantial detail about the lifestyle and beliefs of her people is included. Suitable for young adults and adults and, when excerpted, for young readers.

Oral Expression

◆ COYOTE STORIES

Level: Grades four to eight.

These traditional tales, sometimes categorized as trickster tales, continue to be some of the most popular Native American stories for people of all ages and cultures, due to their humor, wonder, and the irrepressible nature of the coyote. Ask students to read a variety of coyote stories, as retold by Mourning Dove and other writers, as well as about the ways coyote stories are used by various American Indians. Have them learn to retell a favorite one. For guidance on storytelling, see **Storytelling Connections**, chapter 1.

Teaching Advice: In many native cultures in North America, coyote tales are, for a number of sound reasons, told to teach important lessons —and only during the winter. Try to maintain these practices as you use them.

Language Arts

◆ THE VALUE OF A GOOD EDITOR

Level: Grades four to eight.

Thorough editing of a manuscript benefits the literary skills of both the author and the editor. Ask students to write an intentionally poor one- to three-page first draft of an autobiography, leaving out some (but not all) capitalization, punctuation, key words, and important details, names, and dates. Have them exchange first drafts with a cooperative partner, review them, and, in writing, make corrections and improvements for each other's work. Have partners hold a brief conference to discuss editorial changes with the teacher. Ask writers to revise their autobiographies to intentionally improve the finished product.

Social Studies

◆ SALMON

Level: Grades four to eight.

Central to the well-being of the native peoples of the Upper Columbia River in the past and present, salmon are at the heart of a number of contemporary environmental and economic conflicts. There are numerous salmon-related topics for research and reporting, including salmon biology and ecology, Columbia River dams and power generation, salmon art and folklore, commercial salmon fishing, native subsistence fishing today, traditional native fishing practices as described by Mourning Dove and others, fish ladders, hatcheries, and salmon conservation practices today.

GARY PAULSEN

Paulsen, Gary. *Father Water, Mother Woods: Essays on Fishing and Hunting in the North Woods.* New York: Delacorte Press, 1994.

———. *My Life in Dog Years.* New York: Delacorte Press, 1998.

Unlike his frank, full-scale autobiography, *Eastern Sun, Winter Moon: An Autobiographical Odyssey* (San Diego: Harcourt Brace Jovanovich, 1992), which is fascinating, but definitely adult material right from the beginning, Gary Paulsen has never yet written a single personal history for young readers and young adults. (His memoir *The Beet Fields: A Sixteenth Summer* [New York: Delacorte Press, 2000] is best for older teens and adults, as well.) Instead, excerpts from his rugged and remarkable life are found in a number of

242 ADDITIONAL READINGS AND LEARNING EXPERIENCES

books. In *My Life in Dog Years*, Paulsen traces portions of his youth and adult life through stories, both serious and humorous, about his relationships with dogs. We learn a little more about his difficult early life and love of wild country in some of the outdoor essays of *Father Water, Mother Woods*. Much of his realistic fiction has autobiographical elements, too. But until the prolific Mr. Paulsen writes a young adult autobiography, if he ever does, putting the personal pieces together from many sources will have to satisfy his young fans.

Oral Expression

◆ PAULSENTALES

Level: Grades four to eight.

Everyone who enjoys Gary Paulsen's writing has a story of his, a scene from one of his books, that they remember. Ask students to select one favorite episode from his fiction or an essay from his nonfiction work for storytelling. Have them read their excerpt a number of times until they can retell the story in their own words. Have students rehearse the story with a cooperative partner and then present the "Paulsentale" to family and classmates.

Language Arts

◆ SURVIVOR

Level: Grades four to eight.

Brian Robeson, the hero of Gary Paulsen's highly popular *Hatchet* and other books, is marooned in the North Woods with only the clothes on his back and the hatchet of the title. In a one- to three-page piece of imaginative fiction, ask students to decide what one small object (not a hatchet!) they would want with them if they were stranded in an isolated place. Discuss with students the object and the location for the story, if necessary. Have them write the story, describing the setting, situation, and how the object would be used to assist in survival.

Social Studies

◆ CANOE

Level: Grades four to eight.

Plan a one-week canoe trip to Voyageurs National Park or the Boundary Waters Canoe Area Wilderness in Minnesota and the Quetico Provincial Park in Ontario. Using maps and other information from libraries, the Internet, and local sporting goods stores, have student partners plan an achievable route; list all the food, equipment, and supplies needed (including life jackets and an extra canoe paddle each); and estimate the total cost of the adventure, including transportation to and from the trip. Remember, while on the canoe voyage, all transport is muscle-powered. No motors are allowed.

POLINGAYSI QOYAWAYMA

Qoyawayma, Polingaysi, as told to Vada F. Carlson. *No Turning Back*. Albuquerque: University of New Mexico Press, 1977 (1964).

This personal history, in the form of a biography written by journalist Vada Carlson, is subtitled, "A True Account of a Hopi Indian Girl's Struggle to Bridge the Gap Between the World of Her People and the World of the White Man." The first 76 of 180 pages deal with her childhood, a time of great cultural upheaval for the Hopi, and her generally positive immersion in "white man's" education at Sherman Institute, an

American Indian boarding school in Riverside, California. Returning at age 18 to the deeply ingrained traditions of the Hopi culture, Polingaysi must find her own way through personal and societal conflicts. Appropriate for young adults to adults and, when excerpted, for young readers.

Oral Expression

◆ THE QUIET MOON

Level: Grades four to eight.

For the Hopis and other native cultures of the Southwest, the long nights of the winter are the time to tell traditional stories. Plan a special winter evening of storytelling at home or school, based on the American Indian model, in which all generations of family members can share stories together in small groups.

Language Arts

◆ BIOGRAPHY—AS TOLD TO YOU

Level: Grades four to eight.

Using a one- to three-page segment from a favorite writer's autobiography as primary source material, have students rewrite the segment as a biographical passage in the third person. Ask them to add at least one quotation from the autobiography and any other factual information necessary for the biographical segment to make sense.

Social Studies

◆ ANTHROPOLOGICAL RESEARCH

Level: Grades four to eight.

The first 50 pages of *No Turning Back* contain a tremendous amount of information about the little-known traditions of the Hopi people. As a cultural anthropologist would do, while reading this section, maintain a Hopi Cultural Profile, categorized under the headings of Beliefs, Customs, History, and Lifestyle and listing the page number where the information is found. As examples, under History, record "Old Oraibi was built on a rocky mesa top. Page two"; under Customs, record "Hopi villages have hereditary chieftains. Page three."

MARIAN SLOAN RUSSELL

Russell, Marian Sloan, as dictated to Mrs. Hal Russell. *Land of Enchantment: Memoirs of Marian Russell Along the Santa Fe Trail*. Albuquerque: University of New Mexico Press, 1981 (1954). 143 pages.

No young person traveled the Santa Fe Trail by wagon more than Marian Sloan Russell, going five times from end to end with her family between 1852 and 1862. In this glowing memoir, dictated in her last years to her daughter-in-law, Russell recounts moments from her youth and early married life with crystal clarity. The life of the Trail forged the girl into the strong woman she became. Even long after trains and automobiles took the place of the Santa Fe Trail wagons, Marian yearned for the sound of the wagon wheels from her youth. Suitable for skilled young readers, young adults, and adults.

Oral Expression

◆ LIFE ON THE TRAIL

Level: Grades four to eight.
Marian Sloan Russell creates vivid pictures of daily life on a wagon journey that are almost prose poems. Read aloud from chapter 2, the middle of page 18 to the end of page 22 for a prime example. Ask students to look for more evocative passages worth reading aloud in other parts of the book and share them with the class.

Language Arts

◆ MEMOIR—AS DICTATED TO YOU

Level: Grades four to eight.
Winnie McGuire Russell did an admirable job of recording Marian Sloan Russell's reminiscences and editing them for publication. Working with a partner, have students carefully record on audio or video tape each other's brief personal experience stories on any subject. Reviewing the tape on their own, have them prepare an edited transcript of the other's story for presentation to their partner, the teacher, and the class in a display and/or as a read-aloud.

Social Studies

◆ THE STOREKEEPER'S TRAIL

Level: Grades four to eight.
The Santa Fe Trail never carried many emigrants, looking for new homes, as did the Oregon, Mormon, and California trails. It was primarily a trail of trade, sometimes called the storekeeper's trail, and, therein lies much interesting history. Ask students to research and report on some aspect of the history of the Santa Fe Trail. For example, Trail explorers Pedro Vial and William Becknell; oxen, mules, and horses—power providers; Native American responses to the Trail; Trail merchants Josiah Gregg, Jose Antonio Chavez, Ceran St. Vrain, the Bent Brothers; trade between New Mexico and Missouri—a two-way street; everyday life on the Trail.

ERNEST THOMPSON SETON

Seton, Ernest Thompson. *Two Little Savages: Being the Adventures of Two Boys Who Lived As Indians and What They Learned*. Illustrated by the author. New York: Dover, 1962 (1903). 286 pages.

Seton, famed as writer, artist, and cofounder of the Boy Scouts of America, received early inspiration as a naturalist while wandering the prairies and woods of his boyhood Canada. This book is autobiographical fiction, but it is very close to the lively reality Seton lived. Though the title, *Two Little Savages*, and some of the dialogue are stereotypic, Seton's overall intent, through his alter ego Yan, is clearly to emulate and honor traditional Native American culture and values. Seton's personal history is titled *Trail of an Artist–Naturalist: The Autobiography of Ernest Thompson Seton* (New York: Charles Scribner's Sons, 1940. 398 pages). The first 130 or so pages of this book describe the seminal period in his life covered in *Two Little Savages*. Both books are suitable for young adults and adults, and, when excerpted or as a read-aloud for young readers. *Trail of an Artist–Naturalist* is out of print, as of this writing.

Oral Expression

❖ DELVING INTO DIALECT

Level: Grades four to eight.

In part II, chapter IV of *Two Little Savages*, Ernest Thompson Seton introduces the unforgettable Granny de Neuville, the Sanger Witch, and deftly captures in print her Irish brogue and the country drawl of Yan's friend Sam Raften. In readers theater style, ask five readers to take turns with the narration and dialogue of chapter IV to get a feel for the dialects and have fun with the humorous chapter. The characters are Narrator, Yan, Sam, Granny de Neuville, and her granddaughter Biddy.

A tip about reading dialects: Like reading inventive spelling in young children's writing, just read the dialect words the way they are written and they'll come out sounding right in no time.

Language Arts

❖ AUTOBIOGRAPHICAL FICTION

Level: Grades four to eight.

Read aloud or have students read and discuss the first one or two pages of several works of autobiographical fiction, including *Two Little Savages*. Ask students to write the opening one to two pages of their own autobiography. Have them transform the personal history into autobiographical fiction, making either substantial or minimal changes, as the writer desires. Share both versions of the stories aloud with others. (See **Learning Horizons: Transforming Autobiogrpahy into Autobiogrpahical Fiction**, chapter 9, for more detail.)

Social Studies

❖ TRACKING SETTLEMENT IN CANADA

Level: Grades four to eight.

As in the rest of the Americas, emigrants to Canada, like Seton's family, have reasons to settle in particular places. Have students research and map the settlement of peoples from abroad in various parts of Canada and explore their reasons for locating there.

LUTHER STANDING BEAR

Standing Bear, Luther. *My Indian Boyhood*. Lincoln, NE: University of Nebraska Press, 1988 (1931). 189 pages.

Born in the 1860s, Standing Bear, who was the boy named Ota K'te (Plenty Kill), knew the traditional life of the Lakota at the time of his youth, just before his people were moved to reservations. Not to be confused with fellow Lakota Charles A. Eastman's similarly titled memoir, Standing Bear's *My Indian Boyhood* is not so much an autobiography as a factual and informative descriptive of any Lakota boy's life, enhanced with personal anecdotes from his personal history. This book is appropriate for young readers to adults. Raised in traditional ways, he also gives witness to the values of the Lakota in the partly autobiographical *My People, the Sioux* and in *Land of the Spotted Eagle*, both suitable for young adults and adults and for excerpting for young readers.

246 ADDITIONAL READINGS AND LEARNING EXPERIENCES

Oral Expression

◆ LAKOTA STORIES

Level: Grades four to eight.

The three Lakota writers featured in this book have left a great number of Lakota traditional tales for reading aloud and retelling. Look for the stories in Charles A. Eastman's *Wigwam Evenings: Sioux Folk Tales Retold*, Zitkala-Ša's *Old Indian Legends,* and Luther Standing Bear's *Stories of the Sioux*.

Language Arts

◆ PERSUASIVE WRITER

Level: Grades four to eight.

At the time that Luther Standing Bear was writing, many people believed that American Indians were savage, primitive, immoral, untrustworthy, or even less than human. To counter these strongly held beliefs, Standing Bear often attempts to write persuasively about the goodness and value of the Lakota people and their lifestyle. Ask students to review *My Indian Boyhood* to find at least 10 examples of his persuasive statements in favor of the Lakota. Have them analyze the passages and record the trait(s) he is emphasizing. For example, on page 2 Standing Bear states that though his people were full of pride in their power, their women were quiet and gentle and their men were brave and dignified.

Social Studies

◆ CHILDHOOD—THE TIME FOR BUILDING SKILLS

Level: Grades four to eight.

In *My Indian Boyhood*, Luther Standing Bear goes into great detail describing the life skills he acquired in boyhood—making and shooting a bow and arrows, riding, hunting, fishing, plant identification and usage, leather tanning, painting, and others. Charles Eastman (see chapter 1) also writes at length about acquiring life skills in his book, *Indian Boyhood*. Have students identify one of the life skills they have acquired (such as riding a bike, cooking a meal, or using a computer), describe the skill in detail, and tell the story of how they acquired it in the space of two paragraphs to two pages.

LAURA INGALLS WILDER

Wilder, Laura Ingalls. *Little House in the Big Woods*. Illustrated by Helen Sewell. New York: Harper & Brothers, 1932. 176 pages.

This is the first of a long series of memoirs from the writer who is, arguably, the most well-known autobiographer of western childhood and young adulthood. Her style of presentation is highly suitable for young readers and young adults. Because of Wilder's notoriety and the amount of material available by and about her, it seems presumptuous to suggest a few activities related to her books here. Excellent sources of information on Wilder for young readers and young adults are found in books by William Anderson, including *Laura Ingalls Wilder: A Biography, A Little House Reader, A Little House Sampler, A Little House Guidebook,* and others. A worthwhile student activity involves comparing Wilder's life and times with those of the writers in the **Pioneering Young People** section of this book.

RESOURCES FOR EDUCATORS

The following books are fundamental for any adult studying or teaching about young people in the North American West. Both also offer opportunities for excerpted material suitable for student use.

Stegner, Wallace. *Wolf Willow: A History, a Story, and a Memory of the Last Plains Frontier*. New York: Viking, 1962. 306 pages.

In one of the finest evocations of a sense of place in North American literature, Stegner returns to his boyhood home in the Cypress Hills of Saskatchewan, near the Montana border, to recapture the past by retelling his experiences and those of others who lived there. The book is geography, family history, town and regional history, and a multicultural chronicle. In the midst of it all, Stegner recounts the story of the fierce winter of 1906–1907, as seen through the eyes of inexperienced young Englishman, Lionel "Rusty" Cullen, working as a hand on a cattle ranch. Most appropriate for adults or when excerpted in sections for young readers and young adults.

West, Elliott. *Growing up with the Country: Children on the Far Western Frontier*. Albuquerque: University of New Mexico Press, 1989. 343 pages

A scholarly, but very readable work that provides an excellent educational resource for teachers. Elliott West delves into the important, but often ignored, role that children played in the historical West. With each chapter, he includes a brief biographical portrait of a frontier child, including Anne Ellis, Mari Sandoz, and Fiorello La Guardia, among others. The portraits offer good background information for student research.

APPENDIX

TOPOGRAPHIC MAP SYMBOLS

Primary highway, hard surface
Secondary highway, hard surface
Light duty road, principal street, hard or improved surface
Other road or street; trail
Route marker: Interstate; U.S.; State
Railroad: standard gage; narrow gage
Bridge; overpass; underpass
Tunnel: road; railroad
Built up area; locality; elevation
Airport; landing field; landing strip
National boundary
State boundary
County boundary
National or State reservation boundary
Land grant boundary
U.S. public lands survey: range, township; section
Range, township; section line: protracted
Power transmission line; pipeline
Dam; dam with lock
Cemetery; building
Windmill; water well; spring
Mine shaft; adit or cave; mine, quarry; gravel pit
Campground; picnic area; U.S. location monument
Ruins; cliff dwelling
Distorted surface: strip mine, lava; sand
Contours: index; intermediate; supplementary
Bathymetric contours: index; intermediate
Stream, lake: perennial; intermittent
Rapids, large and small; falls, large and small
Area to be submerged; marsh, swamp
Land subject to controlled inundation; woodland
Scrub; mangrove
Orchard; vineyard

Figure App.-1. Topographic Map Symbols.

METERS—FEET CONVERSION TABLE

CONVERSION TABLE

Meters	Feet
1	3.2808
2	6.5617
3	9.8425
4	13.1234
5	16.4042
6	19.6850
7	22.9659
8	26.2467
9	29.5276
10	32.8084

To convert meters to feet multiply by 3.2808

To convert feet to meters multiply by 0.3048

Figure App.-2. Meters–Feet Conversion Table.

AUTHOR AND TITLE INDEX

American Indian Stories (Zitkala-Ša), 24–45
Anaya, Rudolfo, 233–34
Anderson, William, 246

Backes, Clarus, 234–35
Baseball in April and Other Stories (Soto), 206, 215
Bedbugs in Our House: True Tales of Insect, Bug, and Spider Discovery (Dewey), 235
Beet Fields: A Sixteenth Summer, The (Paulsen), 241–42
Bless Me, Ultima (Anaya), 233–34
A Bloomer Girl on Pikes Peak—1858 (Spring), 71–83, 91–92, 101
Borland, Hal, 48, 49–69
Brown, Dee, 234–35
Bueler, Gladys, 91

California Childhood: Recollections and Stories of the Golden State (Soto), 204
Canto Familiar (Soto), 205, 215
Carlson, Vada F., 242
Celebrating the Earth: Stories, Experiences, and Activities (Livo), 126
Child of the Owl (Yep), 223, 231
Cleary, Beverly, 173–74, 175–96
Colorado's Colorful Characters (Bueler), 91
Country Editor's Boy (Borland), 49–69
Covered Wagon Women: Diaries and Letters from the Western Trails, 1840–1890 (Holmes), 101
Cowgirl Dreams (Dewey), 235
Creating Writers Through 6-Trait Writing Assessment and Instruction (Spandel), xx

de Cora, Angel, 34, 45
Dewey, Jennifer Owings, 235
Dog Who Came to Stay, The (Borland), 58
Down the Santa Fe Trail and into Mexico: The Diary of Susan Shelby Magoffin (Magoffin, Drumm), 237–39

Dragon's Gate (Yep), 218, 231
Dragonwings (Yep), 218, 223, 231
Drumm, Stella M., 238
Dry Divide, The (Moody), 104, 112, 122

Eastern Sun, Western Moon: An Autobiographical Odyssey (Paulsen), 241–42
Eastman, Charles A. (Ohiyesa), 3–23, 34, 36, 42, 246
Eastman, Elaine Goodale, 4, 11, 13
Effects of Knut Hamsun on a Fresno Boy, The (Soto), 204
The Elements of San Joaquin (Soto), 203
Ellis, Anne, 235–36
Emily's Runaway Imagination (Cleary), 176, 184, 195

Father Water, Mother Woods: Essays on Fishing and Hunting in the North Woods (Paulsen), 241–42
Fields of Home, The (Moody), 104, 122
Fire in My Hands, A (Soto), 205, 215
Fitzgerald, John D., 236–37
From the Deep Woods to Civilization: Chapters in the Autobiography of an Indian (Eastman), 3–23

Garrard, Lewis H., 237-238
Girl from Yamhill: A Memoir, A (Cleary), 173, 175–96
Great Brain, The (Fitzgerald), 236–37
Great Brain at the Academy, The (Fitzgerald), 236–37
Great Brain Does It Again, The (Fitzgerald), 236–37
Great Brain Reforms, The (Fitzgerald), 236–37
Growing up Western (Backes), 234–35
Growing up with the Country: Children of the Far Western Frontier (West), xv, 47, 247
Guthrie, A. B., 234–35

252 AUTHOR AND TITLE INDEX

Henry Huggins (Cleary), 183–84, 187–89, 195
High, Wide and Lonesome (Borland), 48, 49–69
Holmes, Julia Archibald, 48, 70–102
Holmes, Kenneth L., 101
Home Ranch, The (Moody), 103–23
Horse of a Different Color: Reminiscences of a Kansas Drover (Moody), 104, 112, 122

Indian Boyhood (Eastman), 3–23
Indian Heroes and Great Chieftains (Eastman), 4, 23
Island Between (Murie), 171

Jessie De La Cruz: A Profile of a United Farm Worker (Soto), 215
Junior College (Soto), 203

Land of Enchantment: Memoirs of Marian Russell Along the Santa Fe Trail (Russell), 243–44
Land of the Spotted Eagle (Standing Bear), 245–46
Laura Ingalls Wilder: A Biography (Anderson), 246
Lesser Evils/Ten Quartets (Soto), 204
Life of an Ordinary Woman, The (Ellis), 235–36
Little Britches: Father and I Were Ranchers (Moody), 103–23
Little House Guidebook, A (Anderson), 246
Little House in the Big Woods (Wilder), 246
Little House Reader, A (Anderson), 246
Little House Sampler, A (Anderson), 246
Living up the Street: Narrative Recollections (Soto), 197–216
Livo, Norma J., 126
Lost Garden, The (Yep), 217–32

Magoffin, Susan Shelby, 237–39
McDonald, Margaret Read, 38
Man of the Family (Moody), 103–23
Many Voices: True Tales from America's Past (Holmes, Stansfield), 101
Mary Emma and Company (Moody), 104, 122
Me and My Little Brain (Fitzgerald), 236–37
Momaday, N. Scott, 42, 239–40
Moody, Ralph, 48, 58, 103–23
More Adventures of the Great Brain (Fitzgerald), 236–37
Morris Wright, 234–35
Mourning Dove, 240–41

Mourning Dove: A Salishan Autobiography (Mourning Dove), 240–41
Muir, John, 125–26, 127–50
Murie, Margaret (Mardy), 125–26, 151–72
Murie, Olaus, 152, 160–61, 171
My First Summer in the Sierra (Muir), 137, 147
My Indian Boyhood (Standing Bear), 245–46
My Life in Dog Years (Paulsen), 241–42
My Own Two Feet: A Memoir (Cleary), 176–96
My People, the Sioux (Standing Bear), 245–46

Names, The (Momaday), 42, 239–40
Navajo Summer (Dewey), 235
Neighborhood Odes (Soto), 205, 215
New Read-Aloud Handbook, The (Trelease), 114
No Turning Back (Qoyawayma, Carlson), 242–43

Old Indian Days (Eastman), 4, 16, 23
Old Indian Legends (Zitkala-Ša), 25, 45, 246

"Plain Anne Ellis": More About the Life of an Ordinary Woman (Ellis), 236
Paulsen, Gary, 241–42

Qoyawayma, Polingaysi (Elizabeth Q. White), 242–43

Rattlesnake Dance: True Tales, Mysteries, and Rattlesnake Ceremonies (Dewey), 235
Return of the Great Brain, The (Fitzgerald), 236–37
Rice, Clyde, 234–35
Russell, Marian Sloan, 243–44
Russell, Mrs. Hal, 243–44

Sea Glass (Yep), 223, 231
Seton, Ernest Thompson, 12, 244–45
Shaking the Nickel Bush (Moody), 104, 112, 122
Sister to the Sioux: The Memoirs of Elaine Goodale Eastman, 1885–1891, 13
Small Faces (Soto), 204
Soto Gary, 173–74, 197–216
Spandel, Vicki, xx
Spring, Agnes Wright, 71, 91, 101
Standing Bear, Luther, 245–46
Stegner, Wallace, 234–35, 247

Stickeen (Muir), 137, 147
Story of My Boyhood and Youth, The (Muir), 127–50
Storyteller's Sourcebook: A Subject, Title, and Motif Index to Folklore Collections for Children, The (McDonald), 38
Summer Life, A (Soto), 197–216
Sun Dance, opera (Zitkala-Ša and William Hanson), 35
Sunshine Preferred: The Philosophy of an Ordinary Woman (Ellis), 236
Sweetwater (Yep), 222

This Hill, This Valley (Borland), 58
Thousand-Mile Walk to the Gulf, A (Muir), 129
Trail of an Artist-Naturalist: The Autobiography of Ernest Thompson Seton (Seton), 244–45
Trelease, Jim, 114
Two in the Far North (Murie), 151–72
Two Little Savages: Being the Adventures of Two Boys Who Lived as Indians and What They Learned (Seton), 244–45

Wah-to-yah and the Taos Trail (Garrard), 237–38
Wapiti Wilderness (Murie), 152, 160–61, 171
Waters, Frank, 235–36
Way to Rainy Mountain, The (Momaday), 239–40
Weaver, Mary C., 101
West, Elliott, xv, 47, 247
When the Legends Die (Borland), 50, *69*
Wigwam Evenings: Sioux Folk Tales Retold (Eastman), 4, 13, 23, 246
Wilder, Laura Ingalls, 103, 246
Wolf Willow: A History, a Story, and a Memory of the Last Plains Frontier (Stegner), 247

Yep, Laurence, 173–74, 217–32
Youngest Shepherd, The (Borland), 58

Zitkala-Ša (Red Bird, Gertrude Simmons Bonnin), 1, 13, 24–45

SUBJECT INDEX

Abolitionists, 84
Activities. *See* Learning Experiences, Literature Aloud Experiences, Language Arts Experiences, Social Studies Experiences
Adjectives, 141–43
Alaska, 151–72
American costume. *See* bloomer
American Indians, 1–45, 76, 86, 245–46. *See also* specific tribal names
American Indian boarding schools, 11, 33, 42–44
Anaya, Rudolfo, 233–34
An Appreciation of the Writer
    Borland, Hal, 49–50
    Cleary, Beverly, 175–76
    Eastman, Charles A., 3–4
    Holmes, Julia Archibald, 70–71
    Moody, Ralph, 103–4
    Muir, John, 127–29
    Murie, Margaret, 151–52
    Soto, Gary, 197–98
    Yep, Laurence, 217–18
    Zitkala-Ša, 24–25
Arapahoe Indians, 76, 86
Arizona, 103
Assimilation policy (American Indians), 25, 33
Autobiographical excerpts
    Borland, Hal, 52–54
    Cleary, Beverly, 178–80
    Eastman, Charles A., 4–9
    Holmes, Julia Archibald, 71–83
    Moody, Ralph, 104–7
    Muir, John, 129–32
    Murie, Margaret, 152–56
    Soto, Gary, 198–201
    Yep, Laurence, 218–20
    Zitkala-Ša, 25–32
Autobiography. *See also* each chapter
    autobiographical fiction, 209–10, 245
    events, 161–62

Backes, Clarus, 234–35
Beckman, Hi (cowboy), 109, 110, 118–20
Bent's New Fort, 77, 86
Bent's Old Fort, 238
Biographical Sketches
    Borland, Hal, 54–58
    Cleary, Beverly, 181–84
    Eastman, Charles A., 9–12
    Holmes, Julia Archibald, 84–88
    Moody, Ralph, 108–12
    Muir, John, 133–37
    Murie, Margaret, 157–60
    Soto, Gary, 201–4
    Yep, Laurence, 220–223
    Zitkala-Ša, 33–35
Bison, 74–75, 86
Bloomer, 73, 86, 95–97
Borland, Hal, 48, 49–69
Boy Scouts of America, 12
Brown, Dee, 234–35
Bullying behavior, 198, 200–201, 211–12

California, 128, 136, 175, 183–84, 197–32
Camp Fire Girls, 12
Canada, xv, xvi, 10, 12, 245. *See also specific province names*
Carlisle Indian Industrial School, 34
Character traits, 108
Chautauqua, 59–61
Cheyenne Indians, 76, 86
Chicano/chicana, 205
Cleary, Beverly, 173–74, 175–96
Clinton, William (Bill), 151
Clothing, 95–97
Colloquial language (cowboy), 118–20
Colorado, 49–69, 70, 103–23
Cree Indians, 5–9

Dakota, 3, 13, 36
Descriptive writing, 141–43, 162–64, 225–27, 238
Dewey, Jennifer Owings, 235
Dialogue writing, 118–20
Dogsled, 152, 155–56, 157–58

255

256 SUBJECT INDEX

Eastern Sioux. *See* Dakota
Eastman, Charles A. (Ohiyesa), 3–23, 34, 36, 42, 246
Eastman, Elaine Goodale, 4, 11, 13
Educational background of writers, 173–74
Ellis, Anne, 235–36

Fairbanks, Alaska, 152–54, 157–58
Family history, 213–14
Family migration, 193–94
Family tree. *See* genealogy
First impressions, experiences, 140–41
First Peoples. *See* American Indian
Fitzgerald, John D., 236–37
Flagler, Colorado, 56–58
Fresno, California, 197–216

Gardner, Howard, 125–26
Garrard, Lewis H., 237–38
Genealogy, 190–92
Grasslands. *See* prairie
Guthrie, A. B., 234–35

Hispanic, 205
Historical commentary, 93–95
Historical research. *See* Literature Aloud Experiences, Language Arts Experiences, Social Studies Experiences
History exhibit, classroom, 62–63
Holmes, Julia Archibald, 48, 70–102
Homestead, 54, 55, 64–65
Human necessities, 168–70

In His/Her Own Words. *See* Autobiographical excerpts
Indiana, 24
Indians. *See* American Indians
Inventions, 135–36

Jefferson, Thomas, 64
Johnson, Lyndon B., 160–61
Journal (diary), 92–93, 152

Kansas, 70–102, 103, 104
Kindness. *See* Meanness, kindness discussion

Lakota, 3–45
Lakota-oyate. *See* Lakota
Language Arts Experiences
  adjectives, 141–43
  animal reports, 235
  autobiographical fiction, 209–10, 245
  biography, author, 234, 243
  bullying behavior, 211–12
  business plan, 237
  colloquial language (cowboy), 118–20
  descriptive writing, 141–43, 162–64, 225–27, 238
  dialogue writing, 118–20
  editing, manuscript, 241
  first impressions, experiences, 140–41
  homesteading, 64–65
  ideas for writing, 187–89
  journal (diary), 92–93, 239
  map reading, 65–68, 228
  memoir, 244
  memory, 22, 39, 186–87, 225–26
  metaphor, 226–28
  naming, 16
  organization in writing, 187–89
  persuasive writing, 246
  poetry writing, 208–9
  point of view, 211–12, 240
  script writing, 92–93, 93–95
  senses, 162–64, 225–26
  similes, 116–17
  survival stories, 242
  tall tales, 61–62
  transcribing oral stories, 236
  trickster tales, 40–41
  vocabulary, 165–67
  voice, 211–12, 240
  writing autobiography, 209–10
Latino/latina, 205
Lavender, David, 234–35
Lawrence company, 73–83, 85, 87
Learning experiences, description of, xviii–xix
Learning Horizons. *See* Literature Aloud Experiences, Language Arts Experiences, Social Studies Experiences
Life skills, 19–21, 246
Lincoln, Abraham, 10, 87
Literature Aloud Experiences
  animal stories, 235
  autobiography alive, 161–62
  ballads, 138–40
  book discussion, 184–86
  Chautauqua, classroom, 59–61
  coyote stories, 241

creation stories, 240
cuentos (Spanish American folktales), 233
dialect, 238, 245
family stories, 237
folklore, 37–38
historical comparison, contrast, 239
historical storytelling, 90–92, 93–95
Lakota stories, 246
mistake stories, 236
narrative poetry, 138–40
Newbery Award–winning books, 184–86
oral history, 234
oral interpretation, 239
Paulsen, Gary, 241–42
poetry reading, 206–8
readers theatre, 224–25
reading aloud, 114–15, 244
storytelling, 14–16, 37–38, 90–92, 93–95, 161–62, 243
Lewis and Clark expedition, 54, 64

Magoffin, Susan Shelby, 237–39
Maine, 103, 111
Manitoba, 3
Maps
   Borland homestead area, Colorado, 51
   Fairbanks, Alaska area (Murie), 153
   Fresno, California area (Soto), 199
   Littleton, Colorado area (Moody), 112
   Muir homestead area, Wisconsin, 130
   Redwood Falls, Minnesota area (Eastman), 18
   Central United States, 1859 (Holmes), 72
   San Francisco, California (Yep), 219
   Santee Indian Reservation area, Nebraska (Zitkala-Sa), 26
   Yamhill, Oregon area (Cleary), 177
Massachusetts, 83–84, 103, 111, 112
Meanness, kindness discussion, 212–13
Memory, 22, 39, 140–41 186–87, 225–27
Metaphor, 226–28
Meters—Feet Conversion Table, 250
Mexican, 202, 205
Mexican American, 198, 202, 205
Mexico, *xv*, 205, 238
Migration. *See* Family migration
Minnesota, 3, 9, 10
Momaday, N. Scott, 42, 239–40
Moody, Ralph, 48, 103–23

Morris Wright, 234–35
Mourning Dove, 240–41
Muir, John, 125–26, 127–50
Multiple intelligences theory, 125–26
Murie, Margaret (Mardy), 125–26, 151–72
Murie, Olaus, 151–52, 158–60, 171

Nakota. *See* Lakota
Naming, 10, 11, 16
National parks, 230–31
Native Americans. *See* American Indians
Naturalist, 125–26, 133
Naturalist intelligence, 125–26
Nebraska, 11, 24, 54, 103
New Mexico, 83, 87, 103
Newbery Award–winning books, 184–86, 218
North Dakota, 3

Observation skills, 22
Ohiyesa. *See* Eastman, Charles A.
One-room school, 56, 109, 120–22
Oral expression, xx. *See also* Literature Aloud Experiences, Language Arts Experiences, Social Studies Experiences
Oregon, 175–96
Outsiders, 217–18, 221–22

Paulsen, Gary, 241–42
Personal history, 39, 92–93, 213–14
Pikes Peak, 70, 73, 77, 79–82, 85, 86–87, 89
Pioneers
   ancestors, 175–76
   young people, 47–48, 49–123
Plains. *See* prairie
Poetry
   events, 138–40, 206–8
   narrative and ballad, 138–40
   reading, 206–8
   writing, 208–9
Point of view, 211–12, 240
Portland, Oregon, 181–83
Prairie, 54, 55, 64, 73, 86
Public lands, 64–67
Public domain. See public lands

SUBJECT INDEX

Qoyawayma, Polingaysi (Elizabeth Q. White), 242–43

Readers theatre, 224–25
Reading. *See* Literature Aloud Experiences, Language Arts Experiences, Social Studies Experiences
Reading Aloud, 114–15, 244. *See also* Literature Aloud Experiences, Language Arts Experiences, Social Studies Experiences
Reform dress. See bloomer
Research. *See* Literature Aloud Experiences, Language Arts Experiences, Social Studies Experiences
Rice, Clyde, 234–35
Rocky Mountains, 78–83
Roosevelt, Theadore, 11
Russell, Marian Sloan, 243–44

Santa Fe Trail, 71, 73–78, 85, 87, 244
Santee. *See* Dakota
Santee Normal School, 11, 34
Saskatchewan, 3
Science fiction, 221–22
Scotland, 127, 133, 137
Sense of place, 17, 228, 230, 234<196235
Seton, Ernest Thompson, 12, 244–45
Sierra Club, 137
Sierra Nevada Mountains, 136–37
Similes, 116–17
Sioux. *See* Lakota
Six-trait writing, xix–xx. *See also* Literature Aloud Experiences, Language Arts Experiences, Social Studies Experiences
Slavery, 84, 89
Social Studies Experiences
　American Indian boarding schools, 42–44
　animal raising, 235
　anthropological research, 243
　Bent's Old Fort, 238
　canoes, 242
　family migration, 193–94
　historical comparison, contrast, 239
　history exhibit, classroom, 62–63
　human necessities, 168–70
　clothing, 95–97
　economics, 237
　genealogy, 190–92
　history webbing, 97–100
　homesteading, 64–65
　horses, 240
　life skills, 19–21, 246
　map skills, 65–68, 193–94, 228
　meanness, kindness discussion, 212–13
　mining history, 236
　national parks, 230–31
　New Mexico history, 234
　observation and memory walk, 22
　one-room schools, 120–22
　public lands, 65–68
　salmon, 241
　Santa Fe Trail, 244
　sense of place, 17, 228, 234–35
　settlement (Canada), 245
　wilderness expedition planning, 144–47
　traditional stories, 14–16, 37–38
Soto Gary, 173–74, 197–216
South Dakota, 3, 11, 24
Standing Bear, Luther, 245–46
Stegner, Wallace, 234–35, 247
Storytelling
　autobiographical, 161–62
　educational importance, 1–2
　events, 243
　family stories, 237
　historical, 90–92
　historical in-tandem, 93–95
　personal experience, 39, 186–87, 236
　personal experience in-tandem, 92–93
　skills, 4, 14–16, 37–38
　trickster tales, 40–41
Suffrage. *See* Women's rights movement

Teaching Advice
　Borland, Hal, 58–59
　Cleary, Beverly, 184
　Eastman, Charles A., 12–13
　Holmes, Julia Archibald, 88–89
　Moody, Ralph, 104–7
　Muir, John, 137
　Murie, Margaret, 160–61
　Soto, Gary, 204–5
　Yep, Laurence, 223–24
　Zitkala-Ša, 35–36
Topographic map symbols, 249
Traditional stories (folklore)
　coyote stories, 241
　creation stories, 240
　cuentos (Spanish American folktales), 233
　Lakota stories, 246
　Manitoshaw's Hunting, 5–9
　trickster tales, 40–41
　storytelling, 37–38
　tall tales, 61–62

Utah, 35
Ute Indians, 35

Vocabulary, 165–67
Voice, 211–12, 240

Washington (state), 151, 159
Waters, Frank, 235–36
White's Manual Training Institute, 25, 33–34
Wilder, Laura Ingalls, 103, 246
Wilderness Act, 160
Wilderness expedition planning, 144–47
Wilderness Society, 159
Wisconsin, 127, 129–32, 134–36, 137
Women's rights movement, 71, 84–85, 88, 89
The Writer's Life. *See* Autobiographical sketches
Writers of the New West, 173–74

Writing. *See also* Literature Aloud Experiences, Language Arts Experiences, Social Studies Experiences
  ideas in writing, 187–89
  organization in writing, 187–89
  process, 223–24
  prose forms, xx
  senses in, 225–27
  six traits, xix–xx
Wyoming, 159

Yamhill, Oregon, 177, 181
Yep, Laurence, 173–74, 217–32
Young Naturalists. *See* naturalist

Zitkala-Ša (Red Bird, Gertrude Simmons Bonnin), 1, 13, 24–45, 246

ABOUT THE AUTHOR

Storyteller and writer John Stansfield began exploring the West as a boy in 1960 and has never stopped. He loves hiking and skiing the North American West and telling stories about its diverse lands, wildlife, and people—especially to young people. With the desire to bring people together to share the lore of the region, Stansfield founded the Rocky Mountain Storytelling Festival in 1989. A former elementary schoolteacher, he teaches storytelling on the adjunct faculty of the University of Colorado—Colorado Springs. John and his wife, Carol, live in Monument, Colorado, near Pikes Peak on the high divide between the South Platte and Arkansas rivers.

www.ingramcontent.com/pod-product-compliance
Lightning Source LLC
Chambersburg PA
CBHW080536300426
44111CB00017B/2748